An Education in Facebook?

An Education in Facebook? examines and critiques the role of Facebook in the evolving landscape of higher education. At times a mandated part of classroom use and at others an informal network for students, Facebook has become an inevitable component of college life, acting alternately as an advertising, recruitment, and learning tool. But what happens when educators use a corporate product, which exists outside of the control of universities, to educate students?

An Education in Facebook? provides a broad discussion of the issues educators are already facing on college campuses worldwide, particularly in areas such as privacy, copyright, and social media etiquette. By examining current uses of Facebook in university settings, this book offers both a thorough analytical critique as well as practical advice for educators and administrators looking to find ways to thoughtfully integrate Facebook and other digital communication tools into their classrooms and campuses.

Mike Kent is a senior lecturer in Internet Studies at Curtin University, where his research focuses on disability and the Internet.

Tama Leaver is a lecturer in the Department of Internet Studies at Curtin University. He is also a research fellow in the Australian Research Council (ARC) Centre for Excellence in Creative Industries and Innovation working in Curtin's Centre for Culture and Technology.

An Education in Facebook?

Higher Education and the World's Largest Social Network

Edited by Mike Kent and
Tama Leaver

Routledge
Taylor & Francis Group

NEW YORK AND LONDON

First published 2014
by Routledge
711 Third Avenue, New York, NY 10017

and by Routledge
2 Park Square, Milton Park, Abingdon, Oxon OX14 4RN

Routledge is an imprint of the Taylor & Francis Group, an informa business

Library of Congress Cataloging-in-Publication Data
An education in Facebook? : higher education and the world's largest social network / edited by
    Mike Kent, Tama Leaver.
      pages cm
    Includes bibliographical references and index.
    1. Education, Higher—Effect of technological innovations on.   2. Education, Higher—
Computer-assisted instruction.   3. Facebook (Electronic resource)   4. Social media.   5. Online
social networks.   I. Kent, Mike, 1943–   II. Leaver, Tama.
LB2395.7.E338 2014
378.1'7344678—dc23
2013046246

ISBN: 978-0-415-71317-7 (hbk)
ISBN: 978-0-415-71319-1 (pbk)
ISBN: 978-1-315-88345-8 (ebk)

Typeset in Minion
by Apex CoVantage, LLC

For our students,
Forever partners in learning.

Contents

Part 5
Boundaries and Privacy

Part 6
(Re)Configuring Facebook

Part 7
Conclusion—Beyond Facebook

Acknowledgments

Tama and Mike would like to acknowledge and thank the many students who have been involved in learning and teaching at Curtin University in Internet Studies and Internet Communications. They were the inspiration for this book and their innovation, commitment and interest has been what inspires our commitment to education and the best uses of the Internet as part of that process. Mike and Tama would also like to thank their colleagues in the Department of Internet Studies at Curtin University, debate with whom was the impetus for this book, particularly Clare Lloyd, Kate Raynes-Goldie, Michele Willson, Elaine Tay, Eleanor Sandry, Sky Croeser, Katie Ellis and Matt Allen. The School of Media, Culture and Creative Arts provided both financial support and study leave for both editors without which this collection would never have been possible.

Tama would also like to thank all the teachers who have ever inspired him, but especially Jane Long and Matt Allen, who both championed the idea that the Internet and education are intrinsically intertwined. Tama would also like to acknowledge the support of John Hartley and the Centre for Culture and Technology (CCAT) at Curtin University in which he was a research fellow during 2013, funded by the ARC Centre of Excellence for Creative Industries and Innovation (CCI). Work on this book has coincided with a very challenging year personally, so Tama would especially like to thank his family, Emily, Henry and Tom, for their love, support and patience.

Mike would like to thank his family and friends for their support, and particularly Amanda Ellis for her comments and advice. He would also like to thank his cat Cameron for generously sharing her desk occasionally for him to work on.

Contributors

Kevin F. Adler is an entrepreneur and sociologist who builds ventures to increase human connectivity. He is a Founding Partner of Entangled Ventures, a company that builds companies and instigates change in education. Previously, he co-founded and led alumn.us (acquired) and BetterGrads, and was a Rotary scholar in Mexico. His first book, *Catalyst: How Disasters Can Bring Us Together or Tear Us Apart*, will be published by University Press of America in 2014. He completed his graduate work at the University of Cambridge and was the Culley Award recipient at Occidental College. Say hello at @kevinfad or kevinfadler.com.

Chris James Carter is a PhD Candidate based at the Horizon Doctoral Training Centre for Digital Economy Research, University of Nottingham. His primary research interest relates to digital identity, with a specific focus on how late adolescents and young adults regulate professional image and reputation through their interactions with social media. He also co-manages social media strategy for the *Academy of Management Learning and Education* journal and is co-training and development coordinator for the Organisational Psychology special interest group of the British Academy of Management.

Sky Croeser is an honorary research fellow in the Department of Internet Studies at Curtin University, Western Australia, and is currently based in Toronto. Her research focuses on the ways in which activists and others shape, as well as use, the technologies of everyday life. You can find out more about her research by visiting skycroeser.net.

Katie Ellis is Senior Research Fellow in the Department of Internet Studies at Curtin University. Her research focuses on disability and the media extending across both representation and active possibilities for social inclusion. Her books include *Disability and New Media* (2011; with Mike Kent) and *Disabling Diversity* (2008) as well as the forthcoming *Disability, Ageing and Obesity: Popular Media Identifications* (2013; with Debbie Rodan & Pia Lebeck), *Disability and the Media* (2013; with Gerard Goggin) and *Disability and Popular Culture* (2014).

Janet Fulton is a lecturer at the University of Newcastle, Australia, and teaches media and communication courses in the Communication discipline. Her recent research project was an ethnographic study investigating how print journalists in Australia interact with social, cultural and individual influences when they produce, or create, their work. Her research interests include social media, the use of social media in education, creativity and cultural production, journalism, journalism education and the future of journalism.

Maria L. Gallo is a development manager at St. Angela's College, Sligo at the National University of Ireland, Galway (NUI Galway). She completed her doctorate at the University of Sheffield, the United Kingdom, where she researched institutional advancement in higher education. In 2013, her research on building alumni relationships received the H.S. Warwick Award in Alumni Relations for Outstanding Published Scholarship from Council for Advancement and Support of Education. Follow her at @gallomaria.

Leanne Glenny is Program Director for undergraduate and postgraduate public relations programs at the University of South Australia, teaching across a wide range of subjects including communication and ethics. Her research interests include public relations ethics, technology-enhanced learning, government communication and social media. Her academic positions followed an 18-year military career, which culminated in a position in Defence Public Affairs. She is a fellow of the Public Relations Institute of Australia and a member of its National Education Advisory Committee.

Kerry Gough is a lecturer in Media Theory at Birmingham City University, teaching film and television theory. Kerry has published on comic book culture, and her research interests include crime programming, film and television horror and science fiction. She is actively involved in a number of student/staff partnership projects across the university.

Mona Hajin is a PhD fellow in Media and Communication Studies at Stockholm University and is currently researching the visual and textual use of Facebook among Iranians. Her broader research interests encompass media pedagogy, digital media, social media, visual culture, migration and ethnicity.

Fredrik Hanell is a PhD student in Library and Information Studies at Lund University, Sweden. His research interests include participatory media, learning and information literacy.

Tauel Harper has previously published on the liberating potential of open-source software, the use of games and play in emancipatory politics and the role of online forums in fostering democratic engagement. He has taught extensively through online tools, including a number of units with Open University Australia and is currently a member of the University of Western Australia's Arts Teaching Innovation Committee. His book *Democracy in the Age of New Media* was published in 2011.

David Harte has taught across the media studies subject area for more than 15 years and is currently Award Leader for an MA in Social Media at Birmingham City University. His research interests include citizen and community journalism, and the development of regional creative economies.

Vanessa Jackson is a Senior Lecturer in television at Birmingham City University, teaching practical television production skills to undergraduate students, prior to this she was a BBC series producer, making factual and documentary series.

Pernilla Josefsson is a lecturer with several years of experience teaching in the fields of graphic design and media informatics at University West, Sweden, and with teaching and guest researcher stays in several international universities, including China and South Africa. She is currently working on her PhD in Media Technology and Graphic Art at KTH Royal Institute of Technology, Sweden. Her research interests include e-learning, with special focus on social media.

Mike Kent is a lecturer in the Department of Internet Studies at Curtin University. Dr. Kent's main research interests, as well as online education, focus on people with disabilities and their access to communications technology. His recent book *Disability and New Media* (co-authored with Katie Ellis) was published in 2011. Mike is @cultware on Twitter and can be found on the web at www.cultware.com

Marjorie D. Kibby's research interests are centered on various aspects of online community, particularly on the impact of digital and network technologies on music fans and music consumption and on the use of the Internet in tertiary education. She has a number of publications across these areas. These research areas overlap in the use of the Internet by people of college age and the distinct online practices of those who have grown up with the Internet. Marjorie is head of the Discipline of Film, Media and Cultural Studies, and Director of Student Engagement at the University of Newcastle, Australia.

Tama Leaver is a lecturer in the Department of Internet Studies at Curtin University in Perth, Australia, and is a research fellow in the ARC Centre for Excellence in Creative Industries and Innovation (CCI) working in Curtin's Centre for Culture and Technology. His research interests include digital death, social media, online identity and media distribution, and he has published in a number of journals, including *Popular Communication*, *Media International Australia*, *Comparative Literature Studies* and the *Fibreculture* journal. Tama has won teaching awards from The University of Western Australia, Curtin University and, in 2012, received a national Australian Award for Teaching Excellence in the Humanities and the Arts. He is the author of *Artificial Culture: Identity, Technology and Bodies* (Routledge, 2012). Tama is @tamaleaver on Twitter, and his main web presence is www.tamaleaver.net.

Mark J. W. Lee is an adjunct senior lecturer with the School of Education at Charles Sturt University. He has published widely in the areas of educational technology, e-learning and innovation in tertiary teaching, with almost 70 refereed papers, articles and chapters to his name. He is the editor-in-chief of MERLOT's *Journal of Online Learning and Teaching*, an associate editor of the *IEEE Transactions on Education* and the special issues editor for the *Journal of Computer Assisted Learning*. Prior to entering higher education in 2004, Mark worked in teaching, instructional design and managerial roles at various Australian vocational education and training institutions.

Fergal Lenehan teaches cultural theory and cultural history at the Department of Intercultural Studies and Business Communications at the Friedrich Schiller University of Jena, Germany. Originally from Ireland, he received a PhD in Cultural Studies from the University of Leipzig, Germany.

Clare Lloyd is from the Department of Internet Studies at Curtin University in Perth, Australia. She specializes in mobile communication and mobile media. Her recent publications include the co-authored papers "Seeking Transparency in Locative Media" (2014, forthcoming) and "Consuming Apps: The Australian Woman's Slow Appetite for Apps" (2012).

Xun Luo is a PhD candidate and lecturer at the Department of Intercultural Studies and Business Communication, Friedrich Schiller University of Jena, Germany, where he teaches cultural psychology and Chinese cultural history. His research interests include cross-cultural learning, online learning and intercultural management.

Lee Martin's research explores the development, management and leadership of creativity in the workplace, the recognition of creativity, the development of creative potential, creativity and identity and the role of creativity within education. Lee is chair of the Organisational Psychology special interest group of the British Academy of Management and teaches creativity on the MA, MBA and undergraduate programs at Nottingham University Business School.

João Mattar has a master's degree in educational technology from Boise State University and was a postdoctoral fellow and visiting scholar at Stanford University. He is the author of several articles, chapters and books on educational technology and distance education. He is currently a professor at University Anhembi Morumbi (Brazil)/Laureate International Universities and is a PhD researcher and advisor at TIDD—Graduate Program in Technologies of Intelligence and Digital Design (PUC-SP/Brazil).

Catherine McLoughlin is an associate professor in education at the Australian Catholic University's Canberra campus. She also coordinates the Australian Capital Territory branch of the Research Centre for Science, Information Technology and Mathematics Education for Rural and Regional Australia (SiMERR). With more than 30 years' higher education experience, Catherine has worked in a variety of teaching and learning settings in Europe, Southeast Asia, the Middle East and Australia and has published extensively in the fields of e-learning, innovative pedagogy and emerging technologies. She is an editorial board member for several international journals in these fields.

Claire O'Malley is Professor of Learning Science, School of Psychology, University of Nottingham. She has published more than 150 articles in human computer interaction, developmental psychology and technology enhanced learning. She is on the editorial board of the *International Journal of Computer Supported Collaborative Learning* and the journal *Computers in Human Behaviour*. She is a past President of the International Society of the Learning Sciences and is currently a member of the UK Economic and Social Research Council's Research Committee. She is also co-investigator in the Horizon Digital Economy Research Institute and the Learning Sciences Research Institute at the University of Nottingham.

Kate Orton-Johnson is a lecturer in Sociology at the University of Edinburgh. Her research interests include digital culture and cultures of learning and e-learning. She has published on student identities and technology use, digital mediation and culture and most recently coedited a collection titled *Digital Sociology*, which assesses the conceptual challenges faced by the discipline as it confronts digitalized social landscapes.

Nick Pearce is a social sciences teaching fellow at Durham University (UK). Having previously worked on a Digital Scholarship project at the Open University he now teaches introductory sociology and anthropology courses and researches the use of social media in education. He has worked on a number of social media projects looking at YouTube, Pinterest and Weibo. He has written about clickolage, YouTube and the zombification of higher education. He can be reached at n.a.pearce@durham.ac.uk, @drnickpearce

Kate Raynes-Goldie is a researcher, educator and award-winning game designer working at the intersection of physical and the digital. She is the Director of the interactive program at FTI and a Research Associate at Curtin University's Centre for Sport and Recreation Research, both in Western Australia.

Her focus is games, play, physical space and technology for education, wellness, community engagement and space activation. Completed in 2012, Dr. Raynes-Goldie co-led an action research project with Ryerson University's EDGE Lab (Canada), which was funded by the Office of the Privacy Commissioner of Canada to co-develop a privacy literacy game with a group of children aged 8–10. She has taught extensively online and in the classroom at Curtin University, Open Universities Australia, and the CFC Media Lab (Canada). She has also been following Facebook since 2004, which was the subject of her PhD thesis that examined the company's anti-privacy culture and the subsequent consequences for users.

Collette Snowden has worked as a journalist, media advisor, public relations practitioner and as a freelance writer, consultant and researcher. She is Program Director in Communication and Media Management at the University of South Australia. Her research interests include understanding the consequences of emerging technologies, media processes and practices, the history of the media and the social and political intersection of media communication and policy.

Eve Stirling is a senior lecturer in Design at Sheffield Hallam University, United Kingdom, and is currently undertaking an Economic and Social Research Council (ESRC)-funded PhD at the University of Sheffield researching first-year undergraduates' usage of Facebook in the transition into university life. Her research interests include technology and higher education (HE), the use of social media in HE and the pedagogical impacts of these. She is also interested in design thinking and its influence on the research process and ethnographic research methods and the influence of space and time on the student experience.

Shane Tilton is an Assistant Professor of Multimedia Journalism at Ohio Northern University. He has spoken more than 40 times at a variety of conferences and public forums dealing with issues regarding new media and its social impact. Dr. Tilton was the former chair of the Communication and the Future interest division (National Communication Association) and Two-Year/Small School interest division (Broadcast Education Association). In 2013, Dr. Tilton earned the Kenneth Harwood Outstanding Dissertation Award from the Broadcast Education Association for the best doctoral dissertation in the field of broadcasting and electronic media.

Zara T. Wilkinson is a reference librarian at Rutgers, The State University of New Jersey. She is based at the Paul Robeson Library in Camden, New Jersey.

1

The Revolution That's Already Happening

MIKE KENT AND TAMA LEAVER

Curtin University

To the outside observer, it would appear that online education suddenly appeared in 2012, the year that has been declared in some quarters as the year of Massively Open Online Courses, or MOOCs (Pappano, 2012). However, we have yet to approach the time when universities and corporations try to figure out what exactly MOOCs are good for. Does the provision of units for free simply provide good public relations and advertising for Ivy League instructions? Can meaningful education operate at the scale of thousands or even tens of thousands of participants beyond the banal provision of educational content? What is the value of the tens of thousands of registrations and profiles created by eager students signing up to MOOC platforms? Can student data be mined, producing the educational equivalent of big data (Young, 2012)? Some see these new models of education as a threat to the current structure of universities themselves (Grove, 2013; Shirky, 2013; Zhu, 2012). As institutions and individuals grapple with these questions, a perhaps unlikely source of insight is the history of educational and institutional uses of Facebook.

As Facebook has grown to more than 1 billion users globally, it has entered all facets of society, including education. Facebook has been used widely to advertise colleges and courses and to build the profiles of researchers and teachers. Facebook has been integrated into a wide number of units and courses both informally, often by students (Haverback, 2009), and formally, with specific uses designed and driven by educators (Kayri & Çakir, 2010; McCarthy, 2010; Pimmer, Linxen, & Gröhbiel, 2012; Schroeder & Greenbowe, 2009). Yet, Facebook use is not without its own issues. How do educational institutions reconcile mandating Facebook use in the face of student privacy and copyright when Facebook's Terms of Use explicitly allow data mining, profiling and advertising? Does Facebook being free to use hide the value of personal data being provided when students use Facebook? Is Facebook a viable replacement, at times, for larger corporate learning management systems such as Blackboard or Moodle? Does the context between Facebook as a social and a learning space help or hinder students' work collapse (Nissenbaum, 2009)? All of these questions have been raised via existing Facebook uses by educators and universities, and thus, many of the big MOOC questions have to some extent been explored.

This chapter outlines the broad parameters of that exploration; suggests that rather than seeing MOOCs as entirely novel, they are better understood alongside the long history of distance and online education; and experiments in that field with Facebook as an educational space and tool. It also sets the scene and contextualizes the following twenty-one chapters of this book that explicitly explore Facebook's place and role in higher education.

MOOCs

The history of the MOOC starts more than 150 years ago with the start of distance education. Before the advent of computers and the Internet, in 1858 the University of London's charter was extended to cover offering degrees to people wherever they had studies. This opened the way for the university to be the first in the world to offer distance education. Distance higher education as a supplement or a replacement to more traditional on-campus learning and teaching has been clearly occurring for quite some time. Although these initial forays into distance education were in the form of written correspondence, the adoption and use of new communications technology has always been an integral part of these processes. The radio was adopted in the 1930s to provide education beyond a traditional university campus. Later, this became more customized when students would be sent recordings of lectures and other content on cassette tapes along with written material through the mail. These were later replaced with CDs (Lee & Chan, 2007). In 1969 the Open University in the United Kingdom pioneered using television to deliver lectures and other higher education material to students. Each of these technologies was seen as revolutionary and transformative for higher education.

The first recognized MOOC was launched in 2008 at the University of Manitoba and was based on a premise of connectivism and networking that blended on campus students and students both not studying on the University campus and not formally enrolled in the University—thus, the "Open" nature of the course (Daniel, 2012). The MOOC has been praised as a democratizing higher education (Lewin, 2012) and much like the radio, television, cassette and CD before it has been branded a revolutionary change in the delivery of higher education (Agarwal, 2013; Friedman, 2013). However, the concept has been increasingly commercialized through providers such as edX and Coursera, and the behaviorist pedagogical approach adopted in these more recent offerings has been criticized for being outdated and unable to "teach higher order skills of critical thinking, creative thinking, and original thinking. . . . the very skills that are needed in a knowledge-based society" (Bates, 2012, "Myth 2: New Pedagogy"). There have also been concerns raised at the low completion rates that these units have achieved—typically fewer than 10% of students complete a MOOC. There are also questions about the sustainability of these platforms, as well as the transformative threat they could pose to the university model of higher education (Trounson, 2012). Clearly lessons are still to be learned and implications are yet to be realized from this massification of learning and teaching in higher education.

Online Learning and Teaching

Although it may seem that higher education has only just encountered the Internet through MOOCs, there is a long history of using the Internet to support education, both for distance education students, and, like the original MOOC, for blended learning mixing face-to-face interaction on a university campus and online learning. This has been particularly facilitated by the wide adoption of web-based learning management systems (LMS) such as Blackboard and Moodle. Traditional face-to-face lectures have been recorded and made available online since the late 1990s (Williams, 2006).

The use of online platforms as a space for teaching and learning in higher education is a rapidly growing area (Allen & Seaman, 2010; Allen & Seaman, 2011; Parry, 2010). This growth is occurring for a number of reasons, many of which are focused on convenience and accessibility for students (Ellis, 2011; Fichten et al., 2009; Van de Bunt-Kokhuis & Bolger, 2009), as well as other more practical reasons such as ostensibly to reduce the costs of providing services, or compensation for a lack of physical space for growing student numbers (Craig, Wozniak, Hyde, & Burn, 2009). Much of this growth is in the form of blended learning, of mixing face-to-face and online forms of student learning enabled through dedicated learning management systems such as Moodle and Blackboard. However, there is also increasing use by universities of more common Web 2.0 platforms and social networking sites, such as Facebook (Teclehaimanot & Hickman, 2011). Similarly, there is a growth in the use of these platforms by both students and the wider community. Social networking sites are increasingly a part of people's lives and a part of how they communicate (Ackerman, 2011). However, Liccardi et al. (2007) have cautioned that in this context "the gap that is fast developing between social software and its use in education."

Although having 100,000 students enrolled in a MOOC is an impressive achievement (Carey, 2012), far more pervasive online platforms influence higher education. The largest of these, Facebook, has more than half of all Internet users log into the network each month (Globalwebindex, 2013). Facebook began as a student only space at university campuses in North America before spreading its reach around the world. It still plays a prominent role in higher education, both as a platform for formal and informal learning and teaching and as a platform for students to engage with the broader university environment.

An Education in Facebook

The following twenty-one chapters are divided into the seven parts of this book. This collection brings together a range of perspectives, examples and critiques of the role of Facebook in the higher education environment, from the social network as an advertising, recruitment and transition tool to explicitly mandated uses in the classroom, an informal network building by students, a university-wide communication tool and a core part of college life. Importantly, included work also addresses privacy issues, personal and formal boundaries, copyright challenges in online learning and the overall challenge of education including a for-profit corporate tool largely outside of the control of universities and educators. In an era in which higher education is being rapidly shaped by attention to MOOCs, many of the issues such a focus raises can be meaningfully explored by examining existing uses of Facebook in college and university learning and teaching. Each chapter presents a unique point of view regarding the way Facebook is being integrated into the higher education environment. The different case studies come from a variety of different geographic regions and higher education environments. As Luo and Lenehan illustrate in Chapter 18, these different settings can have a significant impact on the attitudes and approaches to students and staff toward appropriate use of social media in the educational context. By bringing together this diverse set of examples and approaches *An Education in Facebook?* seeks to provide an opportunity to focus on the current research in this field and provide a venue for the information to better inform the use of this platform in a higher education context.

The first part of this book, "Transitions," has three chapters that draw on examples from the United States and Great Britain to explore how Facebook can be used to help students as they transition into higher education and the potential for Facebook to act as a community-building tool in these processes. Chapter 2 looks at how Durham University in the United Kingdom makes use of a Facebook page to engage with its past, current and present students through the university's Foundation Centre. This case study then informs a broader discussion of the challenges and opportunities Facebook presents to higher education institutions. In the next chapter, Stirling looks at an example of a student run Facebook group. This chapter explores how first-year students make use of Facebook to support their transition into the university environment. Stirling observes how this Facebook group is used as a back channel in lectures and how it plays a role in peer support and collaborative learning, as well as social support and integration. Through this group there "is back and forth between the life worlds of the academic and the social within the same space, and this causes the collapse of easily demarked identities and environments" (p. 25). The final chapter in this section continues to explore students' first-year experiences of university life, this time in a US context. Looking beyond specific examples of individual Facebook pages or groups it explores the practices of students' use of Facebook, specifically examining the role the social network plays as a point of engagement between individual students and their community, as a point of awareness for events and issues in that community, and how Facebook acts as a proxy for the larger collegiate community.

In Part 2, "Facebook in Learning and Teaching," McLoughlin and Lee's chapter offers a robust overview of existing literature and research on Facebook as an environment that supports the psychosocial engagement of learners. In particular, they synthesize a wealth of existing studies that largely indicate that the social presence and social capital afforded by Facebook is both valued by students and, when implemented well, offers an additional social layer to the classroom and peer-to-peer learner interaction beyond formalized educational experiences. In "What's on Your Mind? Facebook as a Forum for Learning and Teaching in Higher Education," Kent explores the utility of Facebook groups as an official part of the curriculum, contrasting the more social affordances of the social network with the more rigid forum-based tools in most LMSs. Groups offer a middle ground of sorts, where teaching staff and students can utilize the affordances of Facebook as a communication tool, but not necessarily become 'friends' in order to interact. Although the chapter argues that the affordances of Facebook can facilitate far more fluid and robust conversations, Kent's chapter does raise some important questions about Facebook as a commercially owned and profit-driven platform and the ethical and privacy implications of asking students to interact using Facebook (questions explored in more depth in the chapter by Croeser, in this volume). In Snowden and Glenny's chapter, they utilize the concept of academic armour to explore the way social media challenges and blurs traditional boundaries between university teachers as distant experts and students as learners. After conducting interviews with university educators with experience prior to the introduction of social media, Snowden and Glenny document a casualization and informality that has normalized in contemporary communication between teachers and learners that parallels the emergence of social media, not just Facebook. The always-on nature of social media is also explored in terms of increasing expectations of immediacy in communication between learners and teachers, even outside traditional office hours. In the final chapter in this part, Hajin uses a series of interviews to explore the utility of Facebook groups as supervisory spaces. Groups are found to allow effective supervision to happen at a larger scale and to facilitate lifelong approaches to learning since the spaces involved are not limited to formal educational purposes.

Specific practical and philosophical questions about Facebook as a potential replacement for traditional LMSs are addressed in Part 3. Harper's chapter uses the theoretical work of Hannah Arendt to explore the broader questions raised when education colonizes social spaces such as Facebook, while revisiting some key characteristics of Web 2.0 in terms of meaningful learning experiences.

The possible collapse of public and private spaces into one another is posited as a key concern, raising the specter of private lives being dragged into public conformity due to the normalizing effects of a privately owned platform moderating learning practices. Mattar's chapter tackles the question of Facebook as an LMS using a side-by-side analysis of Facebook and the largest corporate LMS, Blackboard. The students surveyed by Mattar indicated few privacy concerns but tended to use Facebook and Blackboard, with no definitive preference for one over the other; the affordances of both had a role in the learning experience. The chapter by Orton-Johnson also charts the territory where Facebook complements rather than supplants LMSs and other elements of formal education. Orton-Johnson explores Facebook as an ongoing informal learning space in the form of a backchannel that can persist, although not always harmoniously, with more traditional educational tools and practices.

Part 4, "Facebook at College," moves away from formal instruction and the four chapters explore how Facebook is used by students to engage in identity creation, form communities and interact with university libraries as part of the less formal side of higher education. In the first chapter in this section Kibby and Fulton explore students' use of Facebook for mutual surveillance through the Facebook page "People Sleeping at Newcastle University" and how this creates a sense of belonging to the on-campus student community. In the second chapter, Leaver follows this theme looking at how students who are studying fully online utilize Facebook to try to mirror the informal networks and interactions that occur on campus through the "Uni Coffee Shop" Facebook group. The chapter explores how this group provides a place for students to exchange practical advice, social support and develop a sense of community amongst online learners. In the third chapter Gough, Harte and Jackson, drawing back to themes explored in Part 1, look at how students use Facebook to form relationships with newly enrolled undergraduate media studies students before they arrive on campus. They then follow this with an exploration of how that same student body then makes use of Facebook at the other end of their studies to begin to develop links with industry in their professions. Finally, Wilkinson explores how university libraries have made use of Facebook to connect with their patrons through marketing and promoting the libraries' services and resources and delivering online research assistance and to brand the library as part of the university community.

Part 5, "Boundaries and Privacy," turns a more critical eye to Facebook, exploring how the platform can start to blur professional and social boundaries and challenging the privacy of both students and staff. The three chapters draw on examples from Australia, Sweden, China and Germany. In the first chapter Raynes-Goldie and Lloyd, drawing on autoethnographic research in Australia, outline "the challenges of using Facebook for education, from an educator's perspective." This chapter focuses on the blurring of professional boundaries and workload issues associated with using Facebook in learning and teaching, as well as the implications for surveillance, commodification and intellectual property as consequences of Facebook's architecture and policies. In the second chapter of this section Josefsson and Hanell, drawing on the work of Goffman, Hogan and Zhau, explore the renegotiations required when using Facebook as a learning and teaching platform to the relationship between students and teachers, looking specifically at two studies from universities in Sweden. As they observe with the use of Facebook "social roles have become more intertwined than before and the negotiation of the professional role as a teacher and the private role becomes important" (p. 168). In the final chapter in this section Luo and Lenehan explore the differences in approaches to the use of Facebook and similar social media in China and Germany through an empirical study of both staff and students. They observe that "it is clear that a very substantial residue of the respective historical, sociocultural conception of the teacher–student relationship remains evident" (p. 180) with students and staff in these two countries displaying significantly different approaches to privacy and the relationship between staff and students through Facebook and other social media.

The sixth part of the book, "(Re)Configuring Facebook," not only addresses head-on some of the challenges and limitations of using Facebook but also offers strategies for addressing these issues. Croeser's chapter examines the challenges of institutional and platform privacy, along with additional ethical challenges of mandating, or even encouraging, use of an evolving profit-driven platform that utilizes data mining to profile users and thus maximize advertising impact on them. Along with encouraging an approach by educators that includes enhancing student awareness of Facebook's operation and privacy settings, Croeser outlines a number of tools which can allow students, and any user, more fine-grained control and protection from some of the normative data mining Facebook undertakes. Ellis and Kent then turn to the question of accessibility and the challenges faced by many people with disabilities when using various Facebook interfaces, including the mobile apps. For people with certain disabilities, Facebook can offer a space where their impairment is less visible and has less obvious impact, but for learners with visual impairments, the opposite may be true. Ultimately, Ellis and Kent argue that universities need to be mindful of social, ethical and legal concerns in ensuring use of Facebook or any other tool meets the accessibility needs of all teachers and learners.

In the final part of the book, "Conclusion—Beyond Facebook," Gallo and Adler consider the shifting nature of Facebook's dominance as a social network. They examine Facebook's social capital in light of the emerging trend of "Facebook fatigue" in which users, for a range of reasons, are spending less, if any, time on the platform while other social media tools are becoming more popular. Gallo and Adler warn universities about investing all their energy in Facebook when a broader ecology of tools and platforms are available. In the long term, Facebook may prove to be no panacea in attempting to build meaningful alumni relationships that aim to persist for many decades. In the final chapter, Carter, Martin and O'Malley use interviews with UK-based higher education administrators and academics to explore the ecology of social media tools used on a day-to-day basis. Although widely used, Facebook remains among the most contentious tools whereas Twitter, Academia.edu, LinkedIn and other tools have an increasingly central role in higher education in various capacities from education to academic networking. Ultimately, Carter, Martin and O'Malley end the book with a reminder that Facebook's role in higher education will continue to shift and evolve, while a raft of other social media tools exist and will also mature, perhaps, in some instances, providing affordances better suited than Facebook's.

Conclusion

MOOCs may be the current headline technology for delivering higher education through the Internet; however, the area of online learning and teaching is well developed and expanding beyond these massive courses. Facebook in particular has become closely integrated into higher education in many contexts, some deliberate but many just as a consequence of the wide adoption of this platform. As Kift notes, "[l]earning is a profoundly social experience" (Trounson, 2012); thus, it is inevitable that learning would become entangled with the world's largest social network. The use of Facebook is not just changing online education. It also has an impact on traditional campuses of residential and commuter students. This volume outlines what these changes and their implications are. As some of the initial frenzy of activity over MOOCs starts to fade and other modes of learning online gain a greater focus (Kolowich, 2013), it turns out that the revolution in higher education, and how it makes use of the Internet, is already happening.

References

Ackerman, S. (2011, January 28). Egypt Internet shutdown can't stop mass protests. *Wired.* Retrieved from www.wired.com/dangerroom/2011/01/egypts-internet-shutdown-cant-stop-mass-protests/#more-39575

Agarwal, A. (2013, June 16). Online universities: It's time for teachers to join the revolution. *The Guardian.* Retrieved from www.theguardian.com/education/2013/jun/15/university-education-online-mooc

Allen, I. E., & Seaman, J. (2010, November). *Class differences: Online education in the United States 2010.* Wellesley, MA: Babson Survey Research Group and The Sloan Consortium. Retrieved from http://sloanconsortium.org/sites/default/files/class_differences.pdf

Allen, I. E., & Seaman, J. (2011, November). *Going the distance: Online education in the United States 2011.* Wellesley, MA: Babson Survey Research Group. Retrieved from www.onlinelearning survey.com/reports/goingthedistance.pdf

Bates, T. (2012). What's right and what's wrong about Cousera-style MOOCs? Retrieved from www.tonybates.ca/2012/08/05/whats-right-and-whats-wrong-about-coursera-style-moocs/

Carey, K. (2012, September 3). Into the future with MOOCs. *The Chronicle of Higher Education.* Retrieved from http://chronicle.com/article/Into-the-Future-With-MOOCs/134080/

Craig, P., Wozniak, H. M., Hyde, S., & Burn, D. (2009). Student use of web based lecture technologies in blended learning: Do these reflect study patterns? *Same places, different spaces. Proceedings ascilite Auckland 2009,* 26th Annual ascilite International Conference, Auckland,

6–9 December. University of Auckland, Auckland University of Technology, and Australasian Society for Computers in Learning in Tertiary Education (ascilite), pp. 158–167.

Daniel, J. (2012). Making sense of MOOCs: Musings in a maze of myth, paradox and possibility. *Journal of Interactive Media and Education*. Retrieved from http://jime.open.ac.uk/article/2012/18/html

Ellis, K. (2011). Embracing learners with disability: Web 2.0, access and insight. *Telecommunications Journal of Australia*, 61(2), 30.1–30.11.

Fichten, C. S., Asuncion, J. V., Nguyen, M. N., Wolforth, J., Budd, J., Barile, M., Gaulin, C., Martiniello, N., Tibbs, A., Ferraro, V., & Amsel, R. (2009). *Development and validation of the Positives Scale (Postsecondary Information Technology Initiative Scale)*. (Final report for the Canadian Council on Learning). Retrieved from ERIC database. (ED505763)

Friedman, T. L. (2013, January 26). Revolution hits the universities. *The New York Times*. Retrieved from www.nytimes.com/2013/01/27/opinion/sunday/friedman-revolution-hits-the-universities.html

Globalwebindex. (2013, January 22). Social platforms GWI.8 update: Decline of local media platforms. Retrieved from www.globalwebindex.net/social-platforms-gwi-8-update-decline-of-local-social-media-platforms/#Brett

Grove, J. (2013, January 24). V-c warns of massive threat posed by Moocs. *Times Higher Education*. Retrieved from www.timeshighereducation.co.uk/v-c-warns-of-massive-threat-posed-by-moocs/2001080.article

Haverback, H. R. (2009). Facebook: Uncharted territory in a reading education classroom. *Reading Today*, 27(2), 34–34.

Kayri, M., & Çakir, Ö. (2010). An applied study on educational use of Facebook as a Web 2.0 tool: The sample lesson of computer networks and communication. *International Journal of Computer Science & Information Technology*, 2(4), 48–58. doi:10.5121/ijcsit.2010.2405

Kolowich, S. (2013, August 8). The MOOC "revolution" may not be as disruptive as some had imagined. *The Chronicle of Higher Education*. Retrieved from http://chronicle.com/article/MOOCs-May-Not-Be-So-Disruptive/140965/

Lee, M. J. W., & Chan, A. (2007). Reducing the effects of isolation and promoting inclusivity for distance learners through podcasting. *Turkish Online Journal of Distance Education*, 8(1), 85–105.

Lewin, T. (2012, March 4). Instruction for masses knocks down campus walls. *The New York Times*. Retrieved from www.nytimes.com/2012/03/05/education/moocs-large-courses-open-to-all-topple-campus-walls.html?_r=0

Liccardi, I., Ounnas, A., Pau, R., Massey, E., Kinnunen, P., Lewthwaite, S., Midy, M., & Sarker, C. (2007, December). The role of social networks in students' learning experience. *ACM SIGCSE Bulletin*, pp. 224–237.

McCarthy, J. (2010). Blended learning environments: Using social networking sites to enhance the first year experience. *Australasian Journal of Education Technology*, 26(6), 729–740. doi:0.5121/ijcsit.2010.240

Nissenbaum, H. (2009). *Privacy in context: Technology, policy, and the integrity of social life*. Stanford, CA: Stanford University Press.

Pappano, L. (2012, November 2). Massive open online courses are multiplying at a rapid pace. *The New York Times*. Retrieved from www.nytimes.com/2012/11/04/education/edlife/massive-open-online-courses-are-multiplying-at-a-rapid-pace.html

Parry, M. (2010, January 26). Colleges see 17 percent increase in online enrollment. *The Chronicle of Higher Education*. Retrieved from http://chronicle.com/blogs/wiredcampus/colleges-see-17-percent-increase-in-online-enrollment/20820

Pimmer, C., Linxen, S., & Gröhbiel, U. (2012). Facebook as a learning tool? A case study on the appropriation of social network sites from mobile phones in developing countries. *British Journal of Education Technology*, 43(5), 726–718.

Schroeder, J., & Greenbowe, T. J. (2009). The chemistry of Facebook: Using social networking to create an online community for the organic chemistry. *Innovate: Journal of Online Education*, 5(4), 1–7. Retrieved from www.innovateonline.info/pdf/vol5_issue4/The_Chemistry_of_Facebook-__Using_Social_Networking_to_Create_an_Online_Community_for_the_Organic_Chemistry_Laboratory.pdf

Shirky, C. (2013, February 7). Your massively open offline college is broken. *The Awl*. Retrieved from www.theawl.com/2013/02/how-to-save-college

Teclehaimanot, B., & Hickman, T. (2011) Student-teacher interaction on Facebook: What students find appropriate. *TechTrends*, 55(3), 19–30.

Trounson, A. (2012, November 2). MOOCs will drive students away from degrees. *The Australian.* Retrieved from www.theaustralian.com.au/higher-education/moocs-to-drive-part-of-market-away-from-full-degrees/story-e6frgcjx-1226508256465#

Van de Bunt-Kokhuis, S., & Bolger, M. (2009, June). *Talent competences in the new eLearning generation.* (eLearning Papers No. 15). Retrieved from http://openeducationeuropa.eu/it/download/file/fid/19451

Williams, J. (2006, December). *The Lectopia service and students with disabilities.* Paper presented at the Proceedings of the 23rd Australasian Society for Computers in Learning in Tertiary Education Conference: "Who's Learning? Whose Technology?" Sydney. Retrieved from www.ascilite.org.au/conferences/sydney06/proceeding/pdf_papers/p67.pdf

Young, J. R. (2012, December 4). Providers of free MOOC's now charge employers for access to student data. *The Chronicle of Higher Education.* Retrieved from http://chronicle.com/article/Providers-of-Free-MOOCs-Now/136117/

Zhu, A. (2012, September 6). Massive open online courses—a threat or opportunity to universities? *Forbes.* Retrieved from www.forbes.com/sites/sap/2012/09/06/massive-open-online-course-a-threat-or-opportunity-to-universities/

Part 1
Transitions

2

Challenges and Opportunities in Using Facebook to Build a Community for Students at a UK University

NICK PEARCE

Foundation Centre, Durham University

Facebook offers a low-cost scalable platform for interacting with a huge audience. For universities this audience can encompass potential, current and past students, and Facebook has emerged as a key space for informal and formal communication among students and between students and universities. This chapter provides a case study of a formal presence launched three years ago. This experience forms the basis of a more general discussion of the challenges and opportunities Facebook presents.

Facebook is a social network in that it allows individuals to construct a profile and create a network of their connections and view the connections of their contacts (boyd & Ellison, 2007). It is similar to other networks that pre- and post-date it, such as Friends Reunited, MySpace, Twitter, YouTube and LinkedIn, but the key distinctive features of Facebook are that it has rapidly grown to a dominant position, especially within universities, and the range of uses is constantly changing and expanding such as social gaming, chat and the "like" feature.

Facebook has no immediate competitors that pose a threat to its dominant position as one of the most used online services globally. It has nearly 1 billion monthly users as of June 2012, with more than 500 million active daily (Allen, 2012). Facebook has evolved from a social network to a "social service" that encompasses a range of new and emerging features. Facebook allows content to be integrated from other websites, resulting in the user's accessing third-party information through Facebook rather than visiting an alternative website. A user may watch a YouTube video, view an Instagram photo or read a tweet without leaving their Facebook newsfeed.

It is perhaps more useful to think of Facebook as a social medium echoing earlier discourses around Web 2.0 (O'Reilly, 2006; Wilkes & Pearce, 2011). These discourses emphasize the peer-led co-creation of shareable content and thinking of Facebook in this way enables us to foreground the malleable nature of the site, how it facilitates the co-creation of shareable content and the social sharing of external material. This reading would focus on the fact that individual students are free to create their own pages and groups for their classes, cohorts or alumni groups. This leads to an informality about the Facebook space which is popular with students, but which complicates a university's use of it, especially for learning (Madge, Meek, Wellens, & Hooley, 2009; Selwyn, 2009).

One of the newer features to emerge from Facebook is the ability to create pages for companies and organizations in 2010. These pages enable individuals to publicly "like" a brand, an artist or an organization. This not only enables the creators of such pages to use the feature to keep people informed about their latest developments, but it also creates an online space for the fans of the page to share information, photos, videos and so on. It is now common for companies and media organizations to use Facebook pages to interact with their customers and audiences.

A review of 24 leading British research-intensive university's presence on Facebook found that as of August 2012, they all had official Facebook pages, with the number of fans ranging from 3,000 to 600,000 and the group as a whole having more than 1 million total likes (Kelly, 2012). The number of likes is an easily gathered metric for these pages but is not, of itself, a definitive measure of user engagement. This chapter presents a case study of the creation of a Facebook page for the Foundation Centre at Durham University over three years to inform a discussion of some of the issues which arise from creating an official presence on the site. In particular, a case study of this scale enables a discussion of particular groups of students, which would not be feasible with a larger scale, and would no longer be possible with data restrictions from Facebook, outlined below.

The Foundation Centre provides a "year zero" preparation for international and domestic mature students who go on to take the full range of degree programs at Durham University. They therefore represent a particularly diverse group. The center has been operating since 1995 and, in 2012–2013 had 196 students, from 33 countries. This provides a manageable community of present and past students that can be targeted through a Facebook page, as well as provide a potential tool for presenting the center to prospective students (for more on the rationale for setting up the page, see Pearce, 2010). Because this study is over the course of three years, it is possible to observe when students engage with the page and whether they continue to engage past their time with the center.

Methodology

From its outset Facebook has been at the center of debates about privacy (e.g., Albrechtslund, 2008; Grimmelmann, 2009). These debates focus around the extent to which individuals participate in an exchange whereby they agree to give up some of their privacy in order to benefit from the information shared by other in their network. For Albrechtslund this is a new form of participatory surveillance which has positive benefits as "a way to voluntarily engage with other people and construct identities" (Albrechtslund, 2008). Whether this is the case for all individuals on Facebook is open to debate, but the key concern for this chapter is the recognition that individuals knowingly share some of their personal information in order to participate in the social network. From a methodological point of view, the question becomes, To what extent is this information, or a subset of it, a legitimate source of data?

A substantial project which produced a longitudinal data set of Facebook profile and network information of an entire university course, over a four-year period, ignited considerable debate over the ethics of research into this area (see Parry, 2011; Zimmer, 2010). This research used student researchers who made their networks available to researchers, who could then trace the inter-connections of a class. This issue initiated a debate about how the privacy of the members of those networks who had not explicitly consented to taking part in the study and whose anonymity could not be ensured. The analysis carried out in this case study is with the information shared with the page, rather than with another individual, and all of the information taken from Facebook is publicly viewable and therefore does not violate the individual's privacy as such, although no students or staff are mentioned by name in this chapter (Parry, 2011).

One feature of working with social media is the relative ease with which large amounts of data can be gathered, this face this has spawned a new subdiscipline of webometrics (Thelwall, 2008). Once a Facebook page has been set up, the administrators for that page have access to a reasonable amount of anonymized demographic data about the users and quantitative historic information about the interactions such as the number of likes, wall postings or photo views. This data can be exported as a spreadsheet, and these data have been used as the basis for some of the analysis in the next section. This provides a useful starting point for an analysis, but the data were analyzed further in a number of ways to provide more relevant data for this case study.

One key question that this chapter seeks to address is to what extent the page has been successful in engaging with future, current and past students. In order to classify to which community our fans belonged, the fan list was extracted from the page and was cross-referenced against an internal student database in order to identify current and past students. I also identified members of staff and other pages that had 'liked' our page (such as the university's International Office). I made an assumption that the remaining fans would be prospective students. This is likely to be an overestimate and some of these fans may have liked the page for other reasons, but it seems unlikely that there would have been many who would have liked the page for alternative reasons. At some point recently, Facebook stopped making it possible to download a full list of fans for a page, and this has made a comparison across all three years impossible.

Case Study—Foundation Centre on Facebook

My initial proposal for establishing the page suggested that it could create an online community and emphasized three key audiences: prospective students, current students and alumni. This focus on community and range of potential uses, allied with the relative ease in setting up and monitoring the page, led to a laissez-faire attitude when the page was set up in October 2010. The rest of this section outlines who liked the page.

Before the Facebook page was established there had been an effort to establish an online community for current students, through setting up a space in the Virtual Learning Environment (VLE), based on Blackboard, called "Foundation Family" to share photos from social events and comments. This community had struggled to gain momentum and had been abandoned by the time the Facebook page was set up. This highlights a number of issues with attempting to create a community within a VLE. First, the VLE is only generally accessed by students for specific academic-related uses such as downloading PowerPoint slides and is not generally visited on a regular basis. This also means that the environment is closely associated with work, which makes it a difficult location to foster a more informal community. In addition to this, only current students of the university have accounts for the VLE, making it impossible to interact with prospective students and difficult to interact with past students once they have graduated.

Another rationale for establishing the Facebook page was that there was little stopping a third party creating its own page or group for the center over which the staff would have no control. Creating an official page would enable an element of control over its content and direction. Shortly after the page was set up, a group of students established a Facebook group to facilitate organizing social events. This group was clearly targeted at a particular cohort and ran alongside our own page with mutual links between the two.

Figure 2.1 shows the cumulative total likes which the page has recorded to date. This information is only available to download in six monthly chunks, something that has not been consistently done throughout the lifetime of the page, hence the lack of data points in the middle section. The data points shown are for the start of each month for which there are data.

As shown, there was quite a rapid start, followed by steady growth. The page was initially promoted in an e-mail to all students and staff and, since then, has been promoted through a link in the web page (our most common referrer) as well as through Google (our second most common referrer). Obviously given the social nature of Facebook it would be expected that this would be a source of new "likes" as photos have been uploaded and tagged or as items have appeared in the news feeds of non-fans.

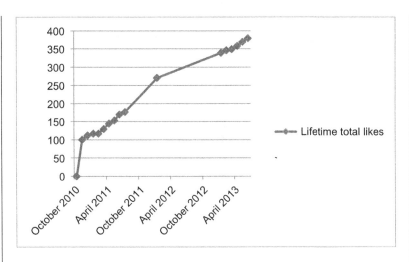

Figure 2.1 Lifetime total likes

Having outlined some general information about the level of use, the next question is, Who is using the site (Figure 2.2)? One consistent feature from the outset of the Facebook page has been a majority (58%) of female users. This has been fairly consistent over the lifetime of the page; the figure was 61% for the previous year. An analysis of the student database suggests that 53% of students since 1997 have been women, but if we take the last four years only, 42% have been women, so female participation with the Facebook page is more than would be expected given the known properties of the current and past student cohorts.

Also, the age demographic is more evenly spread that one might expect for a student group, but this would reflect not only the more diverse student body at the Foundation Centre but also the inclusion of alumni from previous cohorts.

It would have been interesting to explore the nationality of the page fans, but although Facebook provides information on the nationality, this is based on the Facebook settings, which the individual sets and which are clearly vulnerable to international students setting up their accounts on arrival in the UK and appearing as UK based. This effect would be particularly pronounced for students from countries where Facebook and other social media sites are banned (such as China at present), where creating an account prior to arrival is very difficult, if not impossible.

Table 2.1 and Figure 2.3 show different audiences who have liked the page. Over this period the number of students studying with us has been fairly stable (2010–2011: 169, 2011–2012: 182). We can see that for each year the largest group of fans is neither current students nor alumni but

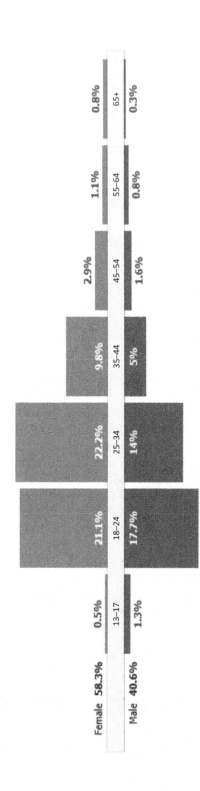

Figure 2.2 Demographic data

Table 2.1 Categories of "likes" over time

| | July 2011 | | August 2012 | |
	Count	%	Count	%
Prospective Student	56	32	119	44
Current Student	50	28	31	11
Alumni	49	28	45	17
Class of 2010–2011	—	—	43	16
Staff	19	11	20	7
Other Pages	3	2	12	4
Totals	177	101*	270	99*

* NB These columns do not total 100 due to rounding.

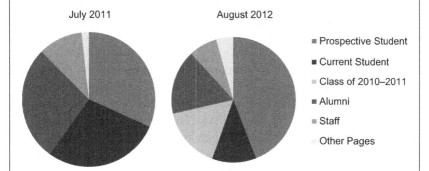

Figure 2.3 Pie chart of "likes" over time

those we have assumed are prospective students. In fact, the proportion of fans who fall into this category has risen, which is surprising, because one might expect it to remain fairly constant.

The number of fans from the current cohort is less for the second year, and has reduced in proportional terms from 30% to 17%. This may be partly due to the count being taken later in the year (the academic year ends in July). We can see that a large number (86%) of the students from 2010–2011 remained fans of the page the following year, and it is unfortunate that there are not data to see how many remained fans the following year, as well as how many of the following cohort stayed.

In summary the page has proved popular, attracting a good number of fans, with female fans overrepresented. The three targeted groups have all liked the pages in broadly even numbers, although there does seem to be scope for increasing the number of likes from current students. Once students like the page, they seem happy to remain connected; however, this may be inertia; we do frequently get interactions on the page from alumni.

Reflections: Challenges and Opportunities

From the start an early concern among staff was about privacy and the blurring of professional boundaries with students. These are two slightly different issues. The first relates to the unease that staff had about the potential for sharing their private profiles with students and about appearing to invade the private space of students; the second is the related but separate issue of how Facebook has established itself as a private, informal space and a worry either that students would resist the Foundation Centre encroaching on this or that the page might be seen to erode the professional standing of staff.

By liking the Facebook page, the individual is not sharing their private information with the page administrators or other fans apart from their username and profile picture. Similarly, when those staff members designated as administrators interact with the page, they do so as being the page itself, rather than as an individual, and therefore, they do not share their personal information (including their username or profile picture) with the rest of the page community. Although the administrator can change whether he or she is interacting with the page in a personal capacity, many forget to do this or are unaware, and this can lead to some personal comments posted as if through the page profile.

As for the Facebook page encroaching on the individual's privacy, the experience to date appears to be the opposite. Clearly, users who felt that liking the Facebook page would share their personal information with it, and who had an issue with this, would not like the page in the first place, so the success of the page in gaining fans suggests that this has not been the case. In fact, an issue that has arisen recently has been prospective students posting inquiries on the wall about their particular applications, which has started conversations that center staff have felt would be better continued in private. It seems that for some prospective students at least they are too keen to share details of their applications and that rather than worry about the page encroaching on their privacy, the page is worried about their lack of privacy. So far the center has responded to this on an ad hoc basis, but it is clear that there is a need for a clear privacy policy that establishes which conversations are best had in private and which are best had in public and takes into account any legal issues (Grimmelmann, 2009; JISC, 2011).

It is important to recognize that Facebook is a business, and this consequently has practical implications. Facebook generates income through placing targeted adverts, and as the Foundation Centre page is recognized as an educational page, frequented by students, the adverts can be from competing providers. A further practical consideration is that the business model for Facebook can change at any time and that if the Foundation Centre is committed to maintaining a presence this may incur additional costs in the future (e.g., if pages became a freemium feature, subject to charges for additional functionality).

Another challenge to creating and maintaining an effective presence on any social media is the time commitment required to post and respond to content. To date this has been managed through staff time, but this is not ideal and as the page continues to expand, and as the center looks to expand its presence onto other media (e.g., Twitter) this is not sustainable. We have decided to employ a student as a social media intern on a part-time contract to assist with this. This is a strategy I know is being used by colleagues across the UK and the US, and it provides for an excellent job opportunity for the student as well as providing an enthusiastic source of content for the page.

A final challenge is to realize that despite the apparent dominance of Facebook its coverage is not total. An increasing number of users have rejected or are rejecting the space and other social spaces exist where students create their own communities (Rainie, Smith, & Duggan, 2013). In the foundation center context, one such space has been created by our students on the website The Student Room (www.thestudentroom.co.uk/showthread.php?t=2328693). Similarly, access to Facebook is restricted in some countries, which is especially important for a center attempting to recruit international students from places such as China and Vietnam.

Conclusion

This case study has been able to provide a snapshot of the way that prospective, current and alumni students connect with the page for a 1-year program over a 3-year period. Future studies will include a content analysis of the ways in which these groups interact with one another and the page. At the moment, there is a good deal of interaction, particularly around photos.

It is clear that Facebook is a useful medium for many students, and for our center to promote itself, although it is important to remember those who are not on Facebook, and to not rely exclusively on this, or any other social media, to interact with these groups. Facebook is a low-cost and attractive platform for interacting with students, but it should not be relied on as the only platform for any community-building strategy.

References

Albrechtslund, Anders. (2008). Online social networking as participatory surveillance. *First Monday*, *13*(3). Retrieved from http://firstmonday.org/article/view/2142/1949

Allen, Matthew. (2012). An education in Facebook. *Digital Culture & Education*, *4*(3), 213–225.

boyd, dana, & Ellison, Nicole B. (2007). Social network sites: Definition, history, and scholarship. *Journal of Computer-Mediated Communication*, *13*(1), 210–230.

Grimmelmann, James. (2009). Facebook and the social dynamics of privacy. *Iowa Law Review*, *95*(4), 1137–1206.

Joint Information Systems Committee. (2011). *Facing up to Facebook: A guide for FE and HE*. Strathclyde: JISClegal.

Kelly, Brian. (2012, August 2). Over one million 'likes' of Facebook pages for the 24 Russell Group Universities [Blog entry]. *UK Web Focus: Reflections on the Web and Web 2.0*. Retrieved from http://ukwebfocus.wordpress.com/2012/08/02/over-one-million-likes-of-facebook-pages-for-the-24-russell-group-universities/

Madge, Clare, Meek, Julie, Wellens, Jane, & Hooley, Tristram. (2009). Facebook, social integration and informal learning at University: 'It is more for socialising and talking to friends about work than for actually doing work'. *Learning, Media and Technology, 34*(2), 141–155.

O'Reilly, Tim. (2006). *Web 2.0 principles and best practices* (O'Reilly Radar Reports). Sebastopol, CA: O'Reilly.

Parry, Marc. (2011, July 10). Harvard researchers accused of breaching students' privacy. *The Chronicle of Higher Education*. Retrieved from http://chronicle.com/article/Harvards-Privacy-Meltdown/128166/

Pearce, Nick. (2010, August 27). Facebook pages in HE [Blog entry]. *Digitalscholarship Blog*. Retrieved from http://digitalscholar.wordpress.com/2010/08/27/Facebook-pages-in-he/

Rainie, Lee, Smith, Aaron, & Duggan, Maeve. (2013). Coming and going on Facebook: Pew Internet Project. Retrieved from http://pewinternet.org/Reports/2013/Coming-and-going-on-facebook.aspx

Selwyn, Neil. (2009). Faceworking: Exploring students' education-related use of Facebook. *Learning, Media and Technology, 34*(2), 157–174. doi:10.1080/17439880902923622

Thelwall, Mike. (2008). Bibliometrics to webometrics. *Journal of Information Science, 34*(4), 605–621. doi:10.1177/0165551507087238

Wilkes, Linda, & Pearce, Nick. (2011). Fostering an ecology of openness: The role of social media in public engagement at the Open University. In C. Wankel (Ed.), *Teaching Arts and Science with the New Social Media* (pp. 241–264). Bingley, UK: Emerald.

Zimmer, Michael. (2010). "But the data is already public": On the ethics of research in Facebook. *Ethics and Information Technology, 12*(4), 313–325. doi:10.1007/s10676-010-9227-5

3

"We Use Facebook Chat in Lectures of Course!" Exploring the Use of a Facebook Group by First-Year Undergraduate Students for Social and Academic Support

EVE STIRLING

University of Sheffield

> The red notification symbol is showing thirty-four notifications. A few are comments in response to a post on my Wall, the majority are activity from the group. It was a busy night, what did I miss?
>
> (Interview with Facebook Friend, January, 2011)

This chapter discusses how a group of students used a Facebook Group for social and academic support and is based on data gathered using a longitudinal ethnographic approach from Facebook in the 2010/11 academic year. The chapter explores some of the opportunities that a student-initiated and -run Facebook Group offers first-year undergraduate students (in this chapter Group with a *G* is used to refers to this Facebook Group). These students are campus based and in their first year at university in the UK. I ask, how does being a member of a Facebook Group support or hinder the transition to university and how does this influence the student life worlds of the social and the academic?

The three themes of the chapter are "the group as a backchannel to lectures," "peer support and collaborative learning" and "social support and integration." The themes are used to describe the functions of this Group space and the practices, which take place therein, drawing upon some examples from empirical research. The work of Doreen Massey (2005) is used as a framework to conceptualize the functions and practices in the Group space. By drawing on Massey's (2005) notions of interrelations, multiplicities and places-within-places, I consider what this Group offers us as a lens to examine contemporary Higher Education (HE). The Facebook Group is bounded, yet flows freely between the social and the academic worlds of the students, and the three themes are used as examples to illustrate this.

A Facebook Group

A Facebook Group is usually a separate private, members' only space within the interface of the social network site (SNS) Facebook. A Facebook Group can be open (anyone can join, all posts made will show up in one's Newsfeed), closed (anyone can join but an administrator has to accept or invite them) or secret (one has to be invited, and this will not show up in his or her Newsfeed).

The Group, which is the focus of this chapter, was a closed Group that was set up in the first few weeks of the 2010/11 academic year and was run by some first year students on a campus-based course. All students of the year-group were members ($n = 80$), and all were aged 18 and 21. The group was of the new group type (in 2010), and this allowed for synchronous group discussions (of more than two members at a time) using the Facebook Chat function. This differentiation is important, because before this Facebook groups did not allow many members to use the Chat function at once.

Social and Academic Support in First-Year Transition to University

Facebook is ubiquitous in many of the lives of young undergraduate students in the UK (Ipsos MORI, 2008). Research in this area shows that Facebook is a key tool in being a student (Selwyn, 2009), both through social support and supporting academic study (Madge et al., 2009). The transition phase of the first year of university within the UK can be particularly challenging. It might involve moving away from home for the first time, making new friends and studying a new academic subject and these influences can have a negative impact on student retention (Wilcox, Winn, & Fyvie-Gauld, 2005; Yorke & Longden, 2008). Wilcox and colleagues (2005, p. 707) findings suggest, "equal emphasis needs to be placed on successful integration into the social world of the university as into the academic world." The focus here is on these two interconnected lifeworlds of the first-year students: the social and the academic.

A Facebook Group as a Space and a Place

Within research into digital spaces I see terms such as *virtual*, *online* and *offline* as unhelpful. I want to draw attention to the real and lived experiences of space. Massey (2005, p. 185) proposes space and place are both "concrete, grounded, real, lived." The digital space of Facebook is not "out there" and unreal but is geographically grounded in our real lived experiences, and attention should be paid to it as such. The Facebook Group in this chapter is conceptualized as a space within the larger interface architecture of Facebook. It sits alongside a students' Facebook Profile and is accessed from the Newsfeed page. Within the larger scale, the Group sits within the digital spaces of students' browser or smartphone apps. Alongside the other websites a student is browsing and alongside the computer programs or apps the student is using. Massey

(2005, p. 184) describes spatialized social practices, which are both open and closed as the "sum of our relations and interconnections." Simply put, the student interactions make space and place. Massey (2005) presents the notion of "places-within-places" (p. 179). These are relational constructions between which there is a back and forth. The Facebook Group could be conceptualized as a place within a place. The Facebook Group conceptualized in this manner offers multiplicities of identities and actions. The back and forth is between a student's Facebook Newsfeed, Friends' Walls and the Facebook Group Newsfeed and interactions within. There is back and forth between the lifeworlds of the academic and the social within the same space, and this causes the collapse of easily demarked identities and environments.

Ethnographic Ways of Seeing

The ideas presented here draw on some of the empirical findings from a study, "Why waste your time on Facebook?" (Stirling, 2014). The study was a multi-sited, connective ethnography (Leander & McKim, 2003) and used an ethnographic approach to explore first-year transition to university. I followed six participants (my Facebook Friends), over the 2010/11 academic year, using the connective approach, which means across both digital (Facebook) and physical (meeting face-to-face on campus) environments. I gained access to the Facebook Group, which is the focus of this chapter, through one of my Facebook Friends (FbF). The data presented here are a mixture of analysis of my ethnographic field notes written during my participant observation, direct quotes taken from the Facebook Group space and direct quotes from participant interviews. The research approach is situated firmly in the realities of Facebook use and the everyday uses and practices of the students. Facebook is a constant in the lives of the students who took part in my study, they engage with the site on a regular basis.

I now move the discussion onto some of the affordances a student-led Facebook Group offers student members. I use Massey's (2005) notions of interrelations, multiplicities and places-within-places in the following examples to discuss the ways in which the students interact across the digital and the physical environments.

The themes I present are "the group as a backchannel to lectures," "peer support and collaborative learning" and "social support and integration." They offer a framework for the remainder of the chapter.

The Group as a Backchannel to Lectures

Eighty students are sat in the lecture theatre waiting for the lecturer to appear. A large-proportion have their laptop out in front of them ready to take notes on what the lecturer will say. Before he arrives emails are checked, Facebook is updated, comments are made and some students

navigate to the Group page. Once the lecture begins the focus of concentration moves to the lecturer, listening, taking notes . . . until . . . a
Facebook Chat box pops up. "What is he on about?"

(field notes, March, 2011)

The term *backchannel* has been associated with the use of social media,
particularly in academic and commercial conferences where twitter is used for
delegates to converse on the topic of which the speaker is presenting. This is
seen as the backchannel to the main presentation. The digital backchannel is
described in relation to learning and teaching in the work of Baumgart et al.
(2012) and Pohl et al. (2011) as a discussion channel of ideas, which takes place
without disturbing the lecturer. In their work, Baumgart et al. (2012) describe
a facilitated formal method of the lecturer supporting what they describe as
the "incoherent backchannel discourse" (p. 364). In this section I discuss these
perceived incoherent discourses, which take place in the digital backchannel of
Group Chat. In this example the lecturer is unaware of the digital chatter, which
takes place alongside his lecture. The Group has a synchronous chat facility
and the students use this to type messages to communicate with each other
throughout the lecture. A Group member described the reason for this activity,
"the problem with most of his lectures is, if you asked a question, if he deemed
it simple he didn't answer it. But the problem was he never went through. . . .
never gave proper working and it ended that you don't understand. So we went
through it on the [Facebook] Group" (FbF interview).

This practice shows the interrelations between the digital space and the
physical lecture theatre (Massey, 2005). The digital backchannel is layered on
the physical space. It is also layered upon other digital spaces in which the students may be visiting: a quick trip to Google for the clarification of a term used
or the university Learning Management System (LMS) to see how this topic
fits with the module assignment. The main foci of the students are on the two
spaces of the Group and the lecture theatre and they supplement each other.
This digital backchannel is an informal, real-time method to get feedback when
something is not clear. This use of peer support in the lecture theater to help
explain what the other students do not understand could be rooted in the power
dynamics of a large lecture theatre and the histories of the delivery method. The
students worry about asking a question in front of a large group and often their
question is left unanswered as it was deemed too simple.

What can we do to respond to this? We all learn at different paces, but
currently we cannot stop or pause the lecturer midpoint like we can with a
YouTube video or with demand TV. The use of the Group as a backchannel
may be seen as incoherent discourse because there is no lecturer involvement,
but in this case it is a useful support mechanism and offers more to the students than does the structured lecture. The flip side of this use of the Group is
that the students may find the information they need from the backchannel,

but at what loss? The learners miss out on the main channel by interacting and concentrating on the backchannel and then the situation is exacerbated and the cycle begins again.

Peer Support and Collaborative Learning

> One of the Group members has a problem with a current assignment. It is 23.07. He explains the problem he has in a Wall post, which the whole Group will see. Within a minute he has two replies and within six minutes, fourteen different comments. These comments range from helpful supportive suggestions on how to work through the problem to funny retorts. Someone jokes, "this isn't the group to get sensible answers from."
>
> (field notes, May, 2011)

Peer support, getting help and feedback from your classmates on assignments is a significant activity, which takes place within the Group and is a practice that many undergraduates take part in. Facebook affords anytime, real-time connection and feedback, which is unrivaled anywhere in the university campus. A one-to-one tutorial with a member of academic staff to go through a difficult element of the module teaching or assignment is invaluable, but what about late at night, when faculty members are not available?

The use of Facebook for learning and its educational value has received much attention (see review by Manca & Ranieri, 2013). This debate shifts between the more formal approaches of Facebook as an LMS (Wang et al., 2012) to the informal use of the site for collaborative classroom activities (Lampe et al., 2011). Research on student views on Facebook for learning has found that Facebook is seen as primarily for social purposes and is sometimes used for informal learning or student-to-student discussions of academic matters but definitely not for formal teaching purposes between staff and students involving formal assessment (Madge et al., 2009). Much of the literature on peer support in HE positions this notion as a formal support mechanism (De Smet at al., 2008). Work by Timmis (2012, p. 4) suggests that peer support is often better placed when it crosses the "formal-informal learning divide," and this can be defined as "offering mutual help and assistance at a social, cultural and affective level, involving both communication and collaboration amongst peers, working together" (ibid). The Group offers this informal, social nature of peer support.

The nature of this Group start-up was to have a shared space, as one member described "where we rant about terrible lectures, make bad course related jokes or talk about the assignments" (FbF interview). The instant and always on nature of the Group encourages its use as a peer support mechanism, as one user describes, "Facebook is left on constantly even if I am not checking it as it is sometimes used as a method of communication for group work in my modules" (FbF interview). The uses of instant messaging communications (such as those afforded by the instant messaging in the Group Chat) are seen as well placed to offer peer support (Timmis, 2012). Other peer support activities, which take place in the Group include using the Wall to ask the group course related administration questions. These range from what are the deadlines for assignments to which readings are required for an upcoming seminar? Much of the Group Wall activity focuses on discussing teaching topics that the students are struggling with, either asynchronously over time or synchronously within a lecture or late at night before a deadline.

The consistency of this Group as a space to return to anchors the class, it binds the group members together through their interrelations (Massey, 2005). These ongoing conversations are important in the students making sense and understanding what is expected of them in the institutional settings. Timmis (2012) suggests that students do not often realize the value of these everyday practices and that they are currently invisible to a large sector of academic and support staff in HE. The always-on nature of digital technologies and the constant feedback offered by peers could influence learning and teaching practices. In the UK the current three-week turnaround for feedback on assessed work seems an age in a space where an unanswered Message on Facebook cannot be left for even a day. The integration of social media into everyday life can mean for some people a blurring between the professional and the personal. As boyd (2013) suggests "the line between what is work and what is fun is often complicated." For undergraduate students this is magnified against what they see as work and fun and what academics view these as. The use of SNS is not something to be kept separate from work, because these are everyday integrated practices.

Social Support and Integration

There is a steady stream of postings and comments on the Group Wall this evening. How to wind up a chatbot is one of these. Thirteen Group members are discussing what they have asked different chatbots and what the bots reply with. I always like it when you ask them the first line of a song and they reply with the next XD.

(field notes, January, 2011)

Within the campus-based environment, the social life is just as, if not more important than the academic life in the first year of university. There is a move in the UK that there should be equal emphasis placed on the social integration into the university as well as the academic and that social support from course mates as well and from those the students live with is vital in supporting student retention (Yorke & Longden, 2008). Student retention is one of the key debates in the current massification model of HE and student departure from university has massive ramifications for both sides of the debate (Tinto, 2007). The social support offered by Facebook starts before the university semester begins (Madge et al., 2009) and the positive way in which Facebook enriches the students' socialization process, through talking about work as opposed to actually doing it, has been noted by a range of scholars (Madge et al, 2009; Vie, 2008; West et al., 2009).

The students of the Group have shared interests and experiences that go beyond the subjects studied in the lecture. The chatbot is just one of these. The Facebook Group space brings people together who do not ordinarily spend time together. The students have the shared experience of meeting face-to-face for lectures or seminars, but within the campus's physical environment there is not always time to chat or socialize. External constraints of other lectures to go to, assignments to complete or employment commitments mean that it is not always possible to have space for the socialization process, which is key here (Wilcox et al., 2005). The Group offers this space for chatter and socializing.

One Group member stated that his time at university would be less social without being a member of the Group: "I think I wouldn't know as many of the people on my course as I do now if it wasn't for Facebook," and he goes on to say, "Like, I know I've made good friends, I know I've made friends who I'm going to be friends for the rest of the time here. I knew I had a chance I was going to find someone who was as crazy as me" (FbF interview). Without the Group the classmates may have met and become friends but this space offers the opportunity to nurture these friendships through constant communication. In this example the Group is a focus of interactions between the classmates. The space is constructed by these "interrelations" (Massey, 2005, p. 8) between the classmates, a comment on a Wall post or an invite to watch TV at a friend's house. The student-initiated nature of this Group could also have a negative impact on students' social integration into the university. The choice to not to be on Facebook or to not to be a member of this Group could potentially mean exclusion from many socialization opportunities, and this would be unknown to the Group members as this person would not exist in that space.

Digital and Face-to-Face Dynamics and Interrelations

This Group is an example of Facebook Group use in campus-based courses. I present the argument that Facebook is geographically grounded in the students' lived experiences and that the Facebook Group has a culture that is both digital and based on "face-to-face" dynamics. The three themes presented here are not activities that take place in isolation; they often take place simultaneously. The interrelations of the three themes are important to note. The Facebook Group offers to the students a space under construction; a space beyond and yet linked to institutional practices. A Facebook Group can be a bounded place but which is in free-flow between the institution (lecture theatre, LMS and curriculum structure) and the individual (a student). The Facebook Group affords communication anywhere, anytime and through this a range of social and peer support (Madge et al., 2009; Wilcox et al., 2005) mechanisms. These range from instant feedback in lectures through Chat and longitudinal conversations and relation-ships built over time through Wall posts.

The use of Facebook in lectures by students is an obvious development of digital technologies and of software and hardware usage. The site affords so many social and cultural practices of student life. Why not use it? The perceived "appropriateness" of the site by faculty is irrelevant to students. When a student is in the first year and is experiencing the transition to university, being a mem-ber of a Facebook Group could be a "betwixt space turning-point" (Palmer, O'Kane, & Owens, 2009, p. 37) between them staying and leaving HE. Facebook is currently ever present in HE, in the lecture theatre, the classroom, the library, the halls of residence and the student union. It is a place-within-these-places (Massey, 2005) interrelated to HE, and as students continue to use the site, we cannot remove the multiplicity of use.

These three examples are some of the Facebook social practices, which come together to create the places of HE. Will these everyday practices of the stu-dents become a challenge to the dominant systems of the university structure and organization of learning and teaching? I believe they already are. In the examples in this chapter, Facebook is the go to place to ask questions when a student does not understand something in a lecture and Facebook is used over the LMS to communicate and collaborate on class assignments.

Both life-worlds of the social and the academic are collapsed into the Face-book Group and these interrelations mean that students are able to interact in both worlds in one place-within-a-place, and this offers what is currently unrivaled, ubiquitous support in their transition to university.

References

Baumgart, D., Pohl, A., Gehlen-Baum, V., & Bry, F. (2012). Providing guidance on Backstage, a novel digital backchannel for large class teaching. In A. Mendez-Vilas (Ed.), *Education in a Technological World: Communicating Current and Emerging Research and Technological Efforts* (pp. 364–371). Badajoz, Spain: Formatex.

boyd, d. (2013). *How would you define work in a networked world?* Available from www.linkedin.com/today/post/article/20130505193508-79695780-how-would-you-define-work-in-a-networked-world?

De Smet, M., Van Keer, H., & Valcke, M. (2008). Blending asynchronous discussion groups and peer tutoring in higher education: An exploratory study of online peer tutoring behaviour. *Computers & Education, 50*(1), 207–223.

Ipsos MORI. (2008). *Great expectations of ICT: How higher education institutions are measur-ing up.* London: Joint Information Systems Committee. Available from www.jisc.ac.uk/publications/publications/greatexpectations.aspx

Lampe, C., Wohn, Y., & Vitak, J. (2011). Student use of Facebook for organizing collaborative class-room activities. *Computer-Supported Collaborative Learning, 6*, 329–347.

Leander, K. M., & McKim, K. K. (2003). Tracing the everyday "sitings" of adolescents on the Inter-net: A strategic adaptation of ethnography across online and offline spaces. *Education, Communication and Information, 3*(2), 211–240.

Madge, C., Meek, J., Wellens, J., & Hooley, T. (2009). Facebook, social integration and informal learning at university: "It is more for socialising and talking to friends about work than for actually doing work." *Learning, Media and Technology, 34*(2), 141–155.

Manca, S. & Ranieri, M. (2013). Is it a tool suitable for learning? A critical review of the literature on Facebook as a technology-enhanced learning environment. *Journal of Computer Assisted Learning, 29*(6), 487–504.

Massey, D. (2005). *For space.* London: Sage.

Palmer, M., O'Kane, P., & Owens, M. (2009). Betwixt spaces: Student accounts of turning point experiences in the first-year transition. *Studies in Higher Education, 34*(1), 37–54.

Pohl, A., Gehlem-Baum, V., & Bry, F. (2011). Introducing Backstage—a digital backchannel for large class lectures. *Interactive Technology and Smart Education, 8*(3), 186–200.

Selwyn, N. (2009). Faceworking: Exploring students' education-related use of Facebook. *Learning, Media and Technology, 34*(2), 157–174.

Stirling, E. (2014). *Why waste your time on Facebook? A temporal analysis of first-year undergraduate students and transition in UK Higher Education.* (Unpublished doctoral dissertation). University of Sheffield.

Timmis, S. (2012). Constant companions: Instant messaging conversations as supportive study structures amongst undergraduate peers. *Computers & Education, 59,* 3–18.

Tinto, V. (2007). Taking student retention seriously, Syracuse University, Syracuse, NY.

Wang, Q., Woo, H. L., Quek, C. L., Yang, Y., & Liu, M. (2012). Using the Facebook group as a learning management system: An exploratory study. *British Journal of Educational Technology, 43*(3), 428–438.

Wilcox, P., Winn, S., & Fyvie-Gauld, M. (2005). "It was nothing to do with the university, it was just the people": The role of social support in the first-year experience of higher education. *Studies in Higher Education, 30*(6), 707–722.

Yorke, M., & Longden, B. (2008). *The first-year experience of higher education in the UK. Final report.* York, England: HE Academy.

4

Facebook as a Student Development Tool

SHANE TILTON

Department of Communication & Media Studies, Ohio Northern University

Facebook is one of the more popular online social networks that took advantage of the computer-mediated communication (CMC) services such as instant messaging, forums and direct messaging with publication services such as blogging and sharing of content to form a service that connected the members within the system to each other. This ability to connect was one of the key aspects leading to the quick adoption of Facebook by Americans ages 15 to 29 (Benbunan-Fich, Adler, & Mavlanova, 2009). This age group forms the primary cohort of students entering most colleges and universities throughout the world. Facebook on college campuses has been a point of interest to student development professionals as it allows those professionals to take a holistic view of how the student survives and succeeds in the higher education environment.

This chapter explores how online social networks, primarily Facebook, can be used by student development professionals as a tool to help understand the needs of college students. The idea of tool in this chapter refers simply as an instrument that allows student development professionals to analyze and communicate with the student body within the campus environment. To discuss the idea of Facebook as a student development tool, this chapter looks at understanding Facebook within the context of the social nature of Facebook interactions. In addition, there is a discussion on some of the key themes present when looking at how some first-year college students use Facebook within the context of the collegiate experience.

Studying Facebook

These themes and discussion points come from a yearlong triangulation study of first-year college students' use of Facebook to cope and adjust to their first 15 months of college (precollege to the end of their "freshman" year). About 180 students filled out an online survey based on standard coping mechanisms/modes of adjustment to see which ones the students used on a regular basis (Schwarzer & Schwarzer, 1996). These coping mechanisms/modes of adjustment were then framed under a social network analysis to see which of the coping mechanisms/modes of adjustment were being aided by Facebook (Ellison, Steinfield, & Lampe, 2007). This survey was followed by interviews with 18 of the survey takers. Those interviews expanded on the themes that were significant from the survey. Those themes were confirmed through a "guided ethnography" between myself and the interviewee in order to determine the validity of the theme. The interviewee was asked to go onto Facebook, and I asked a series of questions based on their actual use of Facebook with me sitting beside the interviewee as she or he was using Facebook (Tilton, 2012).

Presentations and interactions on Facebook by first-year students toward the established network of the campus must pass through the foreignness of the new collegiate environment. The quality of life for the first-year students who attend non-commuter colleges and universities depends on the quality of social relations within the combination of the living environment, classrooms and other communities within the collegiate environment. The social relationships created by first-year students are made complex by "residential mobility, spatially-dispersed relationships and activities [and] instantaneous distance-free communication" (Han, 2001, p. 2). These quality of life factors represent the changes that first-year students could face in their transition from high school life to college. All of the factors could represent foreign concepts to incoming first-year students, especially to students who are coming from smaller towns. The reason these factors could be especially problematic for those coming from smaller towns versus those coming from larger cities would relate to the "culture shock" the students from a small town would feel when encountering a population of people their age nearly the size of their entire hometown, which can potentially lead to digital divide issues for the students coming from these small towns (Gumprecht, 2010).

The Student Online Versus the Reality of Student Life

When talking about the schism between the perception of college life and the reality of college life to the average college student, it is important to note how newer technologies and user interfaces combine together to create a platform of expression and performance. The performance aspect of the platform is the nexus of the discussion. As on any other platform of performance, these performances are a hybrid of the reality of the current culture and the imaginary existence created by the performers. Users of Facebook can utilize the platform to "become the producers and stars of their productions as they create their own profiles and observe those of others" (Pempek, Yermolayeva, & Calvert, 2009). It is through the engagement with others in this realm that a process of "self-image negotiation" is started and maintained. These high-level, detailed cognitive processes force the user of the site to make determinations about not only themselves, but the other "characters on the screen" with regard to the reality of these presentations in the everyday life on campus. Others' behaviors on the site are combined with cross-references from the campus community as a representative model of campus life for the users. In return, the user presents his or her understanding of campus life through the channel of communication that is the personal feed (Rothenbuhler & Coman, 2005).

As newer services are added to Facebook and other online social networks, it is easy to make the argument that those sites go beyond the interpersonal mode of communication to a broadcast model of communication. If it is fair to make the argument that five years ago the foci of communication and community on Facebook was the group page, then now it is also fair to say that the foci of communication are the individual profile page and the construct of community are more loosely based on the informal individual social networks. The profile page has become a hybrid of the newspaper/newsletter model of delivering information post by post and a broadcast channel, allowing the individual user to select and add content in a parallel manner to a traditional broadcast station. The user in effect becomes the station manager with the major exception being the individual user does not have the limitation of time but rather "front page space." Only a few posts can exist on an individual's profile page at one time.

After being embedded within the individual's profile page, group page or other channel of engagement on Facebook, postings are deconstructed by the audience and allowed to create their own meaning from the content based on the content itself, the experience of the individual audience member, the current "cultural status quo" and the nature of the channel of communication (Hall, 1980). The performance becomes more abstract as the relationship between the user and the audience becomes more diffused. The audience of performance on Facebook varies depending on the level of privacy the user has chosen and where the user places artifacts within the walled garden of the user profile. If the user knows the posting will be shared with a selected few, the user would be more likely to narrow the message so the intended audience would be able to understand the message embedded in the artifact.

Key Themes

Regarding understanding Facebook as a student development tool, three key themes are present in the structure and the culture of the site. They are the following: Facebook is a point of awareness regarding events and issues that affected the students' community, Facebook is used as a point of engagement between the student and the rest of their community, and Facebook acts as a proxy for the larger collegiate community. The socio-technical practices of first-year students reinforce those key functional themes present in Facebook. These practices also changed as the interface and structure of Facebook changed throughout the academic year. Socio-technical barriers present in online social networks (persistence, searchability, replicability, and scalability) forced students to adapt to the changes in the online social network. Once a set of changes was finalized through Facebook, the students' ability to adapt to their new environment allowed them to maintain a connection to the large community. These changes also had an impact on how students negotiated key socialization issues, which affected how they presented themselves online (boyd, 2008).

Stream of Awareness

Stories about Facebook, or really any other CMC platforms, go through a series of phases. The new user to the site begins by attempting to become accustomed to the environment of the platform. During the course of getting used to the quirks of any computer program or website, individuals create their own "arrival stories" about getting the hang of using the format. Creating these arrival stories frames the connection between the individual and the platform. As the individuals move on from the initial exposure to the CMC to common use of the platform, the technology and the interface of the platform move to the background of the users' experiences and move out of the way so individuals can simply interact with other users on the network.

The constructed nature of this online social network was aided by the increase of interactions between the members of the network and the rapid spread of membership over the last six years. Facebook, much like other similar services, uses a feed to inform the users about the changes in their connections' status and changes to the overall environment. The changes to the overall environment of an online social network is a composite of structural changes to the network, the addition of groups and other nodes to the networks and mediated content tangent to the traditional status change of individual users. When looking at the first page after logging in or going to the website, the users are exposed to a linear progression of information. Some of this information comes in the form of mediated content and has to go through a level of encoding/decoding between the sender and the receiver. Part of the decoding process by the users comes from understanding not only the content itself but also from reading through all of the other content and information present on an individual's Facebook feed and from understanding the reaction by others to the information and content. An individual user can immediately look at comments and impressions related to an individual post on the feed. The zeitgeist of the users' selected communities is reviewable to all users of the overall network (regarding privacy settings and selective transmission of the user) and can be re-discussed and critically analyzed by others. This zeitgeist is the core connection to coping and adjustment to an online social network. The zeitgeist is better understood in relation to the individual user's "stream of awareness."

The stream of awareness, much like the overall construct of this awareness, has neither a concrete operational definition nor a solid review of literature. However, in this context, the stream of awareness could be considered a multilayered construction. The first layer is the simple structural definition associated with a stream of information. Users are exposed to a wide variety of social information and interactions within the construct of the "News Feed" of Facebook. The stream of information will fluctuate between personal one-on-one communication to the mass broadcasting of information and content for a much wider audience. From this understanding of the basic function of the News Feed, it would be easy to look at the individual users as passive consumers of information and content. However, during the course of this study, some noted differences were above and beyond a simple passive relationship between themselves and their News Feeds (Tapscott, 2009).

The second layer is the convergence between the social structures of campus life and the structure of the online social network itself. This structural point comes from a root change in how college students are more likely to communicate with one another. Within the structure of newer social media services is a type of CMC that allows for "semipublic" communication and social interactions and acts as a bridge between the private life of the individuals and the public displays of the users. Altering the modes of engagement between members of a community of location has led to a type of asynchronous "shared social experiences" that maintains the cohesiveness of the community at large. Short status messages or pointers to resources such as links to articles, photos and videos connect the community and provides a form of social capital for the individuals posting the content and information. If the content is "good" in the eyes of the community, the individuals' status will raise in the community. If the individuals provide valuable information for the community, the members of the community will be more likely to read the information. Because a traditional university setting would be considered a "highly connected social space," the consumption of information in a semipublic environment is a necessary outlet for the community (Naaman, Boase, & Lai, 2010). Regardless of how brief the content is or the issues of rhetoric that are traditionally associated with these types of semi-closed arenas of interaction, the function of such an arena is embedded in the discourse of the community at large and adds to the construct of the "stream of awareness" (ibid).

Point of Engagement

The development of identity in any online environment begins with the user engaging with this stream of information and producing content and artifacts that flow through the stream and potentially change the direction of the discourse. Identities evolve as the user allows aspects of themselves "to step outside" the interactions of the online social network to different environments that are less connected to the normative structure of services like Facebook (Turkle, 1997). This stepping out process reflects the ability to discuss interactions that occur on the network in a real world environment and/or detailing personal real world interactions online.

More important, the collaborative nature of most social networks allows the user of these services to step out from the network and talk with others. The ability to share artifacts outside the confines of these "walled gardens" is available through the link culture of the Internet and the availability of self-published works for general consumption. Groups are formed across platforms based on individual or collective social threads of interest or convenience.

The formation of a collective identity around these threads becomes a super-structure that members of the community can connect with and create points of engagement with others. The platform itself is not a barrier to engagement with other communities of interest, convenience and location but rather acts as another entry point to engage the community at large or parts of the community. The collective social threads are imported into the construction of the community across the different platforms and can allow for a centralized branding or identity of the community regardless of the channel of communication used for the interactions between community members (Kavada, 2009).

Social network sites represent a bridge to cross the social gaps that are present in the modern world. Gaps due to distance between the individual, time, finances or other points of disconnection are irrelevant if the community has a strong sense of identity and cultural ties. As discussed by boyd (2008), the formal or structured activities that students are exposed to at college begins to form the social support structure that helps the first year college student cope and/or adjust to academic life. The dorm environment and social network sites reinforce this skeleton as an unstructured environment that allows the first-year student to engage with peers in an informal manner and forces the student to examine and create his or her own social dynamic structure. The combination of formal and informal structures represents the overall social environment in which college students are engaged and represents a type of training that students must go through to survive real-world interactions.

"Real World" Community Builder

Some college students are able to connect to the day-to-day world of the university through the consistent feed of information about the campus that services like Facebook provide. For any online service to go beyond the structural needs of communication for a given community, the service must provide the elements of engagement that allow users of the service to take the interactions from the service and apply those interactions in the real world. These interactions are more than the simple textual postings found on one's profile page. The artifacts left on one's profile page by another user of the service can reflect a broad spectrum of content from the simple "guttural" expression of a person's existence to the more complex statements of status within the community. Those interactions that extend engagement between classmates from Facebook to campus life helps maintain the sense of community through multiple environments.

For Facebook to assist student development professionals to understand incoming first-year students and the campus community at large, there must be collaboration with others from both within the social network and on campus. Many of the functions embedded within Facebook would be considered community-building features within the site and in the real world. First, a centralized friend management system at the time of this research was relatively simple. Primarily, the friend management system in 2009 was binary within the network. A person was either your friend (a connection) or the person was not your friend (no connection). In addition, a person could be a member of one or more groups that you belong to or he or she belonged to none of your groups. The current version of Facebook, at the time of this writing, supported "friends lists" that allowed the user to organize friends into lists. These lists allowed the user to selectively distribute content to members of one or more lists. This friend management system should be considered as a parallel to the real-world social structure an individual would maintain on a daily basis (Barnes, 1972).

Understanding Facebook Beyond the Campus

Unsurprisingly, the world has changed over the past four years. The transition to a mobile public, at least in the United States, is starting to be seen in the daily lives of Americans and perhaps throughout the world. The allusion to the "ubiquity of wireless computing" that boyd examined in her work in 2008 is becoming part of everyday life. Future researchers should look at not only how the public is using online social networks in coping and adjusting to modernity but should look also at the use of mobile technology as a coping mechanism or mode of adjustment. As these devices are able to act as both the tools of production to create content and the channel of distribution to send information out to the world, these instruments are nodes to the massive mediated world. The thematic issues expressed in this work would be embedded in the overall, everyday norms of a more and more connected society. Even with this change, the understanding of small-town life and life in larger cities can be important to note as the role of socialization still occurs within the confines of the hometown. Social and cultural institutions that currently exist within the students' hometowns will most likely exist in the future. However, the relationships between the student and these institutions have the potential to differ due to the nature of social media and the movement toward a more connected society.

References

Barnes, J. A. (1972). *Social networks*. Reading, MA: Addison-Wesley.
Benbunan-Fich, R., Adler, R. F., & Mavlanova, T. (2009, August). *Patterns of home computer usage among college students: An exploratory study*. Paper presented at AMCIS 2009 Proceedings, San Francisco. Retrieved May 20, 2011, from http://aisel.aisnet.org/amcis2009/112/
boyd, d. (2008). *Taken out of context: American teen sociality in networked publics*. Berkeley: School of Information, University of California-Berkeley.

Ellison, N. B., Steinfield, C., & Lampe, C. (2007). The benefits of Facebook "friends:" Social capital and college students' use of online social network sites. *Journal of Computer-Mediated Communication, 12*(4), 1143–1168.

Gumprecht, B. (2010). *The American college town.* Amherst: University of Massachusetts Press.

Hall, S. (1980). Cultural studies: Two paradigms. *Media, Culture and Society, 2*, 57–72.

Han, B. (2001). *Reweaving the Fabric: A Theoretical Framework for the Study of the Social and Spatial Networks in the Traditional Neighbourhoods in Beijing, China.* Atlanta: Georgia Institute of Technology.

Kavada, A. (2009, September). *Engagement, bonding and identity across multiple platforms: Avaaz on Facebook, YouTube and MySpace.* Paper presented at Proceedings of the 2009 General Conference of the European Consortium for Political Research. Potsdam, Germany.

Naaman, M., Boase, J., & Lai, C. H. (2010, February). *Is it really about me? Message content in social awareness streams.* Paper presented at CSCW 2010, Savannah, Georgia. Retrieved March 20, 2011 from www.scribd.com/doc/23067105/Is-it-Really-About-Me-by-Mor-Naaman-Jeffrey-Boase-Chih-Hui-Lai

Pempek, T. A., Yermolayeva, Y. A., & Calvert, S. L. (2009). College student's social networking experiences on Facebook. *Journal of Applied Developmental Psychology, 30*, 227–238.

Rothenbuhler, E. W., & Coman, M. (Eds.). (2005). *Media anthropology.* Thousand Oaks: Sage.

Schwarzer, R., & Schwarzer, C. (1996). *A critical survey of coping instruments. Handbook of coping: Theory, research, applications.* New York, NY: John Wiley & Sons Inc.

Tapscott, D. (2009). *Grown up digital: How the net generation is changing your world.* New York, NY: McGraw-Hill.

Tilton, S. (2012). *First year students in a foreign fabric: A triangulation study on Facebook as a method of coping/adjustment* (Doctoral dissertation). Retrieved from ProQuest Dissertations and Theses. (Accession Order No. AAT 3561420)

Turkle, S. (1997). *Life on the screen: Identity in the age of the Internet.* New York, NY: Touchstone.

Part 2
Facebook in Learning and Teaching

5

Beyond Friending: Psychosocial Engagement on Facebook and its Implications for Academic Success

CATHERINE McLOUGHLIN

Australian Catholic University

MARK J. W. LEE

Charles Sturt University

Web 2.0 technologies and social networking tools offer alternative ways for conceptualizing and delivering education and are catalyzing shifts in the way learners work, think, and construct knowledge (Lee & McLoughlin, 2010; McLoughlin & Lee, 2010). The advent and growth of these tools and technologies have been paralleled by a heightened emphasis on student-centered pedagogies, and they have garnered much attention among educators, many of whom see them as having the potential to address issues of student demotivation and disengagement with didactic modes of teaching. Facebook, the world's most popular social networking site (SNS) with a reported 1.11 billion active users (Facebook, 2013), is now widely used by students across the higher education sector, and there is substantial research into online behaviors and interaction patterns on this site that yields insight into how identity formation, social connectedness, and informal learning take place (Madge, Meek, Wellens, & Hooley, 2009; Wilson, Gosling, & Graham, 2012; Zhao, Grasmuck, & Martin, 2012). However, enthusiasm and eagerness to adopt Facebook in formal teaching–learning environments may be outpacing our understanding of how it might best be used. This chasm in understanding needs to be bridged if we are to develop effective learning designs and strategies that capitalize on the capabilities and affordances of the technology in pedagogically sound ways.

There is a great deal to be learned from delving into the experiences of students and understanding the learning process from their perspective, including if, why, and how they want to use Facebook. The popular media and academic discourse alike are rife with speculations on the issue of whether Facebook is beneficial for learning. Many hold pessimistic views. For example, Facebook can be seen as a convenient tool for procrastinating, gossiping, and relieving boredom or simply a source of diversion during lectures (Buffardi & Campbell, 2008). Investigations based on self-reported motivations for use of Facebook reveal that relational needs like keeping tabs on one's social network and maintaining relationships are frequently cited; such activities often provide distraction (Madge et al., 2009; Wilson et al., 2012) and can fuel stress and anxiety, together with feelings of insecurity and inadequacy (Donnelly, 2012). Several studies have also pointed to other negative consequences that may arise from Facebook use, including addiction (Andreassen, Torsheim, Brunborg, & Pallesen, 2012) and cyberbullying (Kwan & Skoric, 2013). Nevertheless, there is a consistent thread of research attesting to the fact that social bonding and connectivity are important elements of learning that lead to improved engagement (Kuh, 2009). The work of Cain and Policastri (2011) and Kalpidou, Costin, and Morris (2011), among others, indicates that student-to-student engagement, locus of control, relational communication, and belonging to a community on Facebook can build confidence and foster social engagement in learning through the sharing of ideas and the seeking of assistance from friends and peers. The real value of Facebook is therefore arguably of a psychosocial nature: by establishing supportive links with peers and engaging in constructive dialogue, students become more positive about the learning space and experience a psychological sense of community. Hence, the case can be made for learning as a connected, social, and networked phenomenon. This view is not without its opponents, however. As Friesen and Lowe (2011, p. 190) argue,

> Knowledge is not exclusively embodied in ever-growing networks of connection and affiliation and it does not just occur through building and traversing these proliferating nodes and links. Education is clearly a social process but it is probably much closer to an ongoing discussion or debate than an extended celebration with an ever-expanding network of friends.

The focus of this chapter is on the value and benefits that Facebook networking brings to the psychosocial aspects of learning, which may have an impact on academic performance, persistence, and success. "Psychosocial engagement" is a term used to describe the investment of psychological energy into the social facets of the educational experience (Braxton, Hirschy, & McClendon, 2004). By examining the outcomes of a number of empirical studies and presenting several theoretical frameworks to demonstrate the centrality of networked practices, participation, and peer-to-peer communication, we argue that Facebook interactions are more than just "friending" and can provide emotional support, exchange of resources, and essential socio-cognitive experiences that are pivotal to effective learning. In the ensuing sections, we adopt a synthesis of social presence (Short, Williams, & Christie, 1976) and social capital (Burt, 2005) theories and learning community constructs (Wenger, McDermott, & Snyder, 2002) to show that involvement in Facebook dialogue and connectivity can enable students to engage socially, cognitively, and emotionally and can promote a psychological sense of community. These dimensions of engagement underpin cognitive development and academic achievement.

Fostering Social Presence through Facebook

A key finding reported in the literature on students' experiences in technology-enhanced learning environments is that access to peer support, interaction, and conversation raises both perception of social presence and motivation (Dron & Anderson, 2009). Definitions of *social presence* that have been proposed vary quite significantly, but the term originated in the field of communication psychology and was first characterized as "the degree of salience of the other person in the interaction and the consequent salience of the interpersonal relationships" (Short et al., 1976, p. 65). The array of terms used to portray the topic illustrates the breadth of its scope, and it includes social presence, telepresence, immediacy, transactional distance, and transactional presence—all of which refer to concepts linked to the criticality of interpersonal presence and relational value of communication.

The idea that a sense of personal presence can be conveyed through technology is very relevant to the use of Facebook in learning environments. As e-learning and blended modes of delivery have become more widespread in higher education, students often remain invisible to one another, with limited levels of connectivity (Tu & McIsaac, 2002). Social software tools present interaction affordances that make possible rich and engaging forms of multimodal collaboration, allowing students and instructors to become more directly visible to and socially present with one another. These elements of social presence have been acknowledged to be major motivators for students' use of Facebook to support their university studies (English & Duncan-Howell, 2008). In an Australian study, Wise, Skues, and Williams (2011) found that Facebook played a minimal role in boosting academic achievement, but may indirectly improve academic engagement for passive students by strengthening interpersonal bonds, which can increase participation in collaborative learning. It is this type of affordance—that is, enabling social presence and personalization—that offers the greatest potential to advance learning from a psychosocial standpoint. Evidence from the psychological literature also reflects the notion that social interaction and mutuality positively aid general cognitive functioning (Ybarra et al., 2008). The social presence brought about by Facebook friendships and ties exemplifies the effect that perceived immediacy of peers and instructors has on engagement in online learning, and it adds value to the learning experience by expanding networks of interaction, making the experience more personal and meaningful. The socio-cognitive benefits of Facebook that lend themselves to academic engagement are further analyzed through the lenses of social capital and learning community theories in the sections that follow.

Growing Social Capital with Facebook

Social capital is a multidimensional construct encompassing participation, social and political engagement, life satisfaction, and social trust. The term has two components: *bridging* and *bonding* social capital. The former refers to loose connections between individuals who may supply one another with useful information and/or new perspectives but who are not familiar enough to provide emotional support; the latter is found between individuals in tightly knit, emotionally proximate relationships, such as family members and close friends (Burt, 2005). Studies have shown that social relationships significantly affect the ways individuals seek information and that students are likely to want to communicate with others while learning online or on campus (Kobayashi, Ikeda, & Miyata, 2006). Social capital theory posits that individuals tend to look to existing social networks for information that is easily accessible, relevant, and contextually rich, seeking to gain understandings from others within those networks who are engaged in similar activities.

Social capital theory is useful because it affords a deeper understanding of the connections between individuals on Facebook. In a world where social media are ubiquitous, learning is no longer seen as a purely solitary, individualistic pursuit. Connective technologies such as Facebook enable the generation of social capital through the building of relationships and flow of knowledge between members of the academic community, including friends, associates, and teachers/lecturers. Facebook offers opportunities to create, enhance, and rediscover social ties that make a difference in students' lives, especially when they are in periods of transition, for instance, entering university or living away from home. The connectedness that emerges as a result of online social relationships and activities is important as it signifies the interdependence among people and may lead to offline collaboration, mutual support, and psychosocial wellbeing (Kop, Fournier, & Mak, 2011).

Ellison, Steinfield, and Lampe (2007) looked at the role of Facebook in the construction and maintenance of social capital. Their study examined the relationship between Facebook use and social capital—both bonding and bridging, along with a further dimension called "maintained social capital" (Ellison et al., 2007, p. 1146) that refers to the ability to stay connected. The results signal a clear association between use of Facebook and the three types of social capital, with the strongest relationship being to bridging social capital. In addition, Facebook usage was found to interact with measures of psychological well-being, suggesting that it might provide greater benefits for individuals experiencing low self-esteem. Other researchers claim that web-mediated interaction contributes to the production of what has been termed networked social capital, that is, the accumulation of a stock of knowledge, information, and trust derived within virtual networks themselves (Ginger, 2008; van Bavel, Punie, & Tuomi, 2004). Ellison, Steinfield, and Lampe (2011) and Kirschner and Karpinski (2010) found that passive use of Facebook or simply friending did not have any strong influence on social capital outcomes, but that connection strategies, help seeking, and information sharing were behaviors that would lead to bridging social capital and support socio-cognitive interactions. This view of social networks as valuable resources resonates with Siemens's (2005) connectivist stance on how people learn, communicate, and produce knowledge in the digital age.

Cultivating Learning Communities on Facebook

A learning community is a group of people with common interests, values, and/ or goals, who actively learn with and from one another. This form of participatory learning embodies a culture in which "everyone is engaged in a collective effort of understanding" (Bielaczyc & Collins, 1999, p. 5). It fits in with Vygotsky's (1978) theory of social constructivism, which recognizes students' contributions to and involvement in the learning trajectories of their peers.

Feldman (2000) suggests that in the new millennium, we are witnessing a movement from the "age of the individual to the era of community" (p. xiii). Learning communities, both face-to-face and virtual, supported by social media, are a manifestation of this movement, and we interpret the aim as "to strike a balance between individuality and social connectedness . . . relationship, participation, reciprocity, membership, and collaboration must play [an essential role] in any theory of human development" (Feldman, 2000, p. xiii).

Communities of practice (CoPs) constitute a type of learning community to which the online environment is particularly conducive. According to Wenger et al. (2002), CoPs comprise three elements that are crucial in distinguishing them from other groups and communities. This framework can be used to explain how knowledge creation and sharing occur and are sustained in online social networks:

1. *The domain:* A CoP is something more than a club of friends or a set of connections between acquaintances. In Facebook, the domain is the common ground or space where members share ideas, knowledge, and experiences. This gives rise to personal meaning and a sense of belonging.
2. *The community:* According to Wenger, Trayner, and de Laat (2011), members of the community collectively create value and knowledge though their exchanges and dealings. SNSs such as Facebook can help build community by serving as forums for dialogue, discussion, and debate (Reich, 2010).

3. *The practice:* Whereas the domain denotes the topic or concern that is shared, the practice is the specific knowledge base that the community jointly cultivates and maintains. Facebook offers ways to learn through interactive dialogue and discovery, and can involve multiple viewpoints and levels of expertise. In addition, there is negotiation of meaning as individuals refine and share their ideas and form new understandings. These processes lead to distributed knowledge production (Lee, McLoughlin, & Chan, 2008; Poellhuber, Anderson, & Roy, 2011).

Table 5.1 displays a number of further examples, drawn from the scholarly literature, of the use of Facebook as a platform for building CoPs to meet a variety of goals in different discipline-based university teaching and learning contexts.

Table 5.1 Examples of Facebook-based learning communities/communities of practice in higher education

Source	Facebook Use	Outcomes/Findings
Buzzetto-More (2012)	A Facebook group was used as part of a management course to augment instruction and learning tasks undertaken within the Blackboard learning management system (LMS).	Blackboard was preferred for course announcements and for links to course resources; Facebook was considered overwhelmingly superior for community building and facilitating class discussions.
Cain & Policastri (2011)	Facebook was used for optional activities in a pharmacy management and leadership course to expose students to the perspectives of experts and to issues not covered in the core content of the course.	Students appreciated the informal learning strategy of using Facebook and the optional character of participation with no instructor-imposed interaction requirements. The informality of the learning environment appeared to be one of the primary elements of its success.
Çoklar (2012)	Facebook was used to house a supportive learning environment enabling students in a science history course to share resources about course topics.	Facebook was found to have advantages for sharing information, arousing interest, engendering motivation, offering social interaction opportunities, and facilitating informal learning.

Source	Facebook Use	Outcomes/Findings
English & Duncan-Howell (2008)	Facebook was used to support pre-service teachers undertaking their field practicum.	The majority of communication on Facebook was of an affective nature, for the purposes of group reinforcement, encouragement, and building of community.
LaRue (2012)	Facebook was used in place of an LMS in a graduate-level nursing informatics course.	A peer-to-peer learning environment was established that encouraged student co-creation of knowledge artifacts. Students assumed the roles of both producers and consumers of information, teaching and coaching one another while the instructor served as a facilitator.
McCarthy (2010)	Facebook was used as a platform for an online mentoring scheme linking two digital media student cohorts: an undergraduate cohort in the United States and a postgraduate cohort in Australia.	The US students received valuable guidance and critiques on their work-in-progress imagery from their more experienced Australian counterparts, to which they responded positively. The Australian students obtained support from peers, faculty, and associated professionals in the US as well as from local industry professionals and recent graduates.
Wang (2012)	Facebook was used as a shared virtual space for a cross-cultural project involving Taiwanese students studying a learning technology course and American students studying a computer education course.	Facebook proved to be an ideal venue for intercultural competence development and cooperative learning. Language barriers and social inhibitions were reduced. The site was found to exhibit great potential as a medium for promoting student communication and collaboration, provided it is used within a sound learning design incorporating appropriate scaffolds to stimulate and assist participation.

Conclusion

The impact of Facebook on learning ranges far beyond technological inter-activity and the ability to amass a collection of contacts. Studies reviewed in this chapter indicate that participation in Facebook communities may be an effective means of social integration among higher education students, while belonging to online friendship networks can be associated with positive life satisfaction and sense of connectedness for these students. As social media are now embedded in everyday life and continue to enjoy uptake in academia, tradi-tional teaching methods are being challenged by demand for student-centered pedagogies that place emphasis on knowledge capital emerging through learn-ing communities (Ozturk & Ozcinar, 2013). Students now expect to spend more time engaged in various forms of informal and self-directed learning outside of formal educational settings, and they are increasingly tapping into the vast media-facilitated resources of Facebook, Web 2.0, and the Internet at large. In this chapter, we have made a case for Facebook-mediated interaction, informa-tion sharing, and relationship building as vehicles for socio-cognitive learning and development. More and more, research from the fields of applied psychol-ogy, sociology, and health demonstrates that social supports and transactions on SNSs play a major role in the nurturing and preservation of interpersonal relationships, leading to mutual engagement, social rapport, and a sense of well-being.

It is evident that socially oriented digital media will remain a powerful tool for connecting students and cultivating community among them. Although pedagogical advances are not highly visible in published research or are even advocated (Selwyn, 2009), Facebook and similar social networking platforms would appear to have a future as mainstream communication devices in our society as well as venues for socio-cognitive activity. However, successful inte-gration of Facebook into learning environments is dependent on whether teaching staff have the pedagogical will and the skill to use this tool to its best advantage. This entails promoting peer-to-peer collaboration, encouraging higher order thinking, as well as making students' experiences meaningful and authentic by leveraging opportunities for informal learning and inquiry. In striving to exploit the social and communicative affordances of Facebook, higher educators face the imperative of aligning teaching and learning pro-cesses with social learning outcomes.

In conclusion, Facebook presents opportunities for learner engagement and innovative pedagogy by offering a more accessible and connected world wherein students commune and collaborate with others online. The capacity for students to create and maintain connections, to experience social presence, and to build and partake in a community is an important benefit of Facebook use in higher education. As teaching strategies shift toward more personalized, participatory, and productive learning approaches (McLoughlin & Lee, 2008), SNSs such as Facebook empower students by giving them a voice and medium for self-expression as well as a virtual space within which they can interact and contribute to the generation of shared ideas and resources. These processes can be powerful drivers of psychosocial engagement, which is fundamental to learning and education in the 21st century.

References

Andreassen, C. S., Torsheim, T., Brunborg, G. S., & Pallesen, S. (2012). Development of a Facebook addiction scale. *Psychological Reports, 110*(2), 501–517.

Bielaczyc, K., & Collins, A. (1999). Learning communities in classrooms: Advancing knowledge for a lifetime. *NASSP Bulletin, 83*(604), 4–10.

Braxton, J. M., Hirschy, A. S., & McClendon, S. A. (2004). *Understanding and reducing college student departure.* San Francisco, CA: Jossey-Bass.

Buffardi, L. E., & Campbell, W. K. (2008). Narcissism and social networking web sites. *Personality and Social Psychology Bulletin, 34*(10), 1303–1314.

Burt, R. S. (2005). The contingent value of social capital. *Administrative Science Quarterly, 42*(2), 339–365.

Buzzetto-More, N. A. (2012). Social networking in undergraduate education. *Interdisciplinary Journal of Information, Knowledge, and Management, 7,* 63–90.

Cain, J., & Policastri, A. (2011). Using Facebook as an informal learning environment. *American Journal of Pharmaceutical Education, 75*(10), 207.

Çoklar, A. N. (2012). Evaluations of students on Facebook as an educational environment. *Turkish Online Journal of Qualitative Inquiry, 3*(2), 42–53.

Donnelly, T. (2012, July 8). Facebook and Twitter feed anxiety, study finds. *The Telegraph.* Retrieved from www.telegraph.co.uk

Dron, J., & Anderson, T. (2009). How the crowd can teach. In S. Hatzipanagos & S. Warburton (Eds.), *Handbook of research on social software and developing community ontologies* (pp. 1–17). Hershey, PA: IGI Global.

Ellison, N. B., Steinfield, C., & Lampe, C. (2007). The benefits of Facebook "friends:" Social capital and college students' use of online social network sites. *Journal of Computer-Mediated Communication, 12*(4), 1143–1168.

Ellison, N. B., Steinfield, C., & Lampe, C. (2011). Connection strategies: Social capital implications of Facebook-enabled communication practices. *New Media & Society, 13*(6), 873–892.

English, R., & Duncan-Howell, J. (2008). Facebook© goes to college: Using social networking tools to support students undertaking teaching practicum. *MERLOT Journal of Online Learning and Teaching, 4*(4), 596–601.

Facebook. (2013). Facebook reports first quarter 2013 results [Press release]. Retrieved from http://investor.fb.com/releasedetail.cfm?ReleaseID=761090

Feldman, D. H. (2000). Foreword. In V. John-Steiner (Ed.), *Creative collaboration* (pp. ix–xiii). New York, NY: Oxford University Press.

Friesen, N., & Lowe, S. (2011). The questionable promise of social media for education: Connective learning and the commercial imperative. *Journal of Computer Assisted Learning, 28*(3), 183–194.

Ginger, J. (2008). *The Facebook project: Social capital and the chief.* Retrieved from www.ideals.illinois.edu/handle/2142/3669

Kalpidou, M., Costin, D., & Morris, J. (2011). The relationship between Facebook and the well-being of undergraduate college students. *Cyberpsychology, Behavior, and Social Networking, 14*(4), 183–189.

Kirschner, P. A., & Karpinski, A. C. (2010). Facebook® and academic performance. *Computers in Human Behavior, 26*(6), 1237–1245.

Kobayashi, T., Ikeda, K., & Miyata, K. (2006). Social capital online: Collective use of the Internet and reciprocity as lubricants of democracy. *Information, Communication & Society, 9*(5), 582–611.

Kop, R., Fournier, H., & Mak, J. S. F. (2011). A pedagogy of abundance or a pedagogy to support human beings? Participant support on massive open online courses. *The International Review of Research in Open and Distance Learning, 12*(7), 74–93.

Kuh, G. D. (2009). What student affairs professionals need to know about student engagement. *Journal of College Student Development, 50*(6), 683–706.

Kwan, G. C. E., & Skoric, M. M. (2013). Facebook bullying: An extension of battles in school. *Computers in Human Behavior, 29*(1), 16–25.

LaRue, E. M. (2012). Using Facebook as course management software: A case study. *Teaching and Learning in Nursing, 7*(17), 17–22.

Lee, M. J. W., & McLoughlin, C. (2010). Beyond distance and time constraints: Applying social networking tools and Web 2.0 approaches to distance learning. In G. Veletsianos (Ed.), *Emerging technologies in distance education* (pp. 61–87). Edmonton, Canada: Athabasca University Press.

Lee, M. J. W., McLoughlin, C., & Chan, A. (2008). Talk the talk: Learner-generated podcasts as catalysts for knowledge creation. *British Journal of Educational Technology, 39*(3), 501–521.

Madge, C., Meek, J., Wellens, J., & Hooley, T. (2009). Facebook, social integration and informal learning at university: "It is more for socialising and talking to friends about work than for actually doing work." *Learning, Media and Technology, 34*(2), 141–155.

McCarthy, J. (2012). International design collaboration and mentoring for tertiary students through Facebook. *Australasian Journal of Educational Technology, 28*(5), 755–775.

McLoughlin, C., & Lee, M. J. W. (2008). The 3 P's of pedagogy for the networked society: Personalization, participation, and productivity. *International Journal of Teaching and Learning in Higher Education, 20*(1), 10–27.

McLoughlin, C., & Lee, M. J. W. (2010). Personalised and self-regulated learning in the Web 2.0 era: International exemplars of innovative pedagogy using social software. *Australasian Journal of Educational Technology, 26*(1), 28–43.

Ozturk, H. T., & Ozcinar, H. (2013). Learning in multiple communities from the perspective of knowledge capital. *The International Review of Research in Open and Distance Learning, 14*(1), 204–221.

Poellhuber, B., Anderson, T., & Roy, N. (2011). Distance students' readiness for social media and collaboration. *The International Review of Research in Open and Distance Learning, 12*(6), 102–125.

Reich, S. M. (2010). Adolescents' sense of community on MySpace and Facebook: A mixed methods approach. *Journal of Community Psychology, 38*(6), 688–705.

Selwyn, N. (2009). Faceworking: Exploring students' education-related use of Facebook. *Learning, Media and Technology, 34*(2), 157–174.

Short, J., Williams, E., & Christie, B. (1976). *The social psychology of telecommunications.* New York, NY: Wiley.

Siemens, G. (2005). *Connectivism: Learning as network-creation.* Retrieved from www.elearnspace. org/Articles/networks.htm

Tu, C.-H., & McIsaac, M. (2002). The relationship of social presence and interaction in online classes. *American Journal of Distance Education, 16*(3), 131–150.

van Bavel, R., Punie, Y., & Tuomi, I. (2004). ICT-enabled changes in social capital. *The IPTS Report,* 85. Retrieved from http://ipts.jrc.ec.europa.eu/home/report/english/about/IPTS_report. htm

Vygotsky, L. S. (1978). *Mind in society: The development of higher psychological processes.* Cambridge, MA: Harvard University Press.

Wang, C.-M. (2012). Using Facebook for cross-cultural collaboration: The experience of students from Taiwan. *Educational Media International, 49*(1), 63–76.

Wenger, E., McDermott, R. A., & Snyder, W. M. (2002). *Cultivating communities of practice: A guide to managing knowledge.* Boston, MA: Harvard Business School.

Wenger, E., Trayner, B., & de Laat, M. (2011). *Promoting and assessing value creation in communities and networks: A conceptual framework.* Heerlen, Netherlands: Open University of the Netherlands, Ruud de Moor Centrum.

Wilson, R. E., Gosling, S. D., & Graham, L. T. (2012). A review of Facebook research in the social sciences. *Perspectives on Psychological Science, 7*(3), 203–220.

Wise, L. Z., Skues, J., & Williams, B. (2011). Facebook in higher education promotes social but not academic engagement. In G. Williams, N. Brown, M. Pittard, & B. Cleland (Eds.), *Changing demands, changing directions. Proceedings ascilite Hobart 2011* (pp. 1332–1342). Hobart, Australia: University of Tasmania.

Ybarra, O., Burnstein, E., Winkielman, P., Keller, M. C., Manis, M., Chan, E., & Rodriguez, J. (2008). Mental exercising through simple socializing: Social interaction promotes general cognitive functioning. *Personality and Social Psychology Bulletin, 34*(2), 248–259.

Zhao, S., Grasmuck, S., & Martin, J. (2012). Identity construction on Facebook: Digital empowerment in anchored relationships. *Computers in Human Behavior, 24*(5), 1816–1836.

6

What's on Your Mind? Facebook as a Forum for Learning and Teaching in Higher Education

MIKE KENT

Curtin University

What's on your mind? Facebook confronts users with this question at the top of their home page each time they log in. This call to reflect on our thoughts resonates with questions posed in learning and education. This chapter examines the benefits that can be found in teaching in a venue in which students are already active participants (Bateman & Willems, 2012). While students can create and use their own Facebook groups in relation to their studies (Haverback, 2009), this chapter focuses on the affordances of using this social network as an official space for learning and teaching. As McLaughlin and Lee (2010, p. 28) note, "Students want an active learning experience that is social, participatory and supported by rich media." Facebook is an ideal venue to provide such an experience.

This chapter, following from Allen (2012), explores how Facebook group pages can be used as a venue for learning and teaching in higher education for both fully online courses and for courses that blend on-campus and Internet-based education. It discusses the many advantages to using these groups as a discussion forum, where the majority of students are already familiar with the format and in an online space that they visit frequently (Junco, 2013). It further argues that the use of Facebook changes the nature of the online discussion from a more traditional learning management system (LMS) discussion board. This transformation can lead to a blurring of the traditional understanding of asynchronous communications in these online discussions (see Darics, in press) as well as change the parameters of the discussion to result in a more strongly developed community of learning. While acknowledging that there are significant challenges, including issues of privacy and appropriate boundaries, issues around the copyright of material posted on Facebook and the use of an external privately owned and for-profit online platform for university teaching, the chapter concludes that Facebook does provide a potential in this context that make it a greater opportunity than a threat.

A number of benefits have been identified with utilizing Facebook in learning and teaching in higher education. Facebook has been shown to help students create communities (Cluett, 2010), and act as a venue where students can collaborate and communicate with their peers (Grey, Lucas & Kennedy, 2010). Chang and Lee (2013) noted the positive level of trust developed in Facebook communities in a learning environment, and Ellison, Steinfield and Lampe (2007) also noted its role in helping students develop and maintain social capital. Grey, Lucas and Kennedy (2010) observed that Facebook is easier to use than many existing LMS discussion forums, and similarly, Bateman and Willems (2012) found students access Facebook more than traditional LMS. Dabner (2012) also observed the robust nature of Facebook as a platform for communications in higher education, and Ellis (2011) found that Facebook is the most accessible social network for students with disabilities.

Facebook Groups

Karl and Peluchette (2011) raise pertinent concerns about unequal power relations between faculty and students in becoming Facebook friends in order to better interact on the network. A useful alternative to this is for staff and students in a course of study to share a Facebook group created specifically for the purpose. These groups provide many of the communications and discussion forum benefits of being Facebook friends without the same level of disclosure that comes from access to each individual's private Facebook profile and other information.

Using a closed Facebook group means that each member has to be approved by a moderator before he or she is able to participate. Posts made in the group are not visible to the public. Members of the group are able to see posts, receive alerts when there are new posts and send private messages to other members of the group. However, they do not necessarily provide members access to each other's profiles, thus potentially avoiding access to their Facebook posts outside the forum, photos and other personal information. This provides all members of the group a higher level of privacy and a better separation of a formal learning environment and student and staff's personal online space. As Allen (2012) observes, Facebook groups "are a kind of limited collaboration application, inbuilt within Facebook, but kept somewhat distinct through the capacity to keep group and other activity separate" (p. 215).

Facebook groups provide two different, although complementary, forms of utility as both a method of communications between group members and a forum for discussion and exchange of ideas. Karl and Peluchette (2011) observed that teaching staff found that using Facebook was a much quicker way to communicate with students than was e-mail. This communication can take a number of forms. Overtly it can involve posting in the discussion forum for all to read; it can also involve tagging a particular individual in a post, a link or a picture so that they receive an alert about the posting. Similarly, members of the same group can use the network to send each other a private direct message or engage in real time text chat.

Part of the reason that this method of communication is so efficient when compared to more traditional discussion forums or e-mails is the level of engagement that many of the students have with Facebook (Junco, 2013; Smith & Caruso, 2010). This is partly due to ease of access. Facebook presents a user with a single login. Students accessing a university LMS or even e-mail will often have to navigate a number of screens to log in and access information. Although students and staff may be visiting Facebook for personal reasons, they will also be made aware of any updates to a formal learning group and any messages they may have received. In addition to this, more traditional access through the World Wide Web, Facebook is increasingly integrated into the mobile devices that people carry with them. Shim, Dekleva, Guo and Mittleman (2011) note this integration bridges professional and social contexts and encourages information exchange. Facebook pushes information out automatically to both mobile devices, and its own website alerts users to new posts, comments on their posts and messages. This contrasts with the pull approach of traditional LMSs and e-mail where users need to actively seek out the information.

In addition to this greater access to overt forms of communications on Facebook the network also offers a number of other affordances. Phillips (2011) noted the value of the "Like" function of users' posts as an additional avenue of communications. Similarly, other functions, such as reporting when a message has been seen, or how many in a group have seen a particular post, provides additional texture to these communications that can be particularly valuable in an educational context. Daric (in press) studied corporate instant messaging networks that share many features with Facebook groups and observe that this type of always-on communications can challenge traditional understandings of synchronous and asynchronous communication. Combined with the push approach to content Facebook adopts, it creates a stronger sense of co-presence for participants.

As well as a method of communication, Facebook groups also offer advantages as a venue for online discussion. Gao, Zhang and Franklin's (2013) research suggests that threaded discussion forums—one of the most common discussion environments in traditional LMS—do not foster online discussions naturally. As Dabbagh and Kitsantas (2012, p. 3) observe, traditional learning management systems do not "capitalize on the pedagogical affordances of social media." By providing a single feed of posts and comments, with the most recent activity moving to the top of the page, Facebook group discussions create a different type of forum, that as Kayri and Çakir (2010, p. 56) observes "brings many educational advantages."

This level of engagement is facilitated by the stronger sense of co-presence for participants observed by Daric (in press). This is quite different to the more formally asynchronous communications that are the purpose of threaded discussions. They also mirror the interactions that people engage in as part of their normal online social activity through Facebook, rather than the more artificial threaded discussion forums that are more reminiscent of Usenet or a bulletin board system from the early pre-web Internet, and beyond the experience of the majority of people. As Allen (2012, p. 220) notes Facebook has actually "educated people away from threaded discussion and produced new online conversational conventions." A Facebook group provides a greater ability to leverage student and staff's existing literacies. As a result, their focus can be on the content, rather than learning how to appropriately make use of the online venue.

This combination of communications, co-presence and discussion forum enables a more authentic community of learning. Bateman and Willems (2012) note Facebook creates a social community for a geographically dispersed cohort and engages peer teaching and resource sharing. Bicen and Cavus (2011) similarly note that the use of Facebook in this context can maintain and strengthen social ties that can be beneficial in an academic setting. As Mazman and Usluel (2010) observe,

> Because students complain about lacking opportunities for authentic communications due to non-personalized course content even when alternative delivery methods are employed, providing informal learning contexts by integrating emerging social networks into existing learning practices becomes significantly important to attain more robust learning and teaching opportunities.
>
> (p. 144)

This greater sense of co-presence and community changes the form and content of discussion when a Facebook group is used as a formal online forum. There is a higher level of student activity. Schroeder and Greenbowe (2009) observed that the number of posts that students made increased by nearly 400% when using Facebook. The type of activity also changes. Kayri and Çakir (2010) found that learning was shaped by students and that learning material was developed by students. Similarly, Bateman and Willems (2012) found that the use of Facebook promotes peer teaching and resource sharing.

A recent study comparing the use of both of Facebook groups and more traditional threaded forums through a university LMS confirms these findings (see Kent, in press). Student activity was seen to increase in a Facebook group in line with Schroeder and Greenbowe's (2009) observations. This additional activity also extended across the whole period of study rather than just as spikes in activity and then periods of relative silence found in the LMS-based discussion. The nature of the discourse was also different when using Facebook with students bringing more external material into the discussion, following the findings of Kayri and Çakir (2010) and Bateman and Willems (2012). Much of this additional material consisted of links to other articles and videos hosted on the Internet as students took advantage of the rich media environment noted by McLaughlin and Lee (2010). Although there was an increase in off topic, or social, engagement, the majority of this additional student activity related to course learning activities and discussion.

Cautions

Although there are great potential advantages that can come with the use of Facebook groups, a number of cautions also need to be acknowledged. Although there are advantages that come from using a venue with which both students and staff are familiar, this literacy with the network for all participants is not something that can necessarily be taken for granted. As McCarthy (2010) notes students will have a variety of skills in the use of this type of technology. This will also be the case for teaching staff. Lenartz (2012) found that the most common problems were associated with students and staff posting inappropriate material to their profile page. Although the use of Facebook groups limits the problems this might cause, this requires those involved to have appropriate privacy setting activated. Hew and Cheung (2012) found that most students were unconcerned about privacy, and Facebook's chief privacy officer has reported that only 20% of Facebook users have changed their privacy settings from the default (Stross, 2009). The privacy provided by the use of a Facebook group may be more a potential than actual, or worse illusionary, for the participants without adequate understanding of the privacy settings on their individual Facebook profiles. A further complication with this is that often teachers and students feel the need to self-disclose in order to garner credibility (see Mazer, Murphy, & Simonds, 2009). Despite one of the advantages of Facebook being the level of familiarity that the majority of staff and students will have with the platform, this should not be taken for granted, especially in relation to privacy. The key to ensuring that personal control is maintained over privacy is through explicit education as part of a course's learning material.

Bateman and Willems (2012) noted that Facebook blurs the boundaries between formal and informal education and the professional and social lives of both students and staff. Allen (2012) observed how this can act to challenge the traditional relationships in higher education between students and teachers. Similarly, Best, Hajzler, Pancini and Tout (2011) found that there is resistance from students to faculty intrusion into their 'private' Facebook space. Teclehaimanot and Hickman (2011) note that students might feel it is inappropriate to deal with university staff on Facebook. Using Facebook as an official space for learning and teaching will mean that these boundaries will need to be carefully negotiated and, in some cases, renegotiated between the students and staff involved. Although there have been these observations of initial resistance from students and staff to using Facebook in this way Kayri and Çakir (2010) found that students who have used Facebook as an educational platform develop a more positive view of its use in this manner than those who have not.

An additional concern for both staff and students is the impact on work life balance that having a formal learning and teaching space sit within what would normally be a social space online. Sappy and Relf (2010) noted that the use of information and communication technology (ICT) in general has benefits for both staff and students but teaching labor can become invisible. Similarly, Heijstra and Rafnsdottir (2010) noted both the positive benefits of e-learning and its potential intrusion on people's work–life balance. These problems noted with both ICT in general and more specifically with e-learning is potentially further aggravated when linked to a social networking site frequently visited for personal reasons. It is important to keep both students and staff aware of the need to have boundaries between different parts of their life and need to explicitly acknowledge when they are not available. This process can be utilized in such a way as to have a positive effect as it can draw on a perceived higher level of self-disclosure highlighted by Mazer, Murphy and Simonds (2009), such as when staff post that they are going home for the day and are no longer available for work.

Palloff and Pratt (2009) also note problems of Facebook and copyright. Facebook ultimately holds nonexclusive but perpetual copyright over online discussions that occur in its forums. A related concern is that, because Facebook is a commercial platform, many of the copyright exemptions that exist in different countries in relation to education may not apply when Facebook is used in this manner. Once again addressing this is a matter of awareness and literacy. It is important to keep in mind for both staff and students the type of material that can be posted to Facebook and the consequences.

Finally, Facebook is a publicly listed company with a responsibility to generate profit and provide a return to its shareholders. Although this is also the case with other companies that specialize in educational software and LMSs, such as Blackboard Inc., there is a significant difference in how this money is generated. Although access to a Blackboard Inc. LMS, such as Blackboard or WebCT, might be paid by the university and represent part of the fees paid by students and government investment in higher education, Facebook makes its return on investment more indirectly by building a profile of each user and selling this to advertisers. Thus, the students and staff rather than the LMS become the commodity. Although this is also a feature of other Web 2.0 platforms commonly used in higher education such as YouTube and SlideShare, the more direct link in this forum to a student's personal profile makes this a greater concern in this context. More than 1 billion people are content to use Facebook and to engage in this process; however, it is an area that should be approached with caution when higher education becomes complicit in this commodification (see Croeser, this volume).

Conclusion

Despite these cautions, Facebook can make a valuable addition to both fully online and blended learning environments in learning and teaching in higher education. It allows the existing familiarity that the majority of students and staff have with the network to be leveraged for a higher level of engagement with learning material and encourages students to extend and shape that content online. When engaged in the learning process the question, "What's on your mind?" is one that is asked frequently in relation to what is being taught. This query is the foundation for a discussion of course material and is an important part of the learning process. Its appearance at the start of each Facebook homepage is designed to elicit a response and to encourage the interaction and communication that the network offers. These features can be successfully co-opted for higher education and provide a potent online platform for learning and teaching.

References

Allen, M. (2012). An education in Facebook. *Digital Culture and Education, 4*(3). Retrieved from www.digitalcultureandeducation.com/volume-4/dce1077_allen_2012_html/

Bateman, D., & Willems, J. (2012). Chapter 5 Facing off: Facebook and Higher Education. In L. A. Wankel & C. Wankel (Eds.), *Misbehavior online in higher education* (Cutting-edge Technologies in Higher Education, Vol. 5, pp. 53–79). Bingley, UK: Emerald Group Publishing Limited.

Best, G., Hajzler, D., Pancini, G., & Tout, D. (2011). Being "dumped" from Facebook: Negotiating issues of boundaries and identity in an online social networking space. *Journal of Peer Learning, 4*(1), 24–36. Retrieved from http://ro.uow.edu.au/ajpl/vol4/iss1/5

Bicen, H., & Cavus, N. (2011). Social network sites usage habits of undergraduate students: case study of Facebook. *Proceedia—Social and Behavioral Sciences, 28*, 943–947.

Chang, W. L., & Lee, C. Y. (2013). Trust as a learning facilitator that affects students' learning performance in the Facebook community: An investigation in a business planning writing course. *Computers and Education, 62*, 320–327.

Cluett, L. (2010). *Online social networking for outreach, engagement and community: The UWA Student's Facebook page.* Paper presented at Educating for sustainability. Proceedings of the 19th Annual Teaching Learning Forum, Edith Cowan University, Perth, Australia. Retrieved from http://otl.curtin.edu.au/professional_development/conferences/tlf/tlf2010/refereed/cluett.html

Dabbagh, N., & Kitsantas, A. (2012). Personal Learning Environments, social media, and self-regulated learning: A natural formula for connecting formal and informal learning. *Internet and Higher Education, 15*, 3–8.

Dabner, N. (2012). "Breaking Ground" in the use of social media: A case study of a university earthquake response to inform educational design with Facebook. *Internet and Higher Education, 15*, 69–78.

Darics, E. (in press). The blurring boundaries between synchronicity and asynchronicity: New communicative situations in work related Instant Messaging *Journal of Business Communication.* Retrieved from www.academia.edu/attachments/30730367/download_file

Ellis, K. (2011). Embracing learners with disability: Web 2.0, access and insight. *Telecommunications Journal of Australia, 61*(2), 30.1–30.2.

Ellison, B., Steinfield, C., & Lampe, C. (2007). The benefits of Facebook "Friends": Social capital and college students' use of online social networking sites. *Journal of Computer-Mediated Communication, 12*, 1143–1168.

Gao, F., Zhang, T., & Franklin, T. (2013). Designing asynchronous online discussion environments: Recent progress and possible future directions. *British Journal of Educational Technology, 44*(3), 469–483.

Grey, K., Lucas, A., & Kennedy, G. (2010). Medical Students use of Facebook to support learning: Insights from four case studies. *Medical Teacher, 32*, 971–976.

Haverback, H. R. (2009). Facebook: Uncharted Territory in a reading education classroom. *Reading Today, 27*(2), 34.

Heijstra, T. M., & Rafnsdottir, G. L. (2010). The Internet and academics' workload and work family balance. *Internet and Higher Education, 13,* 158–163.

Hew, K. F., & Cheung, W. S. (2012). Use of Facebook: A case study of Singapore students' experience. *Asia Pacific Journal of Education, 32*(2), 181–196.

Junco, R. (2013). Comparing actual and self-reported measures of Facebook use. *Computers in Human Behavior, 29,* 626–631.

Karl, K. A., & Peluchette, J. V. (2011). "Friending" professors, parents and bosses: A Facebook connection conundrum. *Journal of Education for Business, 86*(4), 214–222.

Kayri, M. & Çakir, Ö. (2010). An applied study on educational use of Facebook as a Web 2.0 tool: The sample lesson of computer networks and communication. *International Journal of Computer Science & Information Technology, 2*(4), 48–58. Retrieved from http://arxiv.org/pdf/1009.0402.pdf

Kent, M. (in press). Changing the Conversation: Facebook as a venue for online class discussion in higher education. *Journal of Online Learning and Teaching.*

Lenartz, A. J. (2012). Chapter 16 Establishing guidelines for the use of social media in higher education. In L. A. Wankel & C. Wankel (Eds.) *Misbehavior online in higher education* (Cutting-edge Technologies in Higher Education, Vol. 5, pp. 333–353). Bradford, West Yorkshire, UK: Emerald Group Publishing Limited.

Mazer, J. P., Murphy, R. E., & Simonds, C. J. (2009). The effects of teacher self-disclosure via Facebook on teacher credibility. *Learning Media and Technology, 34*(2), 175–183. Retrieved from www.tandfonline.com.dbgw.lis.curtin.edu.au/doi/pdf/10.1080/17439880902923655

Mazman, S. G., & Usluel, Y. K. (2010). Modeling educational usage of Facebook. *Computers and Education, 55,* 444–453.

McCarthy, J. (2010). Blended learning environments: Using social networking sites to enhance the first year experience. *Australasian Journal of Education Technology, 26*(6), 729–740.

McLaughlin, C., & Lee, M. J. W. (2010). Personalised and self-regulated learning in the Web 2.0 era: International exemplars of innovative pedagogy using social software. *Australasian Journal of Educational Technology, 26*(1), 28–43.

Palloff, R. M., & Pratt, K. (2009, August). *Web 2.0 technologies and community building online.* Paper presented at the 25th Annual Conference on Distance Teaching & Learning, Madison, WI.

Phillips, N. K. (2011). Academic library use of Facebook: Building relationships with students. *The Journal of Academic Librarianship, 37*(6), 512–522.

Sappy, J., & Relf, S. (2010). Digital technology education and its impact on traditional academic roles and practice. *Journal of University Teaching & Learning Practice, 7*(1). Retrieved from: http://ro.uow.edu.au/jutlp/vol7/iss1/3/?utm_source=ro.uow.edu.au%2Fjutlp%2Fvol7%2Fiss1%2F3&utm_medium=PDF&utm_campaign=PDFCoverPages

Schroeder, J., & Greenbowe, T. J. (2009). The chemistry of Facebook: Using social networking to create an online community for the organic chemistry. *Innovate: Journal of Online Education, 5*(4), 1–7.

Shim, J. P., Dekleva, S., Guo, C., & Mittleman, D. (2011). Twitter, Google, iPhone/iPad, and Facebook (TGIF) and smart technology environments: How well do educators communicate with students via TGIF? *Communications of the Association for Information Systems, 29*(1), 657–672. Retrieved from http://aisel.aisnet.org/cgi/viewcontent.cgi?article=3642&context=cais

Smith, S. D., & Caruso, J. B. (2010). *The ECAR study of undergraduate students and information technology 2010.* Boulder, CO: EDUCAUSE Center for Applied Research (ECAR). Retrieved from http://anitacrawley.net/Resources/Reports/ECAR%20study%20highlights.pdf

Stross, R. (2009, March 7). When everyone's a friend is anything private? *The New York Times.* Retrieved from www.nytimes.com/2009/03/08/business/08digi.html?_r=0

Teclehaimanot, B., & Hickman, T. (2011). Student-teacher interaction on Facebook: What students find appropriate. *TechTrends, 55*(3), 19–30.

7

Academic Armour: Social Etiquette, Social Media and Higher Education

COLLETTE SNOWDEN AND LEANNE GLENNY

University of South Australia

All forms of education are concerned with the communication of knowledge and skill through educational practice and the interaction between academics and students. The complexity of this process and the need for external verification to ensure its validity and authenticity has produced rules, statutes and protocols, which govern the relationship between students and academic institutions. However, the interpersonal nature of communication in the educative process has also produced informal rules and particular academic and institutional cultures, which are transmitted through practice rather than formal codification. The development of such informal culture in organizations is recognized as being equally important as the formal culture (Deal & Kennedy, 1982; Schein 2010).

The culture, subcultures and traditions of the higher education sector have developed over hundreds of years, and modern institutions are modeled on those existing institutions. Even the newest institutions have adopted and appropriated traditional European conventions and practices. Altbach (2004) argues that "this is the case even where, as in China, well-established indigenous academic traditions already existed. The basic structure of the institution and the orientation to teaching, for example, characterize universities internationally and are derived from the medieval European tradition" (p. 4).

Behavioral protocol, or etiquette, influences the manner and form of social interaction and relates to the establishment and maintenance of norms, or the implicit, unwritten rules of behavior (Elias, 1978). All forms of human communication develop associated etiquette that is accepted and widely understood, to the extent that it underpins and defines communication in various social settings and is a component in defining both conformity and deviance (Goffman, 1971). However, social etiquette is culturally and situationally variable, and its nuances are learned through experience, practice and reinforcement. Misunderstanding or the flouting of accepted rules of social etiquette and protocols in various communication environments may lead to conflict and disharmony.

Concerns about the effects of the use of online technology on social etiquette, or the civility and content of communication, began almost as soon as people used it, and persist. In 1978 Licklider and Vezza considered the implications of the new technology of electronic mail and observed that "one could write tersely and type imperfectly, even to an older person in a superior position and even to a person one did not know very well, and the recipient took no offense" (p. 1331). By 1985, Shapiro and Anderson felt compelled to develop guidelines on "the ethics and etiquette" of the use of e-mail and other electronic communication, arguing that guidelines were required to "accelerate the process by which social customs and behavior appropriate to electronic mail becomes established, and thereby to accelerate the effective use of such systems" (p. iii). Subsequently, there has been significant research, media commentary and institutional response to understand and determine online etiquette and implement organizational rules and protocols.

In the daily interaction between students and academics, all communication is influenced by formal and informal codes, rules and accepted etiquette. Lerum (2001) uses the term *academic armour* "to describe the physical and psychological means through which professional academics protect their expert positions or jurisdictions" and further divides these means into three categories, "linguistic, physical, and ideological" (p. 470). Lerum uses the concept of academic armour in the context of the academic as researcher/expert in relation to the subjects of research, in which it describes the process by which academics create distance between themselves and their subjects, to create objectivity, authority and a sense of superiority. We suggest that it can equally apply in the context of the academic as instructor/expert in relation to students. We contend that the etiquette of communication between academics and students has, over hundreds of years, also constructed academic armour, which has assisted academics to be defined and to identify as experts and to differentiate them from the student body. The communication etiquette of the academic/student relationship possesses linguistic, physical and ideological components and, as such, constitutes academic armour.

Additionally, social etiquette in Higher Education institutions produces organizational artifacts (Schein, 2010), and although its material artifacts are more readily identifiable, organizational artifacts include "all the phenomena that you would see, hear and feel when you encounter a group with an unfamiliar culture" (Schein, 2010, p. 23). Therefore, the tone and language, and forms of address, used in oral and written communication can be regarded as organizational artifacts. Schein (2010) further proposes that artifacts are understood as the manifestation of the organization's underlying assumptions and espoused values. The introduction of new forms of communication, especially those less subject to institutional management or control, also affect the organization because they introduce alien artifacts and associated practices, which may not share the same underlying assumptions and espoused values.

Social Media

The use of Facebook in the higher education sector presents an organizational challenge because as an artifact of a particular organization Facebook contains the assumptions and values of the corporation that created and manages it. Although people are accustomed to code switching in different environments and different institutions, Facebook introduces a significant challenge in higher education because the platform is shared with a wider range of people, institutions and organizations. Furthermore, Facebook and other forms of social media open the communication environment in many directions simultaneously and by being accessible, portable and available the social media code is constantly in use. This requires that to communicate a person "must address anybody, everybody, and maybe even nobody all at once," thus creating a process defined as "context collapse" by Wesch (2009). Yet, basic values and assumptions may not be shared, or may be contradictory, and other forms of social etiquette may be breached, causing misunderstanding and conflict.

Similar to other communication platforms Facebook has specific affordances that influence how and when users communicate, as well as the tone and style of language they use. The widespread use of Facebook allows social interaction that not only uses, but also requires, those affordances and their associated forms of communication. Whereas, previously, social interaction and communication were determined by a shared understanding about social etiquette, Facebook has introduced new affordances to disparate groups of people, often with weak ties (Granovetter, 1983; Turkle, 2011). These affordances have resulted in an artifact that is the product of Facebook's organizational values and assumptions and that has been designed to produce specific responses.

In the Higher Education sector the use of Facebook and other social media provides a platform or channel of communication for education purposes, adding to those already used, such as e-mail, internal electronic bulletin boards and the wider range of online learning and teaching tools. Additionally, some academics use social media to promote themselves and to communicate their research. Regardless of how or when it is used, the properties and affordances of Facebook, are imported into the Higher Education sector. In adopting Facebook, academics and higher education institutions thus change and influence existing rules of interaction and etiquette and influence the components of academic armour.

Social Networks and the Academy

Long before the widespread use of social media university academics had created successful social networks. Indeed, academic work has long required social networks to function effectively, as Altbach (2001) reminds us that "from the beginning, universities represented global institutions—in that they functioned in a common language, Latin, and served an international clientele of students.

Professors, too, came from many countries" (p. 4). Consequently, academics have been both innovators and early adopters (Rogers, 2003) of whatever technology or medium allowed them to communicate quickly with colleagues in the global network of the academy.

Online technology, developed significantly by academics working through research communities, created other platforms in the communication repertoire of academics. Among these platforms were e-mail and later forms of social media. The early networks in higher education systems were difficult to access by people outside of those communities and primarily focused on research but in them social and personal communication developed almost immediately. Turkle (2011) notes that "from the very beginning, networked technologies designed to share practical information were taken up as technologies of relationship" (p. 157).

As academics communicated research information, they also exchanged personal greetings, announcements, death notices and gossip. Inevitably, quarrels, disputes and conflict also occurred, and concerns about breaches of professional courtesy and propriety (Sternberg, 2012). From the earliest use of online technology the issue of how social interaction was managed and performed was a topic of interest and concern. Much of this discussion focused on the disruptive properties of technology, especially on language and behavior, and expressed fears or concerns about its use. These fears are counterbalanced by a strong promotional discourse arguing for the adoption of social media to increase business profitability, productivity, enhance sociability and happiness and in the education sector, to improve and facilitate educational outcomes.

In the higher education system the traditional boundary between academics and students is challenged by the use of social media, especially as social media is introduced into educational practice to enhance educational outcomes (Aydin, 2012; Tadros, 2011; Towner & Muñoz, 2011) and used by educational institutions in their own communication practices (Jenkins et al., 2012). The same technology is thus charged with delivering multiple positive outcomes. There is a spectrum of responses observable in the adoption and use of the technology (Rogers, 2003), illustrating the problem that our understanding of the effects and consequences of a technology emerge at the same time as the diffusion of the technology. In *The Medium Is the Massage* (McLuhan, Fiore & Agel, 2008), McLuhan argued that we have an inability to assess the changes happening around us adequately, precisely because we are engaged in them and that "we look at the present through a rear-view mirror. We march backwards into the future" (n.p.). Nonetheless, despite this handicap an assessment of academic use of social media, such as Facebook, provides a useful case study of a population frequently at the vanguard of the introduction of new technology. This is particularly so for academics involved in Communication and Media disciplines who are required to understand and use technology professionally and personally.

Academic Views of Facebook

In an analysis of media accounts of language use in technologies Thurlow (2006) found that the difference between computer-mediated discourse (CMD) and non-mediated discourse was frequently exaggerated and substantially misrepresented. He proposed that the discursive effects of computer-mediated communication (CMC) required "more situated analyses of actual CMD practice" (Thurlow, 2006, p. 690). Following this proposal, perspectives on the use of Facebook in the Higher Education sector of a specific group of academic staff were investigated.

We conducted interviews in order to obtain a practical understanding of how academics regard their professional use of Facebook, and any interaction they have using it with students. This research, using both face-to-face and telephone interviews, gathered data from experienced academic staff working in Communication and Media disciplines in Australian Higher Education institutions. Participants were sought through purposive sampling to locate academic staff with more than 10 years teaching experience, and staff involved in the introduction of Technology Enhanced Learning techniques and tools. The sample was selected because staff members who met the criteria have worked through the period in which online communication technology has been introduced widely in both higher education and the broader community. Consequently, each of the seven participants has worked in the Higher Education sector throughout the period in which social media, and Facebook specifically, were developed, diffused widely and normalized as a communication platform.

Each interview took approximately 30 minutes and used 10 semistructured questions to elicit responses. The interviews also allowed participants to introduce relevant additional material. The interviews were based on three key questions:

- How did etiquette influence the formal communication between students and academic staff in the Higher Education sector prior to the introduction of social media?
- How have the specific affordances of Facebook and other social media platforms challenged these established communication conventions?
- What are the implications of these changes on, and challenges for, the education sector and the professional practices of those involved?

Findings

The effects and consequences of the use of Facebook on student and academic relationships, both formally and informally, were nuanced and were recognized as both positive and negative aspects of the affordances of Facebook. However, interviewees were unanimous in observing that the relationship between students and academics had changed markedly during their tenure. In describing and explaining this change the interviewees related the introduction of less formal interaction between academics and students to the widespread use of communications technology. They also described an accompanying absence of courtesy and professionalism in the use of forms of address, tone of language used, appropriateness of communication and the timing of communication. Although these changes in the nature of academic and student interaction online were not considered problematic or damaging, the interviewees were more concerned about the inconvenience, inefficiency and intrusiveness of much electronic communication.

Although the questions asked were framed to interrogate the use and attitudes of the participants to Facebook specifically, the participants also independently discussed other forms of social media, or volunteered information about multiple forms of social media. Therefore, the specific nature of Facebook was not considered important and Facebook was regarded as one social media platform among a range available. However, opinions about the use of e-mail in the Higher Education sector were expressed vigorously. Similarly, opinions about the negative relationship between communication practices of social media platforms and student communication with academics more generally, including in face-to-face interaction, were also expressed strongly.

Concern was also expressed about the transference of an informal style of communication from Facebook, and other media platforms into the university environment, with four interviewees stating that the tonal and stylistic conventions of Facebook were neither useful for clear communication nor appropriate. However, such concerns were not shared by all interviewees, with three of seven interviewees regarding social media communication styles as similar to e-mail.

All interviewees were clear about their use of Facebook as a personal communication platform, and which they used primarily for private communication, unless a specific group or site was established for teaching or communication purposes. Two interviewees had separate professional Facebook accounts for more public interaction. There was a clear reluctance by interviewees to integrate social and professional relationships and a strong preference for the use of institutional networks for communication with students. This preference was partially due to a recognition that, contrary to the hyperbole about its ubiquity, not every student has a Facebook account, and many do not access it regularly (McAndrew & Jeong, 2012). The use of an institutional platform for contact requires students to use it for institutional communication and for that to be clearly stated and mandated. It is also considered an equity issue, so that all students have equal access to resources and information.

On the specific issue of etiquette and changes in the relationship between students and academics, the interviewees again had mixed views about whether the changes were positive or negative. However, there was a clear concern for what one interviewee called "boundaries" between students and academics: "Uni is where they learn boundaries, the question is how do we help them navigate the blurring [of] boundaries that social media has created." Whereas another mentioned boundaries in relation to the differences between personal and professional communication: "[Students] are very skilled at using [Facebook], but do they understand the boundaries?" This view about the understanding of the boundaries between informal, social use and professional use was also expressed in similar terms by three other interviewees.

In particular, three interviewees said that Facebook and other social media, especially in the mobile environment, created an expectation of 24/7 availability. They perceived that this produced conflict and frustration when messages were not responded to in relatively short time frames. One interviewee noted that it was common to receive communication from students late in the evening, including weekends, and this was one reason why she was not accessible to students outside of the university network. Interviewees also explained that they did not have personal Facebook "friendships" with students because a clear distinction between personal and professional relationships was necessary given their role in assessing and supervising student work.

The use of the concept of boundaries raises Lerum's (2001) concept of 'academic armour,' that is, a need for a barrier or distance between the academic and the student, which was not elaborated. Boundaries may be necessary to maintain the traditional relationship of authority and to acquire social distance, or to assist academics to manage communication with students without it intruding into their personal time. The clear expression of a desire for a distinction between personal and professional relationships with students by academics, however, suggests the consideration of technology as a fourth element to Lerum's concept of academic armour, adding to the linguistic, physical and ideological elements. Regardless of whether it is Facebook or some other form of social media, the affordances of Facebook are being adopted and repurposed in technological "social media" platforms in higher education, both formally and informally. In effect, Facebook establishes the rules and practices for the use of online social interaction, including between academics and students. In doing so it weakens academic armour by overriding the boundaries created by the use of formal language, by the constraints of the physical environment and by the dominant ideology. Referring to situations in which the academic armour of the researcher is breached by experience of intimacy, or subjectivity in field work, Lerum argues that, "in dropping one's academic armour and engaging 'in the moment,' one is required to dance, spar, and negotiate with one's subjects face to face. Although the parameters of these moments may be brief, the content is never neutral, and it often ruins one's sense of control," (2001, p. 481). Similarly, on Facebook the academic student relationship is far more equal, and there is a loss of control as the boundaries that create academic armour are blurred and removed.

Conclusion

Facebook, and other forms of social media, have specific influences on the communication between students and academics. Many of these changes are linguistic, with effects on forms of address, grammatical precision, length and tone of messages. They also have effects in the physical domain, in association with other communication developments, largely in the perception of academic availability and accessibility. These changes can be regarded as chinks in the traditional 'academic armour', which allowed academics to establish and maintain clear boundaries between their professional and personal lives and identities, but which also served as an organizational artifact which contributed to the culture and ideology of universities.

In the context of ethnographic research, Lerum (2001) argues that although "academic armour facilitates researchers' intellectual jurisdiction and privilege, it inhibits the collection of truly subjective, emotionally engaged, embodied data" (p. 479). Similarly, in the context of Facebook, the persistence of a desire by academics to maintain professional boundaries, in effect to wear their armour online, may inhibit the development of relationships that could facilitate both teaching and learning.

Yet, the vulnerability of the contemporary academic to the effects of always-on, always-available expectations that accompany contemporary communications technology use has implications not only for the productivity and the efficiency of academic work in an organizational sense but also for academic identity. There is then a need for the boundaries of academic and student relationships to be reassessed, informed by better understanding of the technology and its affordances. Academics may repair or reinforce their armour with not only the introduction of new rules and processes in relation to the use of Facebook and other social media but also with the development of specific technological responses, including unique software and institutional programs.

Along with transformations in the way that knowledge and information are distributed and shared between networks of connected individuals, Facebook and other social media affect the way we communicate and expectations of how others communicate. It is this point of transformation where the rules and protocols of interaction are in a state of flux. McLuhan, who identified himself as a classical academic with values and beliefs steeped in the Western academic tradition, grasped that managing changes associated with such points of transformation was critical for survival. In the seminal Playboy interview, he said,

> if literate Western man were really interested in preserving the most creative aspects of his civilization, he would not cower in his ivory tower bemoaning change but would plunge himself into the vortex of electric technology and, by understanding it, dictate his new environment—turn ivory tower into control tower.

> (McLuhan, 1961)

Contemporary academics are increasingly taking control of technology rather than bemoaning change, including the changes to longstanding protocols and social etiquette. In this sense, they may drop or redesign academic armour for the battlefield that is contemporary education. Like the technology that has challenged traditional social etiquette, it may be an academic armour that is lighter, flexible and more mobile.

References

Altbach, P. G. (2004). Globalisation and the university: Myths and realities in an unequal world, *Tertiary Education and Management, 10*(1), 3–25.

Aydin, S. (2012). A review of research on Facebook as an educational environment, *Educational Technology Research and Development, 60*(6), 1093–1106.

Deal, T. E., & Kennedy, A. A. (1982). *Corporate cultures: The rites and rituals of corporate life.* Reading, MA: Addison-Wesley.

Elias, N. (1978–1982). *The civilizing process.* Oxford, UK: Blackwell.

Goffman, E. (1971). *The presentation of self in everyday life.* Harmondsworth, UK: Penguin.

Granovetter, M. (1983). The strength of weak ties: A network theory revisited. *Sociological Theory, 1*, 201–233.

Jenkins, G., Lyons, K., Bridgstock, R., & Carr, L. (2012). Like our page—using Facebook to support first year students in their transition to higher education. A practice report. *The International Journal of the First Year in Higher Education, 3*(2), 65–72.

Lerum, K. (2001). Subjects of desire: Academic Armor, intimate ethnography, and the production of critical knowledge. *Qualitative Inquiry, 7*(4), 466–483.

Licklider, J. C. R., & Vezza, A. (1978). Applications of information networks. *Proceedings of the IEEE, 66*(11), 1330–1346.

McAndrew, F. T., & Jeong, H. S. (2012). Who does what on Facebook? Age, sex, and relationship status as predictors of Facebook use. *Computers in Human Behavior, 28*(6), 2359–2365.

McLuhan, M. (1961). The Playboy interview. Retrieved from www.nextnature.net/2009/12/the-playboy-interview-marshall-mcluhan/

McLuhan, M., Fiore, Q., & Agel, J. (2008). *The medium is the massage.* London: Penguin.

Rogers, E. M. (2003). *Diffusion of innovations.* New York: Free Press.

Schein, E. H. (2010). *Organizational culture and leadership.* San Francisco: Jossey-Bass.

Shapiro, N. Z., & Anderson, R. H. (1985). *Towards an ethics and etiquette for electronic mail.* Santa Monica, CA: RAND Corporation.

Sternberg, J. (2012). *Misbehavior in cyber places: The regulation of online conduct in virtual communities on the Internet.* Lanham, MD: University Press of America.

Tadros, M. (2011). *A social media approach to higher education.* Bingley, UK: Emerald Group Publishing Limited.

Thurlow, C. (2006). From Statistical Panic to Moral Panic: The Metadiscursive Construction and Popular Exaggeration of New Media Language in the Print Media. *Journal of Computer-Mediated Communication, 11*(3), 667–701.

Towner, T. L., & Muñoz, C. L. (2011). *Facebook and education: A classroom connection?* Bingley, UK: Emerald Group Publishing Limited.

Turkle, S. (2011). *Alone together: Why we expect more from each other and less from technology.* New York: Basic Books.

Wesch, M. (2009). *YouTube and you: Experiences of self-awareness in the context collapse of the recording webcam.* Retrieved from http://hdl.handle.net/2097/6302

8
Exploring Facebook Groups' Potential as Teaching–Learning Environment for Supervision Purposes

MONA HAJIN

Stockholm University

Facebook as the world's largest social networking site holds significant potential for higher education, which may go beyond socializing, especially when it comes to thesis writing, which is usually considered as an independent task. Using Facebook in higher education may decrease the separation between everyday life and education and may be considered one step toward a lifelong learning approach to teaching and learning (Nicol, 2007; Sharples, 2000). Similar to other studies on higher education, improving students' learning is the foremost aim of this chapter. However, a particular focus is given to exploring the role of Facebook groups as a teaching–learning environment in higher education with a focus on supervision of bachelor's- and master's-level students.

This chapter does not apply the actual uses of Facebook groups, but instead explores and reflects on the views of 5 teachers (advisors) and 10 students in the Stockholm region about using Facebook groups as the main platform for teaching and learning, within the fields of Media and Communication Studies and Social Anthropology for supervision purposes. To provide a basis for the discussion, first students' and advisors' issues and concerns regarding the thesis writing tasks, as experienced in their Thesis Writing course are explored, then the ways in which Facebook groups could be used to address those issues are discussed. Exploring the issues and concerns of the informants related to the course Thesis Writing provided an understanding about the context within which Facebook groups' potential are explored and discussed.

Theoretical Background

The existing body of research on Facebook and education includes a variety of different subjects. Among them, there are many studies done exploring Facebook's potential for education (Bosch, 2009; Kabilan, Ahmad, & Zainol Abidin, 2010; Madge, Meek, Wellens, & Hooley, 2009). However, despite the wide array of active research topics, there are few studies done on how Facebook can be used in higher education with a focus on it as a teaching–learning environment and thesis supervision. There is no current study to date that explores the uses of Facebook groups as teaching and learning environments for supervision purposes and as the main venue of communication, rather than a supplement for the traditional classroom.

A course based on Facebook groups, an online platform in which students and advisors mainly interact and communicate online with one another might be controversial. Because new communication technologies, as Stutzman (2008, p. 7) writes, can be considered a "nascent space" whose functions need to be learned (as cited in Bosch, 2009, pp. 195–196), students and advisors might not be familiar with how these spaces work and with how they can be of benefit for educational purposes.

According to Sharples (2000), technologies can shape an environment for learning and "not only place the learning resources in a familiar context but also provide social environments for engaging with teachers and other learners" (p. 183). As Anderson (2008) writes, the "online learning environment is . . . a unique cultural context in itself" (p. 48). However, a criticism of online learning is that it limits "body languages and paralinguistic clues" (Anderson, 2008, p. 47), which might have a negative impact on formal teaching and learning (Laurillard, 2009, p. 5). According to Anderson (2008) there are scholars who argue that "the unique characteristics that define online learning (appropriate combinations of asynchronous and synchronous voice, text, and video) can actually lead to enhanced or hyper communications" (Richardson, 2000, in Anderson, 2008, p. 47). Also, one can argue that having a course online does not mean that all types of interactions in person disappear. Students have the opportunity to meet in person if they want. According to Madge, Meek, Wellens, and Hooley (2009), "online and offline worlds are clearly coexisting, but used in different ways for developing and sustaining different types of relationships" (p. 145).

Bransford, Brown, and Cocking (1994) "provide evidence that effective learning environments are framed within the convergence of four overlapping lenses," namely, "community-centred, knowledge-centred, learner-centred, and assessment-centred" (as cited in Anderson, 2008, p. 47). In the following, the possibility of using these lenses to explore Facebook groups as teaching–learning environments (Hounsell & Hounsell, 2007; Vermunt, 2007) are discussed.

Facebook groups can be considered as online community-centered environments (Anderson, 2008, p. 51). Facebook groups' access can vary from public to private. Private groups' access is limited to a particular set of members. Such limited access may be more appealing for some students to keep a degree of privacy and to have a chance to separate their everyday life from their educational activity on Facebook. Facebook allows "formation of community" and social "convergence" (Kabilan et al., 2010) and decreases the level of anonymity in larger groups (Bosch, 2009, p. 195), and thus increases motivation among students, and can be more fun for students to use (Kabilan et al., 2010, p. 180). As Anderson (2008) suggests teachers in online learning should make sure to provide opportunities for students to "share their understandings, their culture, and the unique aspects of themselves" (p. 48). Facebook, according to Kabilan et al. (2010, pp. 180–181) motivates "cross-cultural and inter-cultural interactions."

Facebook groups can be learner-centered environments (Anderson, 2008, p. 47), as students can have a central role in expressing themselves and sharing their thoughts, as well as supporting one another, and naturally in these situations the role of the teacher can change from being someone who transfers knowledge to being "monitor" and "supervisor" (Vermunt, 2007, p. 88) where student–student support and approach to teaching and learning is encouraged (Anderson, 2008, p. 57). According to Bosch (2009), Facebook can be a suitable interactive environment for the younger generation to collaborate in (p. 196), which may also provide flexibility in time for teachers and students. Bosch claims that "Facebook may be just the tool we need to stimulate collaborative student-led-learning" (2009, p. 190). Based on a number of ethnographies and interviews, Bosch's study on the use of Facebook in higher education at the University of Cape Town concludes that Facebook can be used for peer review (2009, p. 196), video blogging (2009, p. 192), collaborative classroom environment (2009, p. 191), and has the potential for "breaking down the traditional power hierarchies between student and instructor" (2009, p. 195). Facebook, according to Madge et al. (2009), was considered as a "university thing," which is used "to aid transition to university" (p. 144), because it is mainly used by students in the university to make "new face-to-face friends" (Bosch, 2009, pp. 143–144). A number of studies have thus shown that the use of social networking sites such as Facebook is an "integral part of students life" (Madge et al., 2009, p. 146; see Bosch, 2009; Kabilan et al., 2010), and can be used in higher education.

Facebook groups can provide an assessment-centered environment. On Facebook groups, students can also be assessed based on the quality of their reviews on their peers' drafts. According to Anderson (2008), "quality online learning provides many opportunities for assessment" (p. 49). It is important, as Anderson notes "to create assessment activities that are project- and workplace-based, that are constructed collaboratively, that benefit from peer and expert review, and that are infused with opportunity and requirement for self-assessment" (2008, p. 50). "Peer-marking exercises" suggested in O'Donovan, Price, and Rust's (2004, p. 332) article, is possibly a proper method for making students familiar with the assessment criteria and encouraging them to take an active role on the online platform of the course. In doing so, students should go back to the course intended learning outcomes, assessment criteria and become "more critical and working in more structured ways" (Orsmond et al., 1996, cited in O'Donovan et al., 2004, p. 332).

It may also stimulate learner motivation and engagement, and allow new approaches to pedagogy such as digital pedagogy (ibid., p. 181; Kabilan et al., 2010, p. 181). As Kabilan et al. (2010) write, an indirect type of learning happens on Facebook, which is through networking (p. 180). One could discuss the possibility it may even lead to a lifelong-learning approach toward teaching and learning (Nicol, 2007; Sharples, 2000). Madge et al.'s (2009) study on the use of Facebook showed that a large number of students use Facebook for discussing academic work and assignment related discussion with other students on a daily basis (p. 149). Interestingly, Madge et al. found that even if the students' own use of Facebook is limited to socializing and informal teaching–learning purposes, a wide range of them seem to be positive about the use of Facebook for formal teaching–learning (2009, p. 150).

In all of the reviewed works, Facebook has been used as a supplementary and secondary method for communication with students. However, in this chapter, Facebook groups are explored as a primary form of communication. They are explored as the main setting for communication between students and advisors.

Aim and Research Question

During the past few years, the course Thesis Writing (which was discussed in the interviews) has gradually developed and the number of students attending the course has increased. Due to the large number of students, advisors needed to separate them into smaller groups in which the degree of interaction was increased and students received group supervision, which may also have saved some time. Even if this may sound as an acceptable solution, it might also have decreased the possibility of interaction between students within larger groups. Being separated into smaller groups, students may not get enough knowledge about other research projects that are going on in other groups.

Facebook, writes Bosch (2009), "cannot be ignored as a potential educational tool" (p. 190). Before exploring the potential of Facebook groups for supervision purposes in higher education, the main issues and expectations of students and advisors in relation to thesis writing tasks were explored. The main research question explored here is, How can Facebook groups be used as a teaching–learning environment in higher education for supervision purposes?

Method

To answer the research question, 10 students (5 men and 5 women) who had recently completed their theses in the bachelor or master level, and 5 advisors (3 women and 2 men) were interviewed between 2012 and 2013. The informants were gathered through a colleague network and were kept anonymous. The interviews were then analyzed using thematic analysis (Yin, 2003). Thematic analysis aided the process of analysis, finding similar or different patterns regarding the theoretical discussions in the empirical materials to construct a descriptive approach.

Findings and Discussion

Analysis of the interviews showed that the overall approach toward the use of Facebook groups for supervision purposes is positive, because it could be used to decrease the time pressure and increase the degree of interaction and involvement among students. In addition, the uses of Facebook groups seemed to encourage a lifelong learning approach to teaching and learning and helps in changing the role of the teachers from being the transformers of knowledge to observers and advisors. Students and younger advisors, even if they had not previously used Facebook groups for educational purposes, seemed more optimistic about using them than did the older advisors. However, all of the informants acknowledged the use of Facebook groups as a proper solution for addressing the issues of time pressure and lack of interaction.

Two main themes appeared as important when analyzing interviews: students and advisors both complained about time pressure and lack of interaction in relation to their current Thesis Writing course. The potential of Facebook groups for supervision purposes was explored within a context in which both students and advisors were complaining about time pressure and need for greater interaction. The first two themes are the issues discussed in the interview addressing the Thesis Writing course that the informants have experienced. Finding these issues provided a basis for exploring how Facebook groups can be of benefit in relation to those concerns. Other issues and concerns regarding the use of Facebook groups for supervision purposes are discussed afterward in terms of lifelong learning, the role of the teacher and assessment.

Time Pressure

One of the first themes that appeared as important analyzing the interviews was time pressure. Students and advisors both experienced time pressure in relation to the Thesis Writing course, but in different ways.

The majority of advisors mentioned time pressure, especially when supervising bachelor's-level students who were newer within the field and less familiar with working independently. They mentioned that as well as having many other responsibilities, they usually end up working more than the number of hours for which they were paid. In addition to the number of hours spent in classroom, reading and commenting on the drafts, they spent many hours responding to a large volume of e-mails they received from students on a daily basis, often including similar or repetitive types of questions. Students experienced time pressure too, because they were usually new in the field doing research projects and therefore felt pressure over completion of the task within the course-specific period. They needed to develop their ideas, change their methodologies, and receive feedback from peers and advisors, which could change their approaches, during the process of working on their projects.

As one of the young female advisors (in her 20s) mentioned, some supervision sessions within the course of Thesis Writing are organized in groups of six to nine students, during which students listen to the other student's issues and questions and see how opponents and the advisor comment on their drafts. However, one of the concerns regarding the division of students into smaller groups can be that students with different approaches to teaching and learning would be in the same group. Some may have deep approaches and some surface approaches to teaching and learning (Biggs & Tang, 2009, p. 29). On Facebook, if the groups are not closed—even if students are divided into smaller groups—they would always have the opportunity to move back and forth between different groups and see the advisors' points.

> Instead of traveling back and forth between home and school, students can simply scroll up and down to find out which types of questions are covered and posed previously by others before posing their own questions, which might save some time for advisors not responding to the same types of questions over and over again.
>
> (Female advisor, 20s)

Facebook groups may also encourage a "transparent interaction between students and teachers as all interactions, questions and answers are visible to all group members" (male student, 20s). However, one of the concerns regarding the use of Facebook in higher education was that "using Facebook per se can be time-consuming, and makes students distracted with other notifications appearing on their profiles and they can easily be distracted by socializing uses of Facebook" (male advisor, 30s).

Need for Interaction and Student–Student Support

The second theme was the need for interaction. One of the main issues that advisors mentioned was a low degree of interaction and involvement in the classroom. Students seemed to be passive in the classes, and instead of posing their questions in the classroom, they kept on writing e-mails to the advisors after classes. "If they had posed their questions in the class, we could have answered other students' questions as well and that could have saved lots of time for us as well" (female advisor, 20s). However, from the students' point of view, in each step of thesis writing one was facing new issues and questions, which needed to be clarified, before one goes further: "The new issues and questions were not necessarily happening in the classroom time, but while one was developing ideas, applying methods, working with the materials, analyzing, etc." (female student, 20s).

Lifelong Learning Approach

Lifelong learning is perhaps one of the main missions in higher education (Nicol, 2007). However, a lifelong learning approach can hardly be developed when teaching–learning activities are separated from other aspects of one's life. It seems that Facebook provides a platform in which teaching, learning, and other spheres of one's life may meet: "Even if one supports the idea of drawing lines between learning and other activities, that is also possible on Facebook" (female student, 20s). People can join different groups, which are shaped for different purposes. One of these purposes can be teaching and learning. Facebook has the potential for encouraging a lifelong learning approach to teaching and learning (Kabilan et al., 2010, p. 180; Nicol, 2007; Sharples, 2000). Students and teachers can use the platform, and Facebook group(s) specifically, asynchronously, they can use it whenever they want, independent of any particular time and location (Anderson, 2008, p. 61). "Facebook by keeping different aspects of one's life like education, entertainment, etc. by each other's side may encourage a lifelong learning approach which may be more useful for the younger generation who basically like including them [social media] in their education" (female advisor, 20s).

The Role of the Teacher: Transformer to "Monitor"

Students can support each other and interact with one another (student–student support) using Facebook groups as a learning environment. On Facebook, students can interact through comments, shares, and likes. Students have the possibility of discussing their assignments, asking and answering questions, and supporting each other. Students may be encouraged to collaborate, and take active roles in supporting their peers. Advisors however need to keep an eye on "how students interact with one another and make sure they are on the right path" (female advisor, 20s). "The advisors' role remain crucial though, as they should make sure students do not mislead each other, which might happen for various reasons including misunderstanding of the task" (male advisor, 30s).

Assessment and Peer Marking

"Assessment of interaction on Facebook can be challenging, since some students might look active on the groups, but not be effective or helpful" (female advisor, 30s). Although students in the offered course on Facebook are going to be assessed both based on the quality of their interaction (reviewing other's drafts, responding to questions, etc.) and their final projects, it seems that it is always difficult to assess students' interactions, active roles, and, more importantly, the quality of their interactions. Accordingly, one of the concerns regarding the assessments is "how to make sure that students would keep being active and how to measure or evaluate students' interaction and its quality level" (male advisor, 40s).

Conclusion

The aim of this chapter was to explore the potential of Facebook as a teaching–learning environment in higher education, in particular regarding the supervision of theses. The interview questions first tried to explore the

issues and concerns of students and advisors about the classroom-based Thesis Writing course they have experienced and then explored how they would
consider using Facebook groups as a teaching-learning environment to address
those issues and concerns. Although the overall approach regarding the use
of Facebook groups as teaching–learning environment in higher education for
supervision purposes was positive, some important issues regarding to the use
of Facebook should be mentioned here.

Implementing the proposed form of education on Facebook is a realistic
possibility as long as making new accounts on Facebook is cost-free. The use of
Facebook per se may shift and challenge the issues of time pressure and need
for interaction mentioned by the informants over time. The freshness of using
this platform for educational purposes can be problematic in the beginning,
especially when advisors and students are not completely familiar with how
to use them for their own purposes. Therefore, providing enough knowledge
about the course prior to the beginning of the course is recommended. I also
suggest that students and advisors experience using these groups for educational purposes temporarily to test its potential and drawbacks before actually
taking and presenting a course on them. Facebook can challenge the role of the
advisors and the time they allocate to the course. For instance, the advisors may
end up spending more time on the Facebook groups of the course than in the
classroom. Therefore, making strategies for dealing with these issues prior to
the application of the course is suggested. Facebook per se can be a means of
distraction and might not be suitable for all types of courses and fields. Using
Facebook may be more useful in courses and fields in which a great degree
of interaction is needed. Depending on the field, different approaches may be
taken toward teaching and learning. The role of Facebook may change over
time. This change is not necessarily a negative change; rather, it is a positive one
that is more suitable for educational purposes.

This chapter has focused on providing an understanding from students'
and advisors' perspectives about how Facebook groups may be used in higher
education, before an actual course or thesis supervision was carried out on
Facebook. The findings were limited to a specific context in which a greater
degree of interaction was required and time pressure was experienced by the
informants. This chapter reflected upon the perspectives of a limited number
of informants before the actual uses of Facebook groups in the course were
employed. Therefore, discussing the potential of using Facebook groups in the
interviews can be different from the actual uses of them.

Future studies may explore the actual uses of Facebook groups, exploring
which types of strategies can be made with a focus on the role of the advisors,
and the number of hours they should work in these online environments. More
empirical studies in the future may focus on courses that are actually implemented on Facebook and the result of the course evaluation, reflecting upon
the experiences of teacher and students. Such studies could further explore the

benefits and drawbacks of using a popular social network for educational and specifically supervision purposes.

References

Anderson, T. (2008). Towards a theory of online learning. In T. Anderson (Ed.), *The theory and practice of online learning* (pp. 45–74). Edmonton: AU Press.

Biggs, J., & Tang, C. (2009). *Teaching for quality learning at university.* New York: Society for Research into Higher Education and Open University Press.

Bosch, E. T. (2009). Using online social networking for teaching and learning: Facebook use at the University of Cape Town. *Communicatio: South African Journal for Communication Theory and Research, 35*(2), 185–200. http://dx.doi.org/10.1080/02500160903250648

Hounsell, D., & Hounsell, J. (2007). Teaching-learning environments in contemporary mass higher education. In N. Entwistle & P. Tomlinson (Eds.), *Student learning and university teaching* (pp. 91–111). Leicester, England: Monograph Series II: Psychological Aspects of Education—Current Trends, British Journal of Educational Psychology.

Kabilan, K. M., Ahmad, N., & Zainol Abidin, M. J. (2010). Facebook, social integration and informal learning at University: "It is more for socializing and talking to friends about work than for actually doing work." *Internet and Higher Education, 13,* 179–187.

Laurillard, D. (2009). The pedagogical challenges to collaborative technologies. *Computer-Supported Collaborative Learning, 4,* 5–20. doi:10.1007/s11412-008-9056-2

Madge, C., Meek, J., Wellens, J., & Hooley, T. (2009). Facebook, social integration and informal learning at university: "It is more for socialising and talking to friends about work than for actually doing work." *Learning, Media & Technology, 34*(2), 141–155.

Nicol, D. (2007). Laying a foundation for lifelong learning: Case studies of e-assessment in large 1st-year classes. *British Journal of Educational Technology, 8*(4), 668–678.

O'Donovan, B., Price, M., & Rust, C. (2004). Know what I mean? Enhancing student understanding of assessment standards and criteria. *Teaching in Higher Education, 9*(3), 325–335. doi:10.1080/1356251042000216642

Sharples, M. (2000). The design of personal mobile technologies for lifelong learning. *Computers & Education, 34,* 177–193.

Vermunt, J. D. (2007). The power of teaching-learning environments to influence student learning. In N. Entwistle & P. Tomlinson (Eds.), *Student learning and university teaching* (pp. 73–90). Leicester, England: Monograph Series II: Psychological Aspects of Education—Current Trends, British Journal of Educational Psychology.

Yin, R. K. (2003). *Case study research: Design and methods.* Thousand Oaks, CA: Sage.

Part 3
Facebook as a Learning Management System?

9

How Social Should Learning Be?
Facebook as a Learning
Management System

TAUEL HARPER

University of Western Australia

Education is the point at which we decide whether we love the world enough to assume responsibility for it and by the same token save it from that ruin which, except for renewal, except for the coming of the new and young, would be inevitable. And education, too, is where we decide whether we love our children enough not to expel them from our world and leave them to their own devices, nor to strike from their hands their chance of undertaking something new, something unforeseen by us, but to prepare them in advance for the task of renewing a common world.

—Arendt (1954, pp. 13–14)

While higher education seeks to embrace the many learning advantages brought about by social networking, this chapter illustrates some of the broader issues involved in using Facebook as a Learning Management System (LMS) by teasing out some of the theoretical implications of pursuing education in a social space. I intend to use the work of Hannah Arendt, a renowned theorist of both public debate and education, to explore the reasons students might embrace the use of Facebook as an LMS and to explain why the use of Facebook in this way raises some important questions about the contemporary role of education. I argue that the potential of Facebook as an LMS emerges from its current role as a public space—a space where people can both engage with reasonable discussions and express their identities. However, I also argue that Facebook's public appearance is actually Janus-faced and that the public appearance of Facebook masks the fact that it is a private institution that facilitates social judgment of private issues. Although using Facebook as an LMS opens fantastic opportunities for engaging students in the learning process, the process also engages them in a process of "collateral learning" (Postman, 1985, p. 144), which without careful and extensive moderation will tend to reinforce socially powerful judgments and behavior.

The use of Facebook as an LMS clearly offers a number of benefits for teaching and learning. The use of Facebook in education enables 'constructivist' practices of education that focus on student led inquiry and practice (Rheingold, 2008, pp. 99–101). Some examples of these practices include "learning on demand," in which learning is based on personal motivation, interest and investigation (McGoughlin & Lee, 2010); "seamless learning," which encourages mixed modes of instruction and participation in order to encourage continuous learning (Looi et al., 2010); and the "flipped classroom," where educational content is accessed on the web and class time is used for direct discussion (Norton, Sonnemann, & McGannon, 2013, pp. 23–24). All these practices help to integrate learning with the "lived experience" of the students and can be excellent tools in pedagogical practice for this reason. However, I argue that facilitating such practices through Facebook contains an inherent danger as the platform transgresses the privacy of both the participants and the educational process itself.

The work of Arendt is fundamentally suited to this purpose because she identifies that one of the greatest motivations for engaging in discussions is the disclosure of identity. Drawing on the work of Heidegger and Aristotle, Arendt (1958) claims that every individual has an essence that we strive to express through public engagement (p. 211); we have an inherent desire for self-disclosure "at the expense of all other factors" (Arendt, 1958, p. 194). It is for this reason that the ancient Greeks sought to establish a public realm that would serve to provide a place for people to discuss matters of public importance and, in the process, have the opportunity to express themselves, develop a communal impression of their identity and win a chance at immortality:

> the public realm itself, the polis, was permeated by a fiercely agonal spirit, where everybody had constantly to distinguish himself from all others, to show through unique deeds or achievements that he was best of all. The public realm, in other words, was reserved for individuality; it was the only place where men could show who they really and inexchangeably were. It was for the sake of this chance, and out of love for a body politic that made it possible to them all, that each was more or less willing to share in the burden of jurisdiction, defense, and administration of public affairs.
>
> (Arendt, 1958, p. 41)

It is worth emphasizing that the need to disclose identity preempts the need to create a space where identity can be expressed; the citizens of Athens were prepared to presuppose a certain amount of equality of opportunity and responsibility in order to ensure that they also had the chance to express themselves.

The dynamic success of Facebook, and social networking sites more generally, can be attributed to the fact that such systems re-create this public realm. Whereas our political systems have divorced themselves from our participation, and our public spaces such as shopping malls and sporting contests have long since become privatized, corporatized and sanitized, Facebook and Social Networking Services (SNS) more generally provide us with an opportunity to express ourselves, to establish 'who we really are' and to do so in a forum which valorizes our expression—not just our spending power (Harper, 2011, pp. 85–105). Like the public space of Athens, Facebook provides a somewhat equalizing meeting point, where we can discuss, express and debate while contributing to a public perception of "who we really are." This identity, which inscribes itself on news feeds everywhere, offers us a chance to leave an impression on the world we share. This public valorization of action on Facebook is the key to understanding the attraction of Facebook as an LMS; users feel that their contributions matter, not necessarily just in terms of the ongoing academic discussions but also in terms of their ongoing construction and expression of their identity.

Thus, we can understand that what Facebook offers to education as an LMS is the increased access and engagement, which Arendt associates with the benefits of truly public space. The crux of constructivist teaching practice is to seek to situate students as responsible for their own learning by encouraging them to relate their learning to their own lives. It is clear that the Internet provides a number of forums where knowledge can be collectively established, locally organized and extensively disseminated—essentially increasing the level of personal participation in the construction of communal knowledge and culture. Indeed, the basic characteristics of Web 2.0 reflect both the principles of student centered learning and the architecture of Arendtian public space. We can define these characteristics broadly as centered around encouraging access and engagement, or more specifically as

User-centered Design: The forum is designed in a way that is easy and intuitive for all to use, ensuring the greatest degree of inclusivity.

Crowd-sourcing: The forum gathers information from as many places as possible and most importantly, directly from those who are engaged in the discussion.

Site as Platform: The forum allows for the important processes to be conducted on site, enabling equal access.

Collaboration: The forum recognizes the principle of sharing and working together as producing the best possible results.

Power Decentralisation: The forum is not externally administered but the rules of interaction arise from the participants themselves.

Dynamic Content: The forum should change over time, adjusting to various uses and events and it should be particularly responsive to the activities and expressions of the user.

Rich User Experience: The forum should ensure that the user feels validated through the experience of using the space. (Harper, 2011, pp. 144–145)

When we talk about student centered learning, we are essentially projecting these elements onto the learning experience.

Although a large number of learning platforms enable these characteristics, it is the "ownership"—access and engagement—facilitated by Facebook, which makes it such an attractive tool for teaching. The strength of Facebook as a learning management system arises from its ability to facilitate a feeling of expressive engagement. With Facebook, a user's profile serves as an expression of his or her identity, and thus, the person feels a sense of "network citizenship." Such citizenship can be understood to be a fundamental part of the learning process because it extends the level of student responsibility and investment in that process. Most important, the ubiquity of the Facebook presence offers a forum where users feel that their contributions matter, not only in terms of the discussion taking place but also in terms of their overall identity construction. The extensive identity work that takes place around Facebook, along with its integration with the lived experience of the user, means that it is more likely to stimulate vigorous engagement among students.

However, this does not mean that using Facebook as an LMS is unproblematic, and Arendt also provides some explanation for why we might be wary of understanding Facebook as either a public space or a place suitable for education. The most obvious of these is the infiltration of private concerns into the forum. In fact, we can understand that the main problem with Facebook as an LMS is its inability to distinguish between public and private issues.

The division of "space" into private, public and social "spheres" has always been a central tenet of liberal thought, which argues that people require private space to be free and public space to be equal. Arendt emphasizes the importance of private space for public life by insisting that it is only through the cultivation of individual difference outside of the glare of public scrutiny that allows the difference necessary for public space to flourish:

> Wherever [human life] is consistently exposed to the world without the protection of privacy and security its vital quality is destroyed. In the public world, common to all, persons count, and so does work, that is, the work of our hands that each of us contributes to our common world; but life *qua* life does not matter there. The world cannot be regardful of it, and it has to be hidden and protected from the world.
>
> (Arendt, 1954, p. 8)

Here, Arendt spells out that private matters must remain outside of the scrutiny and judgments of the public debate. Without privacy the individual is never protected from normalizing judgment by the many and, according to Arendt, this situation is detrimental for both public and private space. Under constant scrutiny, the individual no longer experiences freedom from judgment, and because they are then taught to behave, the public space loses its diversity as a result (Arendt, 1958, p. 71). Arendt's conception of public and private space is one of symbiotic co-creation. A public space can only truly be public when it is composed of private individuals who, in turn, are individuals because they have experienced private development, which allows them to celebrate the distinct differences that manifest in their private lives. Privacy gives rise to individuality, which can then be celebrated through its unique contribution to public space. What is critical in this relationship is that the private remains distinct from the public.

Arendt describes the anomie of modern times as emerging as a result of the collapse of the distinction between private and public spaces; instead of a public world enriched by private differences, we have a public world that is obsessed with judging the private lives of its constituents. Arendt's description of this problem has been described as "the occluding of the political by the social and the transformation of the public space into a pseudospace of social interaction, in which individuals no longer 'act' but 'merely behave' as economic producers, consumers and urban city dwellers" (Benhabib, 1990, p. 169). Social space is differentiated from public space insofar as social space is public space utilized for the pursuit of private concerns. Arendt labels private concerns as those that pertain to the maintenance of one's personal life. One's choice of education is, for instance, a private decision and, by extension, should not be publicly mandated; similarly choices about friendships, household economics, sexuality, culture and religion all pertain to the individual's private life and should not be exposed to public scrutiny and judgment. Although there is no doubt that these attributes affect our public performances, our public performances should not be judged on our private attributes. Facebook makes such a distinction between public and private highly problematic.

An example of how the collapse of the private/public distinction can homogenize can be seen in the issue of economics. Arendt (1958) celebrates the fact that in the city-states of classical Greece the concerns of economics were seen to be a matter of private affairs and thus were excluded from public debate (p. 37). Such an exclusion is justified by Arendt because to impose an economic criteria on public space would homogenize the space and make all actors beholden to that one, economic, set of criteria for judgment. It would thus elevate a private issue to become a public concern, marginalizing difference and assuming only the one interest—economic prosperity and capitalism—truly pervades the entire public sphere. With the floating of Facebook on the stock market at a stratospheric $100 billion value, many analysts were quick to point out that Facebook would have to find new ways of monetizing its stated goal of "connecting people and ideas" (Henn & Chace, 2012). As our news feeds are filled with more and more targeted ads, which are leveraged on our trust in the Facebook community, it becomes increasingly clear that one of the major problems with using Facebook as an LMS is that it is actually a private space that simulates public space in order to achieve private goals. Arendt argues that we should not be comfortable with presenting capitalism as an integral part of our shared world because doing so presents capitalism as far more permanent than it actually is and reproduces capitalism and capitalistic modes of being in the process.

In truly public space the individual has an opportunity to be judged according to his or her public performance (whatever that might entail) whereas in social space the individual will be judged based on his or her personal lives, prior to his or her public performance. "Society," Arendt (1958) declares, "expects from each of its members a certain kind of behavior, imposing innumerable and various rules, all of which tend to 'normalize' its members, to make them behave, to exclude spontaneous action or outstanding achievement" (p. 40). The public scrutiny of private issues may establish a tyranny of the majority over individuality, ensuring that even the most personal of events or issues does not escape broad analysis, criticism, and judgment.

Arendt (1958) makes a strong case that many of the crises of modern times directly result from the elevation of private issues to public prominence, replacing in the process truly public debate and, as a result, also allowing invasive "public" judgment of otherwise personal issues (pp. 38–47). The evidence of the occlusion of the public by the social surrounds us—in the prevalence of public figures judged for their personal lives, in the obsession with the intimate goings-on of celebrity figures and, of course, in the prevalence of social networking sites such as Facebook. Just about every criticism of Facebook's impact on our society and selves arises from the inability of Facebook to appropriately distinguish between private and public conversations (Allnut, 2012). It is important to understand that, according to Arendt's schema, the rise of Facebook should be understood as a symptom of the loss of public space, not a cause of it; however, it is also clear that Facebook provides a perfect example of how what appears to be "public" actually works as a system that imposes a series of normalizing judgments on private activities.

It is, of course, possible to suggest that a public/private/social distinction makes no sense in contemporary society, and it is arguable whether education ought to be a private, public, or social endeavor. The strong distinction that Arendt makes between public and private has been criticized by many who argue that the segmentation and removal of certain issues from public discussion does nothing more than propagate a public silence around personal and identity politics (Canovan, 1992, p. 113; Pitkin, 1998, pp. 98–114). If the idea of distinguishing between private and public spaces seems rather arbitrary and nonsensical to us today, Arendt (1958) believes that this is a direct result of the triumph of the normalization of using public space to judge private issues, which she diagnosed as being endemic in society long before Facebook made a business out of the practice (p. 38). When considering how "private issues" might surface and be subjected to "normalizing judgment" while using Facebook as an LMS, it is difficult to think of what might be beyond the auspices of educational discussion, particularly at a tertiary level. The private issues are the ones that trigger the greatest debate and engagement. The personal is political, and in many senses, it is generally only through confronting their personal issues that contemporary students ever come to consider the broader public.

This brings us back to our starting point; the great attraction of Facebook as an LMS is that it encourages access and engagement. If it does so through exposing us to each other's personal and private lives, maybe that is simply a sign of the times. I know that when teaching in person I always try to engage with the "lived experiences" of my students. I am also aware of how important it is to give students an opportunity to express themselves. This is not about subjecting them to observation, normalizing judgment and examination, which Foucault identified as the mechanisms of discipline (Foucault, 2012, pp. 170–192). Rather, it is an opportunity to access that connective energy that arises out of expressing oneself and thus coming to know oneself as related to others and to learning. Public disclosure, however private the subject matter, is one of the great educational incentives, and for this reason, Facebook seems to offer an intoxicating level of potential engagement.

However, such expressive engagement needs to be protected in an educational setting. Without intelligent and careful moderation, the expressive space of education can all too readily become a space of conformity and behavior. Facebook operates extensively as a panoptic system, "a perfect eye that nothing would escape and a centre towards which all gazes would be turned" (Foucault, 2012, p. 173). If we are to encourage academic discussions to take place in such a forum then we should be mindful that extensive moderation is also needed to ensure that the student discussion does not shift from encouraging expression to ensuring behavior. Research on the social effects of Facebook use range from ambivalent to bad. On the positive side, heavy-SNS users have been found to more readily overcome private differences in order to communicate (Burke, Kraut, & Marlow, 2011, p. 2). On the other hand, there is a wealth of evidence of online bullying taking place on the medium, particularly within educational based peer groups, with one study suggesting that 87% of all online bullying takes place on Facebook (Gayle, 2013). When we educate on Facebook, we add a certain normative weight to the discussions and judgments that take place there. Furthermore, by maintaining the continuity of the social space, we fail to provide a separate space where students can escape the social world. Although such an escape might be the last thing on students' minds, it seems important that they know it is possible.

I would like to conclude by reflecting on Arendt's essay on "The Crisis in Education," which is quoted at length at the start of this chapter and which makes a particular point about education and authority. Despite being written more than 50 years ago, it applies to contemporary moves toward "flipped classroom" learning and, by extension, the use of Facebook as an LMS. Discussing the education of children, Arendt comments that the collapse of the distinction between public and private has brought about a lack of faith in authority in general:

> it is obvious that in public and political life authority either plays no role at all . . . or at most plays a highly contested role. This, however, simply means, in essence, that people do not wish to require of anyone or to entrust to anyone the assumption of responsibility for everything else, for wherever true authority existed it was joined with responsibility for the course of things in the world . . . Authority has been discarded by the adults, and this can mean only one thing: that the adults refuse to assume responsibility for the world into which they have brought the children.
>
> (Arendt, 1954, p. 10)

The philosophical move toward postmodern approaches to education encourages teachers to avoid taking responsibility for directing learning, which certainly suits the needs of giving students ownership of their learning but also conspicuously serves the needs of economically efficient education. Leaving education to society will always produce some kind of social consensus, which in its pervasiveness and through its lack of an author, will appear as some divine "invisible hand" of truth (Arendt, 1958, pp. 40–45). In the absence of a strong moderator, the invisible hand of Facebook remains a kind of capitalistic individualism, which is both the reason that Facebook seems so attractive and the greatest threat to the pedagogical purity of educational discussions conducted through the medium.

With the rise of Facebook as an LMS, along with the concurrent flipping of the classroom and rise of peer assessment, we are exposing our educational process to a tyranny of the majority, which has the potential to extend beyond what we learn, to how we live and relate to one another. Although the deeper level of engagement that Facebook offers is attractive because of its ubiquity and depth, the same conditions mean that Facebook moderators must be prepared to "clear a space" for discussions to take place, to arbitrate between the public and the private, and to ensure that public discussions do not become private judgments.

References

Allnut, L. (2012, October 17). Why Do We Hate Facebook? *Radio Free Europe.* www.rferl.org/content/why-do-we-hate-facebook/24742202.html

Arendt, H. (1954). The Crisis in Education. *The Institute of Ideas.* www.instituteofideas.com/documents/PGF_Arendt_Education.pdf

Arendt, H. (1958). *The Human Condition.* Chicago: University of Chicago Press.

Benhabib, S. (1990). Hannah Arendt and the Redemptive Power of Narrative. *Social Research, 57*(1), 167–196.

Burke, M., Kraut, R., & Marlow, C. (2011, May 7–12). Social Capital on Facebook: Differentiating Uses and Users. *Computer-Human Interaction.* www.cs.cmu.edu/~wcohen/10–802/burkeCHI2011.pdf

Canovan, M. (1992). *Hannah Arendt: A Reinterpretation of Her Political Thought.* Cambridge: Cambridge University Press.

Foucault, M. (2012). *Discipline and Punish: The Birth of the Prison.* New York: Knopf Doubleday.

Gayle, D. (2013, March 18). Facebook Is the Worst Social Network for Bullying With 19-year-old BOYS the Most Common Victims. *The Mail Online.* www.dailymail.co.uk/sciencetech/article-2294023/Facebook-worst-social-network-bullying-New-survey-shows-youngsters-targeted-online-else.html

Harper, T. (2011). *Democracy in the Age of New Media: The Politics of the Spectacle.* New York: Peter Lang.

Henn, S., & Chace, Z. (2012, May 15). Is Facebook Worth $100 Billion? *National Public Radio.* www.npr.org/blogs/money/2012/05/15/152736516/is-facebook-worth-100-billion

Looi, C.-K., Seow, P., Zhang, B. H., So, H.-J., Chen, W., & Wong, L.-H. (2010). Leveraging Mobile Technology for Sustainable Seamless Learning: A Research Agenda. *British Journal of Educational Technology, 41*(2), 154–169.

McGoughlin, C., & Lee, M. J. W. (2010). Personalised and self regulated learning in the Web 2.0 era: International exemplars of innovative pedagogy using social software. *Australasian Journal of Educational Technology, 26*(1), 28–43.

Norton, A., Sonnemann, J., & McGannon, C. (2013). *The Online Evolution: When Technology Meets Tradition in Higher Education* (Report No. 2013-3). http://grattan.edu.au/publications/reports/post/the-online-evolution-when-technology-meets-tradition-in-higher-education/

Pitkin, H. F. (1998). *The Attack of the Blob: Hannah Arendt's Concept of the Social.* Chicago: University of Chicago Press.

Postman, N. (1985). *Amusing Ourselves to Death.* Toronto: Penguin Books.

Rheingold, H. (2008). Using Participatory Media and Public Voice to Encourage Civic Engagement. In W. L. Bennett (Ed.), *Civic Life Online: Learning How Digital Media Can Engage Youth* (pp. 1–24). Cambridge, MA: MIT Press.

10
Facebook and Blackboard as Learning Management Systems: Case Study

JOÃO MATTAR

University Anhembi Morumbi

Web 2.0 tools have been continuously integrated into education including social network sites (SNSs), amongst which Facebook is today the largest. This has naturally generated a large amount of research, such as studies on the general use of Facebook by students and teachers, the characteristics of online teacher–student interactions on Facebook, and the uses of Facebook for informal and formal learning. The first section of this chapter reviews the literature on a more specific use of Facebook as an alternative to a Learning Management System (LMS); the second section presents a case in which Facebook was used parallel to Blackboard as an LMS in a higher education course; the next section discusses the results of the study; and the conclusion points to future works.

Facebook as an LMS

Initial research did not find positive results comparing Facebook to LMSs. Parslow, Lundqvist, Williams, Ashton, and Evans (2008) showed that only 7% of the students in their study felt that Facebook was an appropriate place to learn in contrast to 75% who felt the same about Blackboard, whereas DeSchryver, Mishra, Koehleer, and Francis (2009) found no differences on psychology students' perceptions of social presence and the frequency and length of their discussion interactions in Facebook boards and Moodle forums. However, the former study already presented intriguing results: 51% of the students have discussed course work on Facebook, to which they frequently posted, compared to 30% on Blackboard. This kind of result was endorsed and amplified by subsequent research.

Schroeder and Greenbowe (2009) registered that, besides being more complex and detailed, the number of posts by chemistry students on a Facebook group was nearly 400% greater than on WebCT; furthermore, the discussion on WebCT ceased abruptly at a certain point, which did not happen to the Facebook group. Menon's (2012) study with medical students found a high degree of engagement, with 76% of them actively participating in supervised clinical discussions, leading to the conclusion that Facebook groups can enhance experiential learning and stimulate creative clinical thinking. Pellizzari (2012) perceived improvement of qualitative aspects of academic performance of students in a mathematics undergraduate course using a Facebook page, including some evidence of positive correlation of grades and other variables. DiVall and Kirwin (2012) compared the use of Blackboard and a Facebook page in a pharmacy course: 26% of the students contributed with posts or comments on Facebook and an additional 24% by liking, compared to only 11% who posted on Blackboard, and 61% of the students agreed that they were more likely to post (77% to see and read posts) on Facebook than on Blackboard; besides that, 39% of the students reported never looking at the Blackboard discussion board for the course, whereas almost all students followed the Facebook page.

Many results, however, have identified problems and challenges on the use of Facebook as an LMS. Meishar-Tal, Kurtz, and Pieterse (2012) found that although students in a course in education that used a Facebook group experienced contributions to interaction and collaborative learning, communication, learning styles, intensity, and immediacy, they also reported difficulty in locating old items, orientation problems, and workload. Wang, Woo, Quek, Yang, and Liu (2012) showed that students in teacher training courses were satisfied with the use of Facebook groups as LMS, although pointing out some limitations, such as a lack of support for the upload of some format files (overcome today), discussions not being organized in a threaded structure, and students not feeling safe and comfortable with the possibility of their privacy being revealed. Similar to this literature, the following study was interested in comparing students' practices and perceptions on the use of a social network and an LMS to support the teaching and learning process.

Facebook versus Blackboard: A Case Study

A study was conducted with 244 Brazilian engineering freshmen students during the first semester of 2012 at University Anhembi Morumbi (São Paulo, Brazil), a member of the Laureate International Universities. Facebook groups and Blackboard (blackboard.com), the official LMS adopted by the university, were used in similar ways as support online environments for the same Microsoft Excel face-to-face course, in a total of eight classes taught by the same instructor. Eight groups were created on Facebook parallel to eight online classes on Blackboard. The participation on Facebook was not an obligation of the course; that is, these 244 students voluntarily participated on the groups. The instructor (and author of this chapter) had already performed and analyzed similar experiences with the same course during the two previous semesters (2011), however, without having planned and collected data for research, as in this case. Observations on these two previous semesters clearly showed a much higher interaction on the Facebook group than on Blackboard forums. Part of the explanation might be that in these cases a single (and although large) group, contrary to the study here presented, was created for all students, allowing communication by students of different classes, whereas on Blackboard they were separated by classes.

Two questionnaires using Google Docs forms were conducted at both the beginning and the end of the 2012 course, besides the active participation and observation of the instructor in both environments. Answering the questionnaires was part of the students' activities valid for grading. The first questionnaire included general questions (such as name, age, gender, learning styles, and in what course and semester the student was matriculated), questions regarding the previous use and mastery of Excel by the student, and on the student's use of social networks, especially Facebook. More than 90% of the students were younger than 25 years old; 63% were men and 37% women. An insignificant number were not first-year or engineering students. Only five students were advanced Excel users, and most students did not use the software regularly. Most of the students used Facebook every day or almost every day, usually spending from one to two hours a day logged on the network. Other social networks mostly used included Orkut (intensively used by Brazilians), Twitter, and Google+ (although that might have been confused with general Google tools), as expressed in Figure 10.1.

The closing questionnaire included the following questions, which were of direct interest for this study:

1. How did you first receive the announcements of the course?
   Facebook/Email/Blackboard/Class/Friend (one option only)
2. As a support for the course, which did you consider more efficient:
   Blackboard/ Facebook/Both were equally efficient (one option only)
3. How would you grade Blackboard as the support environment for the course?
   0 (bad)/1/2/3/4/5/6/7/8/9/10 (excellent)

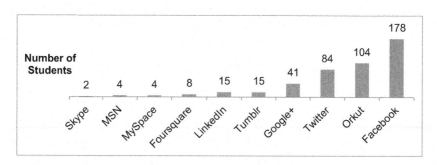

Figure 10.1 Social networks used by students

4. How would you grade Facebook as the support environment for the course?
   0 (bad)/1/2/3/4/5/6/7/8/9/10 (excellent)
5. Please compare Blackboard and Facebook group as support environments for the course—advantages and disadvantages of each, positive and negative points, etc.

About 36% of the students reported having first received course announcements by e-mail, 24% by Facebook, and 10% by accessing Blackboard, as represented in Figure 10.2.

About 60% of the students considered both Facebook and Blackboard efficient as support environments for the course, whereas 25% considered Facebook and 15% considered Blackboard more efficient. Students evaluated the efficiency of Facebook with the average grade 8.56 and Blackboard with 8.40 as support environments for the course.

Students' comments indicate clearly that Blackboard was considered a more structured environment, associated with seriousness, content access, individual study, and student/content interaction, whereas Facebook was seen as space for interaction and communication among students and instructors, and among students themselves. This is even clearer because several students indicated that they preferred Blackboard because there they could find video tutorials, although the same exact tutorials were uploaded to the Facebook group. Students also indicated the tendency for distraction when using Facebook for studying because of different apps and the chat, whereas Blackboard was associated with more focus and concentration. Leisure/Obligation was another dichotomy present on the students' evaluation when defining Facebook and Blackboard as an LMS.

Technical problems, such as being out of order, difficulties in access, and slowness were mentioned about Blackboard, in comparison to the easy and quick access to Facebook, as most of the students are already logged on to the social network during the day, so they could receive announcements of the

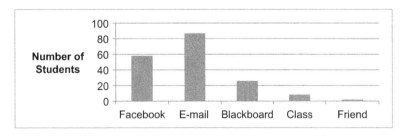

Figure 10.2 Responses to "How did you first receive the announcements of the course?"

course without needing an additional log to Blackboard. Some students, however, also indicated they were not allowed to access social networks at their workplace, making Blackboard the only possible access for studying. Some students also praised the innovative use of a social network for learning purposes. It is important to note that students submitted assignments for the course only through Blackboard, the only online space where they could also see their grades. This was commented by some students on the comparisons, but this is not explored further because it is not of interest for this study.

Discussion

One of the hypotheses of this research was that students would read course announcements initially on Facebook, as they log in daily to the social network. However, e-mail was the first channel for that purpose. Considering that these e-mails were sent through Blackboard, one can state that Blackboard was almost twice as efficient for quickly informing students about the course (46% versus 24%). This is explained by the current pervasiveness of mobile devices and that students did not have the option of blocking Blackboard on sending course announcements, whereas they are allowed to do so on Facebook. So, although students usually rank social networks better than LMS as communication and news tools, Blackboard occupied that role on the course for pushing information to students quickly.

Another hypothesis of this research was that students would better rank Facebook than Blackboard as an LMS. However, this didn't happen. The overall grades (8.56 and 8.40) show a nonsignificant difference and the majority of students considered both efficient learning environments. However, on some specific points, Blackboard was ranked higher than Facebook for learning purposes.

Blackboard was for instance associated by students with organization of information:

> Blackboard is more organized than Facebook; accessing and finding topics is easier. In Facebook students often comment on unneeded things and end up leaving the topic slightly shifted, a little confused.
>
> (F. H. G., male)

> Blackboard is more organized, you just need to click on the course and you see the announcements posted by the teacher and we can communicate with him by email, but it is not good to communicate with classmates (not sure if you can do it there) because generally we do not access it every day.
>
> (P. B. S., female)

Consequently, whereas Facebook was seen as a space for communication, Blackboard was seen as a space for study:

> Blackboard is more formal, so when we access it we are seeking information that would assist us on activities, a time that we have booked for the study; Facebook, on the other hand, is more relaxed, it is a time we take to communicate with friends and have fun.
>
> (I. B. C., female)

Facebook's potential for distraction was also compared negatively to Blackboard's appeal for concentration:

> For better learning, Blackboard is more useful than Facebook, where there are many distractions that draw our attention.
>
> (F. S. S., male)

> Blackboard's advantage is that, compared to Facebook, you have more concentration on what you are doing, because it does not have a chat, which is what harm performance on Facebook, as we are distracted with other information.
>
> (W. M. G., male)

These results validate what previous literature (Meishar-Tal et al., 2012; Wang et al., 2012) identifies as difficulties in finding information, orientation, and organization of content on Facebook, which Blackboard seems to offer with better quality.

Bypassing these advantage/disadvantage comparisons, students showed a clear and impressive consciousness that both environments might have different purposes and function complementarily, allowing different types of interaction.

Moore's (1989) article introduced a taxonomy of types of interaction covering learner–content, learning–instructor, and learner–learner interactions: "The first type of interaction is interaction between the learner and the content or subject of study" (Moore, 1989, p. 2). Thurmond (2003) found that the most significant predictor of student outcomes was students' perceptions regarding their interaction with instructors, whereas Yacci (2000) emphasized the importance of instructor's feedback. Learner-learner or interpersonal interactions (Berge, 1999) foster cooperative and collaborative learning and create a sense of belonging to a community.

Other types of interaction were added to these three initial ones proposed by Moore. Hillman, Willis and Gunawardena (1994) added the interaction between the learner and the interface. Called by some authors *learner–self-interaction*

(Soo & Bonk, 1998), *intrapersonal interaction* (Berge, 1999), or *internal learner interaction* (Hirumi, 2011), self-interaction emphasizes the importance the internal dialogue students have with themselves during engagement with content. Learner–other (Hirumi, 2011) adds the interactions a learner might have with people outside the course; Xenia and Christos (2012) use the expression *community–student interaction*.

A rich imaginary showed up in some of the students' reflections on learner–interface interactions: on one hand, Blackboard is described as a space for individual study, self-education, self-interaction, and learner–content interaction, whereas, on the other hand, Facebook is described as space for communication among students and instructor (learner–instructor interaction), among students themselves (learner–learner interaction), and with others (learner–others interaction):

> Blackboard is something more private, for personal use. Facebook makes you able to interact more with other students, teachers, and other members of the college.
>
> (Y. C. F., male)

> Facebook was positive for me for asking questions, super fast return. Blackboard was used more for access and download posted materials and for studying.
>
> (A. M. A., male)

The positive results of social networks compared to LMS might be explained by the fact that previous studies measure mainly learner–instructor and learner–learner interactions, giving little attention to self-interaction and learner–content interaction. The present study shows that the taxonomy of types of interactions might add interesting dimensions to the body of knowledge that has already been established by this tradition of comparative studies.

It is notable that no single student comment expressed any fear of invasion into his or her personal online space by institutions or instructors, in contrast to the literature (Stoerger, 2013; Towner & Muñoz, 2011); on the contrary, Facebook is praised when compared to Blackboard exactly because of its possibilities of learner–instructor interactions:

> On Facebook I was able to ask questions directly to the teacher, while on Blackboard I asked questions to videos and explanations available there.
>
> (J. M. S. O., male)

> On the Facebook group, one of the great advantages is that I was able to ask questions directly to the instructor and students online!—but some information was missing. On Blackboard, on the other hand, all the

missing information was there with the help of videos and corrections by the teacher.

(W. D. S. G., male)

Leaving the academic environment, in Facebook the contact with the teacher is closer, allowing students to clarify doubts and deadlines, as well as stimulating the mutual interaction among colleagues of the same course.

(K. F. V., male)

No comments of the students expressed either that the merging of the social with the educational environment was perceived as a violation of privacy, also common in the literature (Stoerger, 2013; Towner & Muñoz, 2011). That is, the results of this case study not only do not show that students prefer a separation between learning space and social space but, on the contrary, also show that students see a clear distinction of Blackboard and Facebook as learning environments and—the most impressive—that they clearly argue for the advantage of fusing both spaces for learning. Differences in the methodologies of the studies might explain these contrasts, which might also reflect the dynamic changes on privacy issues and personal/social uses of networks. No comments of the students expressed a sense of information overload with the use of Facebook, common in the literature of the use of social networks for learning (Stoerger, 2013). The way in which students used both environments simultaneously and for different purposes, cleverly distributing knowledge, might explain these results.

Conclusion

Although some authors (Wang et al., 2012) argue that Facebook may be used as an alternative to an LMS with major advantages for learning, other authors (Towner & Muñoz, 2011; Stoerger, 2013) point out that students prefer keeping their online social spaces (such as Facebook) separated from their learning spaces (LMS). The overall results of this study suggest neither that social network sites should replace LMSs nor that we should not use social network sites for formal teaching purposes. This study validates the use of Facebook as an LMS in formal learning and shows that there is a place for the integration of Facebook into higher education. However, the results also indicate that higher education students clearly position traditional LMSs and social networks as complementary learning environments, associating Blackboard with structure, learner–content interaction, and self-interaction and Facebook with communication and learner–instructor, learner–learner, and learner–other interactions. That is, from the students' perception, there is a space for integrating social networks into formal learning in higher education, however, without putting aside traditional LMSs.

In the same direction, further analysis could try to identify if there is an additional student imaginary that connects learning and leisure spaces, as discussed by Parslow et al. (2008). It is important to note that the data discussed in this case were not correlated with gender and learning-style results (from the first questionnaire), but such refinement could generate interesting additional discussion.

Future works might include comparisons of (a) the efficiency of LMS and Facebook chats or other synchronous tools; (b) the specific dynamics of LMS forums and Facebook discussions, including the levels of instructor/students control, content organization and retrieval, and the fact that newer posts (or commented posts) are pushed to the top on Facebook; (c) the fact that content and interaction are usually separated in an LMS, whereas on Facebook both, are inevitably created together, being interaction though inherent in the content (Meishar-Tal et al., 2012), and how this might be associated with workload; and (d) if social network sites, such as Facebook, haven't developed to a level at which they can play the role of managing course and learners, producing reports, offering feedback, assessing students, and grading, which Meishar-Tal et al. (2012) associate with LMS.

References

Berge, Z. L. (1999). Interaction in post-secondary web-based learning. *Educational Technology, 39*(1), 5–11.

DeSchryver, M., Mishra, P., Koehleer, M., & Francis, A. (2009). Moodle vs. Facebook: Does using Facebook for discussions in an online course enhance perceived social presence and student interaction? In I. Gibson et al. (Eds.), *Proceedings of Society for Information Technology & Teacher Education International Conference 2009* (pp. 329–336). Chesapeake, VA: AACE. Retrieved from www.editlib.org/p/30612

DiVall, M., & Kirwin, J. L. (2012). Using Facebook to facilitate course-related discussion between students and faculty members. *American Journal of Pharmaceutical Education, 76*(2), 32. Retrieved from www.ncbi.nlm.nih.gov/pmc/articles/pmc3305941/

Hillman, D.C., Willis, D. J., & Gunawardena, C. N. (1994). Learner-interface interaction in distance education: An extension of contemporary models and strategies for practitioners. *The American Journal of Distance Education, 8*(2), 30–42.

Hirumi, A. (2011). *Applying grounded strategies to design and sequence e-learning interactions.* Manuscript submitted for publication.

Meishar-Tal, H., Kurtz, G., & Pieterse, E. (2012). Facebook groups as LMS: A case study. *The International Review of Research in Open and Distance Learning, 13*(4), 33–48. Retrieved from www.irrodl.org/index.php/irrodl/article/view/1294/2295

Menon, V. (2012). Using a Facebook group for interactive clinical learning. *International e-Journal of Science, Medicine and Education, 6*(1), 21–23. Retrieved from http://web.imu.edu.my/imuejournal/approved/5.Original_Menon_p21-23.pdf

Moore, M. G. (1989). Editorial: Three types of interaction. *American Journal of Distance Education, 3*(2), 1–6.

Parslow, P., Lundqvist, K. Ø., Williams, S., Ashton, R., & Evans, M. (2008, September). *Facebook & BlackBoard: Comparative view of learning environments.* Paper presented at SSE Systems Engineering Conference 2008, The University of Reading, Berkshire, England. Retrieved from http://centaur.reading.ac.uk/1105/

Pellizzari, P. (2012, February 1). *Facebook as an academic learning platform: A case study in Mathematics.* (Research Paper Series No. 01/WP/2012). Venice: University Ca Foscari of Venice, Department of Economics. Retrieved from http://dx.doi.org/10.2139/ssrn.2016139

Schroeder, J., & Greenbowe, T. J. (2009). The chemistry of Facebook: Using social networking to create an online community for the organic chemistry laboratory. *Innovate: Journal of Online Education, 5*(4). Retrieved from http://gator.uhd.edu/~williams/AT/ChemOfFB.htm

Soo, K., & Bonk, C. J. (1998, June). *Interaction: What does it mean in online distance education?* Paper presented at the *ED/MEDIA/ED-TELECOM 98* World Conference on Educational Multimedia and Hypermedia & World Conference on Educational Telecommunications, Freiburg, Germany.

Stoerger, S. (2013). Making connections: How students use social media to create personal learning networks. In H. Yang & S. Wang (Eds.). *Cases on formal and informal e-learning environments: Opportunities and practices* (pp. 1–18). Hershey, PA: IGI Global.

Thurmond, V. A. (2003). *Examination of interaction variables as predictors of students' satisfaction and willingness to enroll in future web-based courses while controlling for student characteristics.* (Doctoral Dissertation, University of Kansas). Retrieved from www.bookpump.com/dps/pdf-b/1121814b.pdf

Towner, T. L., & Muñoz, C. L. (2011). Facebook and education: A classroom connection? In Wankel, C. (Ed.), *Educating Educators with Social Media* (pp. 33–57). Bingley, England: Emerald Group Publishing Limited. doi:10.1108/S2044-9968(2011)0000001005

Wang, Q. Y., Woo, H. L., Quek, C. L., Yang, Y. Q., & Liu, M. (2012). Using the Facebook group as a learning management system: An exploratory study. *British Journal of Educational Technology, 43*(3), 428–438. doi:10.1111/j.1467-8535.2011.01195.x

Xenia, Z., & Christos, G. (2012). Open source computer-mediated collaborative community learning. *International Journal of Computer and Information Technology, 01*(01), 67–76.

Yacci, M. (2000). Interactivity demystified: A structural definition for online learning and intelligent CBT. *Educational Technology, 40*(4), 5–16.

11

Rethinking Community? Facebook as a Learning Backchannel

KATE ORTON-JOHNSON

University of Edinburgh

In the context of Higher Education the use of Facebook as part of teaching and learning has stimulated debates about the pedagogical potential of social networking sites (SNSs) to offer collaborative and reflexive spaces for active and participatory scholarship (Bateman & Willems 2012). The well-documented ubiquity of Facebook and its role in the everyday lives of university students have prompted educators to focus on the possible benefits of the site as a tool for encouraging and (re)engaging students in creative ways. Proponents point to the ability of SNSs to support informal learning communities (Yardi 2006), to engage students as active learners (Maloney 2007) and to enhance communication between staff and students (Lemeul 2006). More cautious analyses point to the distracting nature of a network of entertainment in the lecture theatre and to the mismatch between multimedia-multitasking and traditional pedagogical objectives of deep, critical engagement (Bugeja 2006). There is evidence to suggest that students' use of Facebook sits somewhere between these poles, acting as an informal backchannel to the more formal activities of the academy (Selwyn 2007, 2009). As a learning backchannel Facebook gives students the opportunity to take an active and critical role in their learning as well as providing a social space to share information, "banter" and personal experience.

This notion of a backchannel as an ongoing conversation around formal teaching is not a uniquely technological phenomena and the exchange of chat and experiences with peers has long been a part of the student experience. What is interesting about the use of Facebook as a backchannel is the growing emphasis on spaces and "communities" of informal learning and on the value of diverse networks of knowledge consumption, construction and production. Meyers et al. (2013: 12) define these activities and spaces as "learning ecologies" that, in turn, rest on new conceptions of digital literacy and demands the ability to navigate and manage activities and forms of sociality that take place across a range of media and across formal and informal contexts.

This chapter explores the use of Facebook as an informal learning community and as a backchannel that sits, sometimes quite uncomfortably, alongside more formal channels of academic teaching, disrupting the boundaries between spaces of learning, creating opportunities for new forms of mediated interaction and demanding new types of digital and pedagogical literacies.

Research Context

The chapter draws on data exploring student use of Facebook as part of an introductory sociology course at a UK university. The large team-taught course is required for first-year sociology students but is also available to students from across the university. The course is designed with two formal lectures per week supported by small-group tutorial sessions. The 2012/13 cohort consisted of 450 students (83 of whom were sociology students) following degree programs in the social sciences, geosciences, humanities, business, languages, engineering and mathematics. Student feedback mid-semester indicated that the large and interdisciplinary nature of the group meant that the students lacked, and desired, a sense of course belonging and "community." In part the response to this, a private Facebook group, was established by the course convener to act as an informal space for students to discuss course content and to interact with each other, the course tutors and course lecturers. All students on the course were invited to join the group, and for the duration of the course, the group averaged around 200 members. Data collection took place over a period of 12 weeks, covering the second half of the course and key events in the academic cycle, including the submission of an assessment and the exam diet. Data collection techniques flowed through online and offline spaces and included e-mail and Skype interviews, the exchange of Facebook messages and face-to-face interactions with 43 students during the fieldwork period.

As a lecturer on the course I was active as a group member and used the Facebook wall as a space to post questions in preparation for and to follow up on lecture material, to solicit student examples and experiences to include as part of future lectures, to pose questions and prompt debate and to answer student questions and respond to posts and comments. At the end of the course I posted a request for permission to use the posts and interactions as part of the research and asked for student comments on a set of questions about how they used the group and what they thought of the use of Facebook as part of the course. I invited those interested to participate in further research and advised that they were free to opt out and for their posts and comments to not be used. This request was posted after the assessment of the course was complete to ensure that students did not feel that they would be disadvantaged from asking not to be included in the study, and so that there was no longer a direct teacher–student relationship with the author.

The "like" and "seen by" functions of the wall showed that 209 of the group members had seen the post, and in an attempt to ensure that de facto consent was not assumed by the lack of an opt-out option, I sent a follow-up e-mail reiterating the post to all of the students in the group. This does not necessarily mean that group members would wish to be the individual focus of research and in online spaces with fluctuating memberships informed consent is temporal and shifting (Markham & Buchanan 2012: 9). Accordingly, the analysis presented here draws on overarching themes rather than individual practice and potentially identifying posts and details have been adapted to preclude the risk of author identification.

Informal Community? The Facebook Wall as a Symbolic Marker of Connectivity and Engagement

The students' use of the Facebook group created a sense of connectivity and engagement, outside of the formal contact hours of the lectures and tutorials, that maps onto definitions of learning communities as informal, social and participatory (Brown & Adler 2008). The group wall was used by staff and students to post links to a range of media including YouTube clips, images and news stories that were related to or were exemplars of issues covered in the course. Although the "like" feature of the wall was heavily used by the students in response to posts, there was little interaction or ongoing discussion about these substantive types of post, and the wall acted more as a notice board or repository of links than a space of debate or exposition about course themes. Although challenging notions of a Facebook "learning community," the lack of interaction did not mean that the group was not engaging students in meaningful ways, and the sense of ongoing involvement in the course that the wall fostered was keenly felt.

> It did make me kind of constantly "on", in a good way, so that there was like a continual link between lectures. Usually outside of the lecture you are on your own but it kind of kept the momentum up.
>
> (Tom)

This continuity between face-to-face sessions was described by students in terms of "belonging," "connection" and "membership" and acted as a meaningful quasi-academic social space and set of practices "talking," "social stuff," and "kind of study stuff."

The notion of "stuff" is important here as aside from wall posts on specific examples, focused tasks or responses to questions posed by lecturers and tutors, the group primarily acted as a space for rather mundane and routine enquiries and discussions about workload, assessment, room locations and accessing course materials. This mirrors the findings of research that has noted the gap between the purported affordances of collaborative informal learning spaces and the more banal realities of student use (Madge et al. 2009; Selwyn 2007, 2009). However, it would be inaccurate to conclude that in deviating from more traditional or formal academic objectives the group lacked educational value. The group opened up and made visible existing student backchannels and was an important site for support and encouragement, providing a familiar space to 'be a student' with a wider network of peers:

> *I suppose I have though[t] of it as somewhere where I can have an academic version of the kind of chat I have in the rest of my Facebook or the chat I'd have after a lecture or tutorial with friends. It's like a really really informal on going [sic] tutor group that rumbles away in the background.*
>
> (Anna)

This informality played a valuable role for students who, as first year undergraduates, were insecure about learning to learn in a university environment. The Facebook group was positioned as a familiar space in which they were able to comfortably contribute to and feel part of the course in ways that were defined as social *and* academic. Facebook as a backchannel acted as a symbolic space of "doing work" and was a site that represented a convergence of the academic and the everyday. The notion of a symbolic space points to the students' cognizance of the ambiguities surrounding their definitions of what academic study was, and where it takes place, and their reflections on "figuring out" and "moaning" about the amorphous nature of their intellectual endeavor.

For the students the integration of an academic activity into their existing social network created a powerful sense of discursive connectivity and, in blurring the boundaries of the academic and the social, provided a space in which these identities could comfortably merge. This integration of familiar social networking practices with new academic activities represented a significant but unremarkable environment that was embedded in the local offline contexts of undergraduate life and that acted as a site for the "cultural learning" of what it is to be a student (Selwyn 2007:18).

The spaces and activities of formal study (the library and the lecture hall) were diversified into spaces and interactions that the students recognized were not "intellectual" or "proper" but were valued for the intangible sense of "engagement" and "involvement" that they created:

> *Obviously [the wall is] not a place of lively intellectual discussion but it is a place that didn't really exist anywhere before, it's a space where the day-to-day stuff can happen as a group and that does feel like something different and of value in a learning sense.*
>
> (James)

The Facebook group mapped onto and reinforced existing patterns of informal student interaction while at the same time extending the boundaries of this interaction in ways that fostered a sense of trans-temporal engagement and connectivity across online and offline spaces. I use the term *connectivity* to emphasize the social functions of the group without drawing on notions of community, which evoke meanings, images and emotional responses that do not resonate with the more utilitarian use of Facebook outlined here. If we take the meaning of a backchannel to be the maintenance of a behind the scenes conversation about a core activity, one that creates and sustains a community through shared discussion and expertise (Yardi 2006), then the use of Facebook, in this context, did little more than make visible the everyday activities that have long been a feature of student life. Facebook acted as additional "social glue" (Madge et al. 2009) for informal interaction but its role in the creation of 'community' was more closely related to a vague sense of being part of a wider body of people that were connected *by* and *through* the group. Membership in this group was not marked by active and critical learning practices but by more passive acts of social networking, "liking stuff" and simply "being there."

Rather than a coherent set of informal learning practices in a well-defined learning community the Facebook group connected and was sustained by this kind of "active lurking" (Orton-Johnson 2008) on the wall and through the maintenance of a "social presence" in the group (Bateman & Willems 2012). While friendship, shared connections and community have commonly been defined as the central metaphors of SNS (boyd & Ellison 2007) as a learning backchannel, Facebook use appears to be more akin to passive interaction opportunities (Baym & Leadbetter 2009) grounded in pragmatic approaches to the demands of study. In this sense "learning community" is more accurately defined as "learning connectivity" as students engage in a range of formal and informal activities and do so across different offline and networked spaces. Learning connectivities then refer to a continuum of participation practices that are indistinct but can be understood as having some sense of obligation, ongoing participation and self-identification as "member" (Kozinets 2010). This provides a more fluid understanding of community formation and maintenance and enables us to think beyond narratives of community in defining educational uses of SNS.

Negotiating Digital Literacies

The previous section emphasized issues of connectivity, sociality and engagement in arguing that Facebook acted as a symbolic marker for doing academic work. Although the social and symbolic importance of the group as part of a wider learning ecology was clear, this should not preclude an analysis of its pedagogical value. Although the role of the group as a tool for learning was more difficult for the students to articulate its scholarly importance was evident and the source of ongoing reflection: "*It was more than just a meeting place, it did tick a learning box but it's hard to really define what that box was*" (Angus).

The meaning of this equivocality demands a more refined analysis of the ways in which students understand Facebook as part of learning and a reflection on the ways in which students manage and negotiate their learning ecologies. In this section I argue that in blurring the social and the academic, the Facebook group also challenged the digital literacies of students and disrupted shared understandings of teaching and learning spaces.

The Backchannel to the Backchannel: Managing Digital Literacies

One of the oddities of the group activity was the contrast between the fairly static and mundane nature of the wall posts and interactions and the dynamic and prolific interactions that occurred in and via an additional layer of learning backchannel. Although my public wall posts, questions, requests and provocations would receive many likes and views, they did not regularly attract more than a few responses or stimulate ongoing interaction. However, alongside this public lack of dialogue private e-mails and Facebook messages proliferated. This created a backchannel to the backchannel as students messaged and contacted me "off group" in private responses to my own group-directed wall questions and posts. In contrast to the more informal chat and discussion on the group wall, these private messages were overwhelmingly substantive comments and critical reflections on lecture content, messages sharing relevant personal experiences and suggestions of examples that I could include in future lectures or post on the group wall myself. "Academic" staff–student interaction about substantive course content was conducted in an additional backchannel of private messages that were prompted by public wall posts in the Facebook group. Perhaps most interestingly these messages were frequently prefaced with acknowledgments that they "should" be wall posts: "I know you wanted us to post on the wall but . . ."; "I realise that I should share this with the group but wanted to message you directly . . ."; "You should probably post this for everyone but . . ." Students displayed an awareness of the collaborative and participatory conventions and expectations of the Facebook group as a Web 2.0 environment but chose to participate *publicly* in what they defined as more social ways and *privately* for what they defined as academic interaction. In the subsequent interviews and discussions with students, this kind of management of public/private and academic/social in and across mediated spaces was a salient issue, relating to issues of emerging and conflicting understandings of learning spaces and digital literacies.

Research has highlighted the willingness of students to use SNS backchannels to perform social identities that align with narratives of "the student" as passive, critical and disengaged rather than educational identities of intellectual enthusiasm or immersion (Selwyn 2009). This performative tendency finds some support here with students comfortable in engaging in low-stake social, everyday interactions but less willing to be visible in higher stake academic performances that risk exposure and critique.

Here the shift from learning *community* to learning *connectivity*, suggested earlier in the chapter, is key. Although students did feel belonging and membership in the group, this did not extend to a perception of the spaces as a supportive, bounded and collaborative community in which more exploratory, uncertain and hesitant interactions could be facilitated.

These academic insecurities are nothing new and are not unique to mediated environments, but they highlight a need for analytical attention to be paid to the ways in which students are managing sometimes quite contradictory digital and pedagogical literacies and expectations. As educators we may embrace innovative and creative ways of delivering course content and supporting and interacting with our students, but these do not always sit comfortably alongside the formal requirements and regulatory structures of our higher education institutions. Encouraging use of social networks and informal teaching backchannels may conflict with student understandings of the demands of assessment and of course participation and requires them to draw on a range of new digital literacies to engage with new learning spaces.

These new literacies require students to balance the boundaries of the personal and the private, as social spaces of play, procrastination and leisure merge with academic spheres in ways that may be challenging and counterintuitive. Facebook is a place of narrative and performance and of the tensions between constructing academic and personal experiences, and making sense and meaning of these experiences for the self means that students are both familiar and out of place when using Facebook as a learning backchannel. In presenting students with an academic version of their embedded and everyday Facebook activities, we fracture understandings of where the academic is:

> I think that Facebook is just so normal and being a first year it's university that isn't normal yet, so what is being described as a new space for learning to me is just same old Facebook, its university that is the innovative and alien learning space.
>
> (Nick)

It is in navigating these "alien" spaces of ambivalence that the backchannel(s) opened up avenues of communication that students would otherwise not have pursued. For the students the Facebook group created a sense of increased lecturer presence and accessibility and a perceived flattening of the hierarchies of communication. They used both backchannels to redefine and reconfigure their learning spaces and their access to the lecturer.

Some research has suggested that while Facebook plays an important role in social and academic interactions between students it does not open channels of communication between academic staff and students in the same way (Hewitt & Forte 2006; Madge et al. 2009). Recognizing the value students place on the additional backchannels, and the increase in communication, challenges this and raises important questions about the nature of peer-to-peer interaction, academic-to-student interaction and course design as part of increasingly mediated learning ecologies. These kinds of extensions to learning spaces and channels of communication may have the potential to enrich the student experience, but they also create their own tensions and demands as narratives of student consumerism combine with digital technologies to weigh heavily on academics as digital labor and connectivity proliferate (Selwyn 2013).

Conclusion

The growing body of literature that has concerned itself with the potentials and perils of SNS in education presents a picture that is far from clear. Research outlining active, collaborative learning communities populated by engaged and reflexive students is balanced by enquiry that reveals a much less dramatic and less transformative empirical reality.

Perhaps one point of commonality is that students that are active (however broadly defined) and connected via Facebook are able to engage with the process of learning as something broader than face to face teaching and individual study. As I have suggested in this chapter even seemingly limited engagement and mundane interaction encouraged students to identify themselves as participatory agents enjoying an increased sense of connectivity with staff and peers. In blurring the boundaries between well-established social networking practices and academic activities, Facebook acted as a space in which emerging identities and practices of 'student' could be explored and negotiated. In providing an informal backchannel to the more formal activities of teaching and learning it enabled students to develop new digital literacies and new understandings of the spaces and boundaries in which scholarship takes place.

Given the nature of the students' more social and informal use of Facebook, there is logic in treating it as little more than a technological expression of 'business-as-usual' activities that are on the periphery of formal education: not requiring or being appropriate for teaching or pastoral interventions (Madge et al. 2009) and continuing and developing 'unabated and firmly "backstage"' (Selwyn 2007:21). This is particularly important if we understand student use as the more passive and proxy involvement suggested in this chapter. As Selwyn (2013: 3) argues, we need to avoid technology use becoming little more than "techno-erotica," appealing to students rather than providing genuinely enabling and empowering opportunities for participation and collaboration.

In engaging with Facebook as part of informal or formal teaching and learning activities we are in danger of valorizing and privileging SNS as a medium that is only one of many contexts through which and in which learning occurs. Conversely, can we afford to ignore powerful social networks such as Facebook that may have the potential to act as a mezzo level of connectivity between informal and formal learning activities in a changing and increasingly mediated landscape of Higher Education?

References

Bateman, D., & Willems, J. (2012). Facing off: Facebook and higher education. In L. C. Wankel (Ed.), *Misbehavior Online in Higher Education* (Cutting-Edge Technologies in Higher Education, Vol. 5, pp. 53–79). Bingley, UK: Emerald Group Publishing Limited.

Baym, N., & Leadbetter, A. (2009). Tunes that Bind? *Information, Communication & Society, 12*(3) 408–427.

boyd, d., & Ellison, N.B. (2007). Social network sites: Definition, history and scholarship. *Journal of Computer Mediated Communication, 13*(1), 210–230.

Brown, J. S., & Adler, R. P. (2008). Open education, the long tail, and learning 2.0. *Educause Review, 43*(1), 16–20.

Bugeja, M. (2006). Facing the Facebook. *Chronicle of Higher Education, 52*(21), C1–C4.

Hewitt, A., & Forte, A. (2006, November). *Crossing boundaries: Identity management and student/faculty relationships on the Facebook.* Paper presented at the CSCW Conference, Banff, Alberta, Canada.

Kozinets, R. (2010). *Netnography: Doing ethnographic research online.* London: Sage.

Lemeul, J. (2006). Why I registered on Facebook. *Chronicle of Higher Education, 53*(1), C1.

Madge, C., Meek, J., Wellens, J., & Hooley, T. (2009). Facebook, social integration and informal learning at university: "It is more for socialising and talking to friends about work than for actually doing work." *Learning, Media and Technology, 34*(2), 141–155.

Maloney, E. (2007). What Web 2.0 can teach us about learning. *Chronicle of Higher Education 53*(18), B26.

Markham, A., & Buchanan, E. (2012). *Ethical decision-making and Internet research recommendations from the AoIR Ethics Working Committee (Version 2.0).* http://aoir.org/reports/ethics2.pdf

Meyers, E., Erickson, I., & Small, R. (2013). Digital literacy and informal learning environments: an introduction. *Learning, Media and Technology, 5*(1). doi:10.1080/17439884.2013.783597

Orton-Johnson, K. (2008). "Give me a website and I'll wipe out a rainforest." Student constructions of Technology and learning. *The International Journal of Learning, 14*(12), 161–166.

Selwyn, N. (2007, November). *"Screw blackboard . . . do it on Facebook!" An investigation of students' educational use of Facebook.* Paper presented to the Poke 1.0—Facebook Social Research Symposium, University of London.

Selwyn, N. (2009). Faceworking: Exploring students' education-related use of Facebook. *Learning, Media and Technology, 34*(2), 157–174.

Selwyn, N. (2013). Digital technologies in universities: problems posing as solutions? *Learning, Media and Technology, 38*(1), 1–3.

Yardi, S. (2006, June). *The role of the backchannel in collaborative learning environments.* Paper presented at the Proceedings of the 7th International Conference of the Learning Sciences (ICLS'06), Indiana University, Bloomington.

Part 4
Facebook at College

12

Facebook at Uni: Mutual Surveillance and a Sense of Belonging

MARJORIE D. KIBBY

Humanities and Social Science, The University of Newcastle

JANET FULTON

Design Communication and IT, The University of Newcastle

Surveillance usually has negative connotations of intrusion, control, and privacy invasion. However, participatory surveillance can be seen as empowering rather than violating users (Albrechtslund, 2008) in that it provides information that can increase cultural capital. Mutual surveillance on Facebook is a social act that facilitates connections and an analysis of the discourse on the "People Sleeping at Newcastle University" Facebook page shows students choosing social cohesion over privacy in a number of ways. They identify themselves in anonymous photographs, respond to posted images with explanations and excuses for their on-campus naps, and share advice on the most comfortable sleeping spots and the most ennui-inducing courses and lecturers. Students offer themselves up for surveillance and in doing so establish a presence in the university community.

Social network use has been identified as serving a number of functions for users. Social media can provide users with social and emotional support through the creation and maintenance of ties to people they know (Ellison, Steinfield, & Lampe, 2007; Wellman & Gulia, 1999). Facebook, in particular, is a platform for self-affirmation where users can preserve perceptions of self-worth (Lewis, Pea, & Rosen, 2010; Toma & Hancock, 2013). An information resource, it can provide users with social capital (Ellison, Heino, & Gibbs, 2006) by building an understanding of networks, norms, and expectations that facilitate social interaction. In the case of students, it can foster a sense of community (O'Shea, 2013), and it is a place where students can "become versed in 'identity politics'" (Selwyn, 2009, p. 171) and learn how to be a student. Facebook is also used for social browsing, where users of the site seek to develop new connections, and social searching, where Facebook is used to find out more about people met offline, such as in a class or at a social function (Lampe, Ellison, & Steinfield, 2006). Many users describe their use of social networking as "keeping in touch," seeing what friends and acquaintances are doing, with or without maintaining communication with them (Lampe et al., 2006). The different uses of Facebook have been summarized as "virtual people watching" (Joinson, 2008).

People watching, or surveillance, has become a widespread cultural practice. Students, in particular, are accustomed to official surveillance practices that range along a spectrum from care to control. They are watched for their own protection, and they are observed in order to enforce discipline (Lyon, 2001). Their behavior is monitored through devices such as customer loyalty cards with their consent (Monahan, 2011) and reality television, in exposing the everyday life of celebrities and housewives to casual view, creates an unconscious desire for surveillance (Pecora, 2002). Part of this culture of surveillance is the expectation of a right to spy on others—people watching is not only socially acceptable; it is also a social imperative.

Facebook developed from the paper "face books" of cohort photographs and brief biographies circulated amongst commencing students at some universities, and it was originally restricted to users with an "edu" e-mail address, which has contributed to its high use by students. Although the user demographics have broadened since Facebook's original restriction to users with an "edu" e-mail address, this group is still dominant. In Australia, for example, 49% of Australian users are aged between eighteen and thirty-four, and 57% are university or college educated (Queensland Government, 2013). This group continues to impact the way in which Facebook is developed and used, including its use as a mechanism for peer surveillance, and its use in conjunction with face-to-face interactions to provide additional information on friends and fellow students and on university and college life. For social networks to function, users must submit information, and in doing so they make otherwise transient activities and thoughts permanent and available to others. Facebook is composed of users seeking out and watching over each other (Trottier, 2012). Students are aware that they are both spies and spied on, but see the lateral information exchange as a necessary component of a desired visibility (Trottier, 2012), and users maintain a trade-off between ensuring privacy and maintaining public exposure (boyd & Hargittai, 2010). Users come to see peer-to-peer surveillance as a condition of social media use, further normalizing surveillance (Murakami Wood & Webster, 2009).

Facebook users seem willing to perform themselves online and offer that performance up for surveillance on their personal home pages (Westlake, 2008, p. 38). However, on their own pages they have a degree of control over what is retained and who accesses the information. Pages established for the express purpose of exchanging information on others raises different questions on self-presentation and lateral surveillance. One example of this type of page is "Stalkerspace," Facebook pages at a number of Australian universities on which users post photos of badly parked cars and campus oddities or enquire after the details of someone they'd like to meet. "Stalkerspace" pages are overt about obtaining and/or sharing information about others without their consent, and although there are concerns about the legal and ethical implications of such unofficial university sites (Woodley & Beattie, 2012), these sites offer students the opportunity to engage informally with the university environment. Another example is the "People Sleeping" pages on which students post photographs taken of their peers asleep in the libraries, classes, and grounds of their campuses, posting them as anonymous or tagged images. Others can tag the images and can like, share, and comment on them. Page administrators can highlight contributions by reposting them.

Some academic institutions for which there is a "People Sleeping" Facebook page include Rocky Mountain College Montana (RMC), Boise State University, Cedarville University Ohio, Colorado Christian University (CCU), Liberty University Virginia, Adelaide University South Australia, Griffith University Queensland, and the University of Newcastle, Australia (UoN). The pages have a range of levels of engagement, with some pages showing an active moderator who has provided detailed information including, in some cases, the real names of the page administrators. The pages also have a range of levels of student engagement, with pages established in 2010 or 2011 having around 3,000 to 5,000 subscribers and newer 2013 pages having 200 to 300 page likes. Some pages provide guidelines for use, advising posters that all submissions are moderated, and that people can have photos of themselves immediately removed on request, whereas others simply warn that "Anything goes. Let the payback begin!" (such as the "Sleeping students of RMC" Facebook page). The "About" sections of the pages include descriptors such as

> Post your pictures of those sleeping in class, chapel, on roadtrips, couches, from all around campus. Anything goes.
> ("Sleeping students of CCU" Facebook page)

> To all you head bobbers in class, snoozers, and droolers . . . You might wanna nap or start drinking Rinnova, so BEWARE. Students of CU start snapping pics of sleepers, upload, and let the laughing begin. One rule . . . Pictures cannot be of students sleeping in their beds in their dorms . . . thats [sic] not interesting lol.
> ("Sleeping Students of Cedarville" Facebook page)

> "Nap and you'll get snapped" Fan participation welcome. Mission: to create a uni wide sleeping student database.
> ("The Notorious Sleeping Students of
> Adelaide University" Facebook page)

> Pictures of people. Sleeping. If you have a photo of yourself on this page made for FUN ONLY and wish to take it down please don't hesitate to message admin and prompt action will be taken.
> ("People sleeping at Macquarie University" Facebook page)

The "People Sleeping at Newcastle University" Facebook page is the most active of those reviewed. Established at the beginning of the 2010 campus year, it had more than 7,000 subscribers at the beginning of 2013, at which point it had a change of moderators after the graduation of the original administrator. Detailed page information encourages students to get involved, photographing sleepers on campus and uploading or sending the photos to the moderators, tagging sleeping students and other people in the image, commenting, and contributing relevant media clips. Contributions to the site include all of these types of involvement, with many of the posts having more than 1,000 interactions (given in the "People Talking About This" count).

This exploration of the "People Sleeping at The University of Newcastle" page used what Hine (2007) describes as connective ethnography, a method that integrates research across online and offline spaces, taking into account the offline contexts of individuals' production of online texts. Leander and McKim (2003) explain how connective ethnography analyzes users' experience of online tools/environments in terms of "flow," which describes "not merely a networked structure, but rather, the performance of individuals of and through that structure" (p. 226). Connective ethnography allowed an investigation not only of the exchanges between users of the Facebook page but also of the ways in which these exchanges reflected offline practices and attitudes and in turn helped to constitute these practices. Drawing data from a discourse analysis of the public Facebook page, from interviews with users on both their use of the page and their experience of the university environment, and from participant observations of the university community, this method provided cumulative layers of information about the university experience, and an understanding of the role of Facebook in that experience. Our primary interest was the diffusion of surveillance practices across people and online/offline spaces, and the impact of these practices on students' sense of belonging to the University community.

Although posts to the page are primarily photographs of people asleep on campus and comments on those images, a significant number of posts go beyond the immediate focus of the page, broadening its scope to a university community page. Users share relevant clips from the media including *Daria*, *The Simpsons*, *Ferris Bueller's Day Off*, *For Better or Worse*, Internet memes, and Imgur images. Some posts are comments on the features and milestones of university life:

- Congratulations to all those that just received offers to complete a sleep filled degree at this uni.
- It's usually around this time in the semester, people start teaching themselves the courses they are enrolled in.
- Best wishes for all those starting exams this week.
- REST2020 is my favourite class.
- Having four exams in one week > Nickelback

There are the usual games of social networking sites:

- Describe your year at uni, using only the title of a movie.
  - Dude, Where's my Car [park]?
  - Dazed and Confused.
  - While You Were Sleeping!
  - Bad Teacher.

Many of the posts are immediate status updates, or shout-outs to others in a similar activity:

- [Ferris Bueller] is on GO at the moment. I might treat myself to a day off tomorrow; this week has been tough so far.
- Hey, I just met you, and this is crazy, but we're in CT202 so wake me, maybe?
- Anyone awake in STAT1070?
- I'm falling asleep in this lecture, someone should set the fire alarm off.
- Anyone at uni meant to be working but streaming Coachella?
- About half of GENG1803 is asleep. Someone with a quiet camera shutter get on that.

Students also use the page as a source of information on university administrative requirements rather than accessing formal information sources. In this way, the page can contribute to the development of cultural capital and enhance students' feeling of belonging. Dalton and Crosby (2013) contend that social media are now the primary gatekeepers of a student's experience at college, and evidence of this contention was found on the "Sleeping" site:

- Does the saf fee just defer to hecs or do I have to pay it separately and by this Friday?
  - You must complete a new eCAF to defer this charge to an SA-HELP loan. This can be done through myhub.
  - Thankyou!

Students seem to trust the information on the site, to the extent that when a surveillance society course posted an image of the whole class posed asleep, few recognized it as a setup until the students involved explained how it came about:

- How is the lecturer still lecturing?! Surely they would play a prank on all the sleepers?
- Wow haha man that lecture must be so boring haha.
- What subject was This! Awesome!

During an interview, one student (Alyshia) said the informal university sites were her preferred way to get information because of the tone used on the sites: 'I use more of the student-run ones [Facebook sites] because they're a bit more informal' (interview May 14, 2013). Additionally, Alyshia commented on how she has become aware of information about lecturers, courses or programs via the "Sleeping site" and acknowledged, tongue-in-cheek, that this knowledge assisted her choices at university: 'I know that I should never take Stats because a lot of photos are taken in Stats' (interview May 14, 2013). Postings by others on the page also demonstrate how the site is used to share evaluations of teaching spaces, courses, and professors:

- INFT1004 in what would go down as a joke of a lecture.
- CT202 is like sleep headquarters; they schedule the most boring lecturers in there year after year.
- Marcus is AWESOMELY enthusiastic. You only need to be in Marcus's lecture for 30 minutes to see how enthusiastic he is! I do better in his class than any other.
- James makes the lectures entertaining . . . i can see it now. Educational Psychology: The Musical!!!
- Didn't take long for POLI3001 to claim its first victim—living up to its reputation.
- STAT1070 . . . Enough said.
- Get ready for another victim in V107. It won't be long. This teacher is boring as batshit.

Other posts demonstrate a sharing of the chat, gossip, and community mythology that forms the basis of friendship ties in online spaces. The "Sleeping Dude" is a man who is regularly seen, and photographed, asleep on campus:

- This is the Sleeping Dude isn't it? I've seen a few photos of this guy on here.
- This guy used to be a regular on this page. At least 5 photos of him floating around from the past.
- I saw him awake this morning!!!! at gloria jeans
- He probably does Mechatronics or Mechanical or something similar, because he's in my Comp Eng lectures, but nothing else.
- Sleeping dude—sleeping!!!
- [This] looked like the guy we used to call 'Sleeping dude'.

Posted images of sleepers attract a range of comments:

- [He] looks like he travelled all the way from the 90s, no wonder he needed a nap!
- He's / She's a pro. Wish I'd thought of a blanket for my sleeps.

- Amazing that he can sleep without the drone of a lecturer in the background.
- Maybe they're passed out after a big night and never made it to the train . . .

And university events are discussed:

- It was good to see a bed entered, at the Autonomy Day billy cart races.
- Frenzel Rhomb at Bar on the Hill Goodbye my Liver
- It's Cultural Awakenings next week at Uni food fair friday!!

Users recognize the surveillance that the page facilitates, but seem to have an ambivalent attitude towards spying and being spied on. Although fearing or resenting being monitored by parents, employers, or university staff, some seem to welcome the minor celebrity attached to peer surveillance. Users will comment on having had a nap on campus that was not photographed and posted:

- So glad no one caught me taking a nap in my car this morning in the main carpark . . . woke up in a panic expecting someone to be peering in the window with a camera :p
- Looks like nobody was quick enough to snap a photo of my nap in CT202

However, users frequently identify themselves in photographs posted by others:

- That guy looks awfully familiar . . . *cough*
- Yes, that's me and yes, that couch is amazingly comfortable.
- That's me. A big week with assessments and exams, few late nights and early mornings . . . figured whilst the lectures being recorded I would have a nap lol
- Hahaha mate that's me my last night on that library for this year . . .
- Me! That couch just sucks the life out of you.

There is no expectation of anonymity, and users regularly identify sleepers:

- That looks heaps like a guy named alex!
  - Elyse, i agree with you !, i rekon [sic] it looks like alex
  - Alex, agreed.
  - Looks like Alex, and has an army bag. Yeah, that's Alex.
  - yeah that's him. I must be just left of frame haha (on the other side by about 2–3 rows)—Thats [sic] Alex alright.
  - yep . . . that's Alex lol

Some posters are reluctant to be identified as the snapper, sending their images to the page administrators to be posted:

- Sent in by one of many photo ninja's [*sic*] at the Uni
- The rare double, taken by a prolific photographer who wishes to remain anonymous

Others acknowledge reticence when posting images of friends:

- I know she's going to kill me.. but I couldn't resist LOL! Brennan Room
  - Tag her in it!
  - Ahaha she'll kill me.. haha oh well "Abby"

Or reluctance to take photographs of sleepers:

- I feel too creeper taking a photo, but the back of GP201 is full of sleeping kids. Apparently HIST1080 is a bit tiring.

There is some suggestion that users change their online and offline behaviors as a result of their awareness of personal surveillance (Trottier, 2012). One of the concerns about social networking is the later consequences of current posts, as transient activities are made permanent, searchable, and replicable (O'Shea, 2013; Paradise, 2012). Some users express a fear of having an image of them asleep posted on the page, and their efforts to avoid being caught napping:

- The reason I am terrified to go to lectures when I'm tired without a coffee—those with cameras and internet D:
- I'm terrified I'm going to end up on this page.
- Desperately trying to stay awake. Girl in front just had her photo taken.

However, during her interview, Alyshia laughed when asked if she would mind if her photo was taken and posted and said she was "not too worried. I know I've been asleep in a few different places around Uni but no-one's caught me yet" (interview May 14, 2013). Alyshia also said she would have no hesitation putting a photo of a sleeper up on the site but only if she knew the person and "I'd think they'd be OK with it" (interview May 14, 2013), although, when asked if she would then tag the person, she laughed and answered with an emphatic "Yes." Alyshia is an intermittent user and initially discovered the "Sleeping Page" via other UoN informal Facebook sites such as "The Dapper Gentleman of the University of Newcastle," a tribute page to a staff member who is "regularly seen strolling the grounds of the University of Newcastle" in "sartorial splendour," and Newcastle's "Stalkerspace" page and thought the

"Sleeping" site was funny. She first posted on the site after seeing a photo of "someone asleep in a subject I would find equally as boring, or sleep inducing" (interview May 14, 2013) and it made her laugh. Alyshia's comment demonstrates that she identifies with others on the site: she has found a sense of camaraderie with others in the university community and a further comment during the interview confirmed that idea:

> The Sleeping one [site], that's more like a friendly, poking fun at people falling asleep, when we all know that we've probably all done the same thing. It's more just, not like a friendship kind of thing, but all knowing that we're in this together.
>
> (interview May 14, 2013)

Although there are concerns about how and what users share on Facebook, particularly when it comes to privacy and self-disclosure and the negative consequences that may come from these practices (Paradise, 2012; O'Shea, 2013), it would seem from this analysis of Newcastle's "Sleeping" site that the "negative consequences on users' academic and professional lives" (Paradise, 2012, p. 263) is not of a high concern to the users. Rather, the students use the site to learn about the interests, actions, and values of the community, thus providing a sense of belonging. This analysis has found evidence of students using the site to connect with other users via chatting about events and experiences, searching for and sharing information about courses and teachers, and, of course, posting and tagging photos and liking and commenting on them. In other words, engaging in surveillance practices. Furthermore, the site has expanded from its original purpose of being a place where people are gently mocked for "getting caught" sleeping in public spaces to a place where students can begin to negotiate the University community and become part of that community. As Hilton and Plummer (2012) noted, "Facebook has the potential of assisting students in settling into University life" (p. 204), making them feel, as Alyshia said, "all in it together."

References

Albrechtslund, A. (2008). Online social networking as participatory surveillance. *First Monday, 13*(3). Retrieved from http://firstmonday.org/htbin/cgiwrap/bin/ojs/index.php/fm/article/viewArticle/2142

boyd, d., & Hargittai, E. (2010). Facebook privacy settings: who cares. *First Monday, 15*(8). Retrieved from http://firstmonday.org/ojs/index.php/fm/article/view/3086/2589

Dalton, J. C., & Crosby, P. C. (2013). Digital Identity: how social media is influencing student learning and development in college. *Journal of College & Character, 14*(1), 1–4.

Ellison, N., Heino, R., & Gibbs, J. (2006). Managing impressions online: Self-presentation processes in the online dating environment. *Journal of Computer-Mediated Communication, 11*(2), 415–441.

Ellison, N., Steinfield, C., & Lampe, C. (2007). The benefits of Facebook "Friends": Social capital and college students' use of online social network sites. *Journal of Computer-Mediated Communication, 12*(4), 1143–1168.

Hilton, J., & Plummer, K. (2012). To Facebook, or not to Facebook? *Digital Culture and Education (DCE), 4*(2), 203–217.

Hine, C. (2007). Connective ethnography for the exploration of e-Science. *Journal of Computer-Mediated Communication, 12*(2), 618–634. Retrieved from http://jcmc.indiana.edu/vol12/issue2/hine.htm

Joinson, A. N. (2008). Looking at, looking up or keeping up with people? Motives and use of Facebook. In *Proceedings of the twenty-sixth annual SIGCHI conference on human factors in computing systems* (pp. 1027–1036). Florence: Association for Computing Machinery (ACM).

Lampe, C., Ellison, N., & Steinfield, C. (2006). A Face(book) in the crowd: social searching vs. social browsing. In *Proceedings of the 2006 20th anniversary conference on computer supported cooperative work* (pp. 167–170). Alberta: Association for Computing Machinery (ACM).

Leander, K. M., & McKim, K. K. (2003). Tracing the everyday 'sitings' of adolescents on the Internet: A strategic adaptation of ethnography across online and offline spaces. *Education, Communication & Information, 3*(2), 211–240.

Lewis, S., Pea, R., & Rosen, J. (2010). Beyond participation to co-creation of meaning: mobile social media in generative learning communities. *Social Science Information, 49*(3), 351–369.

Lyon, D. (2001). *Surveillance society*. Buckingham, England: Open University Press.

Monahan, T. (2011). Surveillance as cultural practice. *The Sociological Quarterly, 52*(4), 495–508.

Murakami Wood, D., & Webster, C. W. R. (2009). Living in surveillance societies: The normalisation of surveillance in Europe and the threat of Britain's bad example. *Journal of Contemporary European Research, 5*(2), 259–273.

O'Shea, J. (2013). The role of social media in creating a 21st century educational community. *Journal of College & Character, 14*(1), 39–45.

Paradise, A. (2012). Picture perfect? College students' experiences and attitudes regarding their photo-related behaviors on Facebook. In L. A. Wankel & C. Wankel, C. (Eds.), *Misbehavior online in higher education* (pp. 261–292). Bingley: Emerald Group Publishing Limited.

Pecora, V. P. (2002). The culture of surveillance. *Qualitative Sociology, 25*(3), 345–358.

Queensland Government. (2013). *Business and industry portal: Who uses Facebook*. Retrieved from www.business.qld.gov.au/business/running/marketing/online-marketing/using-facebook-to-market-your-business/who-uses-facebook

Selwyn, N. (2009). Faceworking: exploring students' education-related use of Facebook. *Learning, Media and Technology, 34*(2), 157–174.

Toma, C. L., & Hancock, J. T. (2013). Self-affirmation underlies Facebook use. *Personality and Social Psychology Bulletin, 39*(3), 321–331.

Trottier, D. (2012). *Social media as surveillance: Rethinking visibility in a converging world*. London: Ashgate Publishing, Ltd.

Wellman, B., & Gulia, M. (1999). The network basis of social support: A network is more than the sum of its ties. In *Networks in the Global Village: Life in Contemporary Communities* (pp. 83–118). Boulder, CO: Westview Press.

Westlake, E. J. (2008). Friend me if you Facebook: Generation Y and performative surveillance. *The Drama Review, 52*(4), 21–40.

Woodley, C., & Beattie, S. (2012). Treading carefully in stalk space: social media and risk. In M. Brown, M. Hartnett, & T. Stewart (Eds.), *Future challenges, sustainable futures. Proceedings ascilite* (pp. 1091–1095). Wellington, NZ: Australasian Society for Computers in Learning in Tertiary Education.

13

Facebook, Student Engagement and the "Uni Coffee Shop" Group

TAMA LEAVER

Curtin University

The version of the Internet Communications degree offered by Curtin University taught via the online education provider Open Universities Australia (OUA) poses specific challenges in terms of facilitating student engagement and informal learning. Student engagement, although a somewhat nebulous term, generally refers to the idea that student learning is best facilitated by the inclusion of not just academic elements, but also nonacademic and social activities somehow related to learning activities or learning spaces (Krause & Coates, 2008). Indeed, informal learning—those unplanned interactions, exchanges and connections that broadly contribute to meaningful learning without being explicitly driven by curriculum (Greenhow & Robelia, 2009)—often occurs when students are simply in the same physical spaces. Although the design of campuses, including the provision of social spaces in libraries, coffee shops and even building foyers can facilitate unplanned social interaction for students (Matthews, Adams, & Gannaway, 2009), comparable spaces are more difficult to find for online learners, if they exist at all. Indeed, online learners frequently choose that mode of study out of necessity due to restrictions in terms of time, financial resources or the physical distance to relevant learning institutions; these challenges can exacerbate a sense of disconnection and distance from learning as a process and as a shared environment.

Although the lecturers and tutors teaching Internet Communications via OUA have been engaging with students for a number of years using the microblogging tool Twitter (Leaver, 2012), in the past Facebook has been largely left alone because this was viewed as a more casual space where students might interact with each other, but not with teaching staff. However, since 2010 an increasing number of students have created Facebook groups to use as a discussion space about their units, often attracting a significant proportion of students from that unit. At times, but not at others, members of the teaching staff have been invited by students to participate in these groups; both options present opportunities and challenges in terms of boundaries and related issues. Although unit-specific Facebook groups and the discussion boards and other functions of formal Learning Management Systems (LMSs) may facilitate some informal interaction for online learners, these spaces usually disappear at the end of a specific unit or course. Whereas LMSs tend not to afford ongoing communication and connectivity, social networking services (SNSs) such as Facebook can provide spaces that are not necessarily bounded by the duration of a specific unit, course or even degree of study and may facilitate more persistent informal learning opportunities (Chen & Bryer, 2012). This chapter seeks to investigate one such persistent space, an ongoing, student-run Facebook group dubbed the "Uni Coffee Shop (a place to unwind and let it all hang out)" (hereafter abbreviated to UCS).

This investigation draws on three primary sources: an online survey of UCS members, combining quantitative and qualitative questions about student activities and perception of the group; in-depth structured interviews with the two student administrators of the UCS; and informal ethnographic observation by the author as an invited member of the UCS in his role as lecturer and unit controller in the Internet Communications degree. Although this chapter mainly utilizes the first two sources, the fact that the author was a member of the UCS, and made contributions including responses to student queries and more general responses, should be taken into account as it informed the discussion and investigation outlined in the following. After reviewing current literature situating Facebook in terms of student engagement, this chapter introduces the UCS and then focuses on three main areas: practical support within the UCS, social support within the UCS and the influence and role of teaching staff within a student-led space. The importance of practical and social support are focal points for gauging student engagement, while the focus on the influence and role of teaching staff explores the way that engagement is situated in terms of distance from formal learning and teaching spaces.

Facebook and Student Engagement

At the time of writing, the SNS Facebook has more than 1.10 billion monthly users, with more than 650 million of those users logging onto Facebook each day, while more than 750 million accessed the platform using mobile devices (Facebook, 2013). Facebook fulfills the widely cited basic features of an online social network in that it allows users to "(1) construct a public or semi-public profile within a bounded system, (2) articulate a list of other users with whom they share a connection, and (3) view and traverse their list of connections and those made by others within the system" (boyd & Ellison, 2007). Although earlier studies have often situated Facebook as one SNS among a sea of similar services, the sheer size and breadth of Facebook users means that for many people it is not just a SNS but more a platform through which a great deal of their online communication, interaction, news and media flows. Facebook has also been instrumental in moving away from treating digital spaces as distinct from offline ones in large part by insisting on the continuity of using of real names and identities. In terms of the number of users, as well as increasing dominance in the mobile media landscape, as Matthew Allen argues (2012), "Facebook is no longer one of several competing but similar online services: it is unique" (p. 214).

Given Facebook's early history as a university-based networking tool, and its current dominance of the SNS landscape, a number of studies have addressed Facebook's utility for enhancing student learning. Early work by Ellison, Steinfield and Lampe (2007), for example, demonstrated that Facebook use increased social capital for undergraduate students, allowing them to maintain or strengthen relationships that had usually started face to face, or had some offline component. Research by Selwyn (2007, 2009), focusing on public Facebook posts by students, concluded that students use the SNS to actively engage in many informal learning strategies around education, from resource sharing and collaborative negotiation of common dilemmas to social bonding, but warned that students appeared unlikely to welcome forced formal education on Facebook. A study examining Facebook use by UK students found that it provided an important space for informal learning and social interaction while at university, but also highlighted the role of the platform in allowing students to seek out initial online connections with fellow students before beginning their studies (Madge, Meek, Wellens, & Hooley, 2009).

Although a cultural myth persisted for some time that Facebook and other social networks were draining time students should otherwise have dedicated to their studies, early research challenged this myth (Pasek, more, & Hargittai, 2009), although subsequent work (Junco, 2012a, 2012b) has shown negative correlations between certain types of Facebook use and grade point averages (GPA) for US university students. Highlighting the complexity of treating Facebook activity as single measurable act, Junco (2012b) found that the relationship between social networking and co-curricular activities, which broadly align with informal learning, can differ depending on the particular activities; playing games on Facebook was shown to have a negative impact on informal learning, whereas time spent commenting on Facebook was shown to have a positive impact. These results serve as a reminder that Facebook is not a single tool, but a platform encompassing many tools, and those different tools and activities can have quite different impacts on formal and informal learning. In general, however, existing research has shown that Facebook can be a very effective space for student engagement and informal learning, although most of these studies have investigated Facebook use when there is some face-to-face interaction among students. However, this chapter now turns to a Facebook group with a membership of students who are exclusively online learners.

The "Uni Coffee Shop" Group

The UCS is an open Facebook group that was created in early 2011 by two students undertaking an Internet Communications degree from Curtin University via the online education provider OUA. Although the initial membership was exclusively Internet Communications students, the two administrators made the group open to any OUA student, and students from a number of other OUA degrees have joined the group, although it maintains a core of students either taking the Internet Communications degree or taking units from within that degree as options within a different degree structures. Student numbers grew over each study period (OUA has four consecutive 13-week study periods each year), and during the period this chapter investigates (August and September 2012), the UCS had approximately 300 members (the number fluctuated, although not by much) with approximately 100 of those members actively posting during the two months in question.

In September 2012 the two students who administer the UCS group participated in structured interviews which, in part, outlined the impetus and philosophy behind the group. As the first administrator (A1) describes the rationale behind the group:

> I initially set up the group because when I started my degree there was an intense feeling of being alone with online study even though there were pre-existing groups both on Facebook and Skype, but for me there was no real sense of community. Study can quite stressful and I needed to talk to others outside of a designated unit group who were also experiencing similar stress responses. Having studied physically on a university campus, knowing that there is a strong community bond amongst students, I felt disconnected online from those who were also studying. By having the Coffee Shop, the continually growing group has enabled students to share experiences, help those who are struggling, talk about things that are not unit orientated and connect with others from a variety of universities.

A1's description of the UCS outlines the group as an explicitly situated space for student engagement, highlighting the importance of social connectivity in ongoing learning experiences. Moreover, because A1 had previously experienced face-to-face study, she sought to facilitate the informal learning opportunities present on a university campus, evident even in the naming of the groups as the Uni Coffee Shop, the most iconic of informal learning spaces. Both A1 and the other student administrator (A2) outline that they maintain and enforce specific standards in the UCS, including a no swearing rule, except in a specific thread once each study period. Although such guidelines can be a cause of tension, A2 explains that the aim is to ensure that the UCS feels open and inclusive:

> there is the occasional situation where students can become too political on certain topics and begin to degrade the knowledge of others . . . The result of this, is that a few students leave the group. . . . By keeping the

conversations regulated to an extent, there is a more welcoming atmosphere, and less apparent degradation of others—as there is less chance for degrading text to be taken offensively.

Unlike many Facebook groups, the administrators explain they take a very active role in reinforcing particular standards for their group, which does function as a community on some level. Although any standards or rules governing online communication may feel too restrictive to some people, groups will often develop their own internal tensions and disagreements, depending on the personalities within the group, the sort of decisions the student administrators make in running the group, and how inclusive and open the group is to members (Goodband, Solomon, Samuels, Lawson, & Bhakta, 2012). Both administrators mentioned that moderating the group took considerable time, especially when there was a disagreement about how the community standards should be enforced, but for both, maintaining the openness of the community was paramount.

In order to analyze the usefulness of the UCS for the members and not just the administrators, in August 2012 all UCS members were invited to complete an online survey that combined quantitative and qualitative questions. The survey was available for a period of 10 days across late August and early September 2012 and in total received 47 responses across a total membership during that period of approximately 300 students, representing 16% of the total membership of the UCS. It is worth noting that during August and September 2012 no more than 100 students actively participated in the UCS, so the survey respondents arguably represent closer to 47% of the active UCS membership at that time. In gender terms, 87% (41) of respondents identified as female, 11% (5) male, and one person identified as other, meaning that the responses are heavily skewed in gender terms. In age, one person was under 18 years of age, one in the 18- to 21-years-old range, whereas 23% (11) were 22 to 30 years old, 32% (15) were 31 to 40, 30% (14) were 41 to 50 and 11% (5) were 51 or older. Significantly, respondents appeared to be mainly mature age students, with only one student of a direct from school entry age. Only 11% of respondents were in full-time employment, with the majority (13) identifying as self-employed, 23% (11) split between part-time or casual work, 15% (7) stay-at-home parents and 23% (11) unemployed.

All respondents were long-term Facebook users, with the vast majority (72%, 34 respondents) indicating they had used Facebook for more than 3 years, 23% (11) for 2 to 3 years and 4% (2) for 1 to 2 years; no one indicated they had been using Facebook for less than a year. Similarly, the majority of respondents spent a considerable amount of time on Facebook in the average week: 28% (13) spent more than 20 hours a week on Facebook, 28% (13) spent 11 to 20 hours, 17% (8) spent 2 to 5 hours, only 4% spent 1 to 2 hours and no one spent less than an hour a week using Facebook (see Figure 13.1). The majority of respondents had been

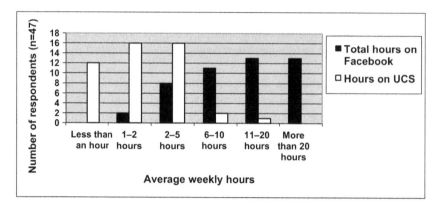

Figure 13.1 Average weekly hours spent on Facebook in total versus hours in the Uni Coffee Shop (UCS)

members of the UCS for a considerable period: 57% (27) had been members for a year or longer, 17% (8) for 7 to 12 months, a further 17% (8) for 2 to 6 months and 9% (4) for 4 weeks or less. However, despite the long-term membership, or perhaps because of it, in an average week UCS members spent a relatively small percentage of their Facebook time in the UCS: 26% (12) spent less than an hour in the UCS; 34% (16) spent 1 to 2 hours; a further 34% (16) spent 2 to 5 hours; whereas only 6% (3) spent 6 hours or more a week in the UCS. Given that Facebook is a diverse platform, even those UCS members spending less than an hour a week may still be making considerable contributions as it is entirely possible to skim the contents of a Facebook group, make a couple of comments, make a new post and like a few other posts in 5 or 10 minutes. From the responses it seems unlikely that many respondents are using Facebook exclusively or even primarily for engaging with their studies. With this framing information in mind, the next two sections turn to the important questions of what UCS members perceive to be the benefits of being part of the group.

Practical Support

In response to statements in the survey regarding the importance of practical support, 76% (35) either strongly agreed or agreed that *receiving* practical support was a key reason they participate in the UCS, with 20% (9) people giving a neutral response, whereas only 4% (2) either disagreed or strongly disagreed. Similarly, 70% (32) strongly agreed or agreed that *giving* practical support was a key reason they participate in the UCS, with 21% giving a neutral response and 9% (4) disagreeing or strongly disagreeing (see Figure 13.2). In the 40 comments made on a qualitative question about the types of practical support given or received, five main areas were mentioned: technical support, either using LMSs, especially Blackboard or specific software such as Endnote; administrative advice, including

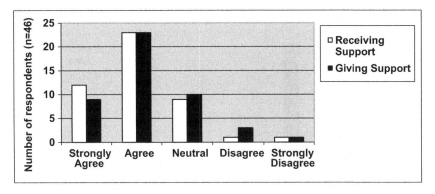

Figure 13.2 Importance of receiving and giving practical support in the Uni Coffee Shop

handling late enrollments, navigating course structures and finding the right contact person (an especially difficult challenge for OUA students who are sometimes enrolled in units managed by two or three different universities at the same time); writing guidance, including general tips on essay writing and overcoming procrastination; guidance on doing online research and navigating different library collections and databases; and a significant number of people mentioned the importance of assistance with referencing (again exacerbated by enrollment across multiple universities or units utilizing different scholarly referencing styles). The majority of survey responses indicated that both giving and receiving practical support are key elements of the UCS. The range of types of practical advice at hand and the peer support offered in the Facebook group is clearly significant in scope and important to members. It is also important to note that almost as many people mentioned that giving support was as important as receiving it, demonstrating a breadth of support and interest in giving it. Moreover, the forms of practical support and the peers offering it epitomize the best of informal learning, deepening meaningful discussions about academic work and related issues. However, an important caveat arises in that several responses indicated that practical support given regarding unit information and assessment details turned out to be incorrect. Apparently the student offering advice had taken a previous version of the unit in question and the details had either changed or been remembered incorrectly. Although peer advice and support are important, ideally it should be balanced with students still seeking out formal advice within the support and information in unit material or official university documentation.

Social Support

With regard to the importance of social support in the UCS, 78% (36) agreed or strongly agreed that *receiving* social support was a key reason they participated in the Facebook group, with 15% (7) giving a neutral response and

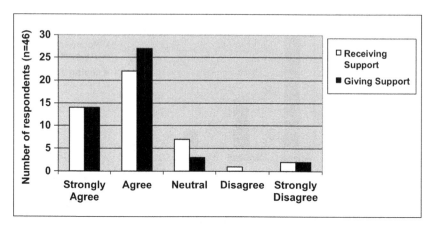

Figure 13.3 Importance of receiving and giving social support in the Uni Coffee Shop

7% (3) disagreeing or strongly disagreeing (see Figure 13.3). Notably, even more respondents ranked *giving* social support as important, with 89% (41) of those surveyed either agreeing or strongly agreeing that giving social support was one of the main reasons they participated in the group, with 7% (3) selecting a neutral response and 4% (2) strongly disagreeing. Both receiving and giving social support ranked more highly than the comparable questions regarding practical support, indicating the importance of communal ties to the success of the group. Reinforcing the centrality of social support, when interviewed, both A1 and A2 stated that a sense of community was the single most important thing generated by the UCS, with both administrators mentioning that protecting and perpetuating that community was their most significant role.

In the 36 qualitative responses made outlining the sorts of social support given and received, the vast majority of respondents cited three main areas of importance: the building and maintenance of a sense of community between online learners that was not available elsewhere; the sharing of the challenges, burdens and eventual successes of online learning; and the importance of shared humor both relating to their studies and in general. Emotional support in relation to studying and the broader social sphere were of key importance for respondents. Reinforcing success with learning and assignments, as well as lamenting less successful efforts and offering supporting in dealing with less stellar marks was also widely mentioned, with one respondent describing the group as "virtual cheerleaders" for one another. As with many communities, shared humour leads to in-jokes, and a number of comments mentioned specific reoccurring jokes that had emerged from various conversations in the UCS. Shared pictures, online memes and other media also featured frequently in the group. As one commentator succinctly summarized the social support

offered by the UCS: "encouragement, commiseration, humour (very important!), knowing other people are in the same mindset, place, under the same
stress = belonging." Not only is this comment representative of the vast majority
written, but it also reads as an exemplary list of the important social elements of
student engagement; bonds are built by the shared joys, pains and development
of learning together.

Students as Leaders, and Teachers as Peers

When examining a space like the UCS, an important question to consider is
whether such a group could be run and administered by a university or an
academic staff member. Shedding some light on this question, when asked
whether it was important that the UCS was run by students (not a specific university teacher) 89% (41) of respondents agreed or strongly agreed, with 7% (3)
being neutral regarding the question and only 4% (2) disagreeing or strongly
disagreeing. In qualitative comments about overall perceptions of the group,
many students commented that a student-run space for students meant that
they could be more open, honest and less formal in their discussions. The personalities and time commitment of student administrators of the group may
also make a significant impact on the success and coherence of the community.
In the interview, A1 indicated that it was very important that the UCS was
student run, because she believed it facilitated a more social and less formal
atmosphere. Moreover, A1 indicated that teachers were welcome as participants, who could also answer questions if needed, but not set the agenda: "The
ideal role for academic staff is what is happening currently, allowing students to
have their own voice while still being easily accessible when needed, while not
being an overbearing 'paternal' voice" (A1).

When asked whether the presence of university tutors and lecturers as group
members influenced what group members were willing to say in the UCS, 33%
(15) agreed or strongly agreed, 13% (6) were neutral and 54% (25) disagreed
or strongly disagreed. Whereas the majority did not indicate that the presence
of teaching staff influenced what they were comfortable saying, nevertheless,
a significant minority who did feel teacher presence had an impact. Whether
that impact is negative or positive is hard to judge, but it does suggest that
the UCS is still seen as an academic space, not a purely social space, by some
members, although this may be entirely in keeping with the design and administrators' views of the UCS. For academic participants, being a member of the
group does allow them to provide information, and correct information, where
required, although negotiating the exact boundaries is important as well. Many
academics have concerns about engaging with students on Facebook (Chen &
Bryer, 2012; Heiberger & Harper, 2008; Lloyd & Raynes-Goldies, this volume),
although the affordances of Facebook groups are better than some spaces allowing teachers to be part of the group without explicitly "friending" students, thus

allowing SNS based interaction without having to make a formal or explicit SNS connection.

Conclusion

Consistent with the ideal form of student engagement, the student-run Uni Coffee Shop Facebook group provides a space for practical and social support and interaction above and beyond any institutionally provided scaffolding. Moreover, the role of the UCS as a community of learners is the single most important facet it offers members with 95% (42) of the final comments summarizing the importance of the group explicitly stating that what mattered most was social support, including "a sense of belonging," "community" and "friendship and belonging." That said, activity within the UCS does not represent the only informal learning spaces for most members; 87% (39) of those surveyed were also members of unit-specific Facebook groups, with only 13% (6) not participating in groups relating to the specific units they were studying. Thus, the UCS may provide the connective social tissue—the space that persists and maintains ties, support and a sense of community across the length of a degree—while the majority of UCS members have a broader ecology of Facebook groups in which they participate. As the space that students return to during and between discrete units and courses, the UCS allows online learners to support each other with practical advice, social cohesiveness and allows the participants to make the most of Facebook as an online social networking service meaningfully supporting student engagement online.

References

Allen, M. (2012). An education in Facebook. *Digital Culture & Education, 4*(3), 213–225.

boyd, d., & Ellison, N. (2007). Social network sites: Definition, history, and scholarship. *Journal of Computer-Mediated Communication, 13*(1). Retrieved from http://onlinelibrary.wiley.com/doi/10.1111/j.1083–6101.2007.00393.x/full

Chen, B., & Bryer, T. (2012). Investigating instructional strategies for using social media in formal and informal learning. *The International Review of Research in Open and Distance Learning, 13*(1), 87–104.

Ellison, N. B., Steinfield, C., & Lampe, C. (2007). The benefits of Facebook "Friends:" Social capital and college students' use of online social network sites. *Journal of Computer-Mediated Communication, 12*(4), 1143–1168.

Facebook. (2013). Facebook Newsroom. Retrieved June 11, 2013, from http://newsroom.fb.com/Key-Facts

Goodband, J. H., Solomon, Y., Samuels, P. C., Lawson, D., & Bhakta, R. (2012). Limits and potentials of social networking in academia: case study of the evolution of a mathematics Facebook community. *Learning, Media and Technology, 37*(3), 236–252. doi:10.1080/17439884.2011.587435

Greenhow, C., & Robelia, B. (2009). Informal learning and identity formation in online social networks. *Learning, Media and Technology, 34*(2), 119–140. doi:10.1080/17439880902923580

Heiberger, G., & Harper, R. (2008). Have you facebooked Astin lately? Using technology to increase student involvement. *New Directions for Student Services, 2008*(124), 19–35. doi:10.1002/ss.293

Junco, R. (2012a). Too much face and not enough books: The relationship between multiple indices of Facebook use and academic performance. *Computers in Human Behavior, 28*(1), 187–198. doi:10.1016/j.chb.2011.08.026

Junco, R. (2012b). The relationship between frequency of Facebook use, participation in Facebook activities, and student engagement. *Computers & Education, 58*(1), 162–171. doi:10.1016/j.compedu.2011.08.004

Krause, K., & Coates, H. (2008). Students' engagement in first-year university. *Assessment & Evaluation in Higher Education, 33*(5), 493–505. doi:10.1080/02602930701698892

Leaver, T. (2012). Twittering informal learning and student engagement in first-year units. In A. Herrington, J. Schrape, & K. Singh (Eds.), *Engaging students with learning technologies* (pp. 97–110). Perth, Australia: Curtin University. Retrieved from http://espace.library.curtin.edu.au:80/R?func=dbin-jump-full&local_base=gen01-era02&object_id=187379

Madge, C., Meek, J., Wellens, J., & Hooley, T. (2009). Facebook, social integration and informal learning at university: "It is more for socialising and talking to friends about work than for actually doing work." *Learning, Media and Technology, 34*(2), 141–155.

Matthews, K. E., Adams, P., & Gannaway, D. (2009). The impact of social learning spaces on student engagement. In K. Nelson (Ed.), *Proceedings of the 12th Annual Pacific Rim First Year in Higher Education Conference* (pp. 1–10). Brisbane: Queensland University of Technology. Retrieved from www.fyhe.com.au/past_papers/papers09/content/pdf/3A.pdf

Pasek, J., more, e., & Hargittai, E. (2009). Facebook and academic performance: Reconciling a media sensation with data. *First Monday, 14*(5). Retrieved from www.uic.edu/htbin/cgiwrap/bin/ojs/index.php/fm/article/view/2498/2181

Selwyn, N. (2007, November). *"Screw Blackboard . . . do it on Facebook!": An investigation of students' educational use of Facebook.* Presented at the Poke 1.0—Facebook social research symposium, University of London. Retrieved from www.scribd.com/doc/513958/Facebook-seminar-paper-Selwyn

Selwyn, N. (2009). Faceworking: Exploring students' education-related use of *Facebook. Learning, Media and Technology, 34*(2), 157–174.

14

"I Think It's Mad Sometimes"—Unveiling Attitudes to Identity Creation and Network Building by Media Studies Students on Facebook

KERRY GOUGH, DAVID HARTE AND VANESSA JACKSON

Birmingham City University

This chapter presents research that sheds light on the ways in which students use Facebook during the transition to university life as a *social experience* through to the culmination of their university degree as a *professional endeavor*. We draw on findings from two case studies by Birmingham City University's School of Media and reveal the value that students place on Facebook in a learning context. In doing so we examine notions of the "networked audience" (Marwick & boyd, 2011) whereby users of social media platforms "navigate multiplicity" (Marwick & boyd, 2011, p. 123) as they communicate to diverse audiences. We first explore how Facebook was used to support students prior to their enrollment in an undergraduate Media Studies course. Second, we draw on interviews with existing students who utilize social media platforms as tools of engagement in developing a professional network. The chapter argues that students create significant personal and professional capital from the strategic ways in which they put Facebook to use.

Social Capital and Identity Creation

Many scholars have noted the ways in which the Internet, and particularly social media, goes beyond a place for communication and self-expression, and instead allows for a performance to support self-promotion. Van Dijck (2013, p. 210) notes that platforms such as Facebook and LinkedIn: "cajole users into releasing information about themselves, both consciously and unconsciously." Drawing on Goffman's (1959) theory of "self-performance," he describes how even the displaying of "signs" about oneself, intentional or not, is part of an increasingly strategic use of Social Networking Sites (van Dijck, 2013, p. 201). Sun and Wu (2012) explore various "traits" in Facebook users' perceived ability to manage their online identify. These include a general awareness of oneself as a social object with the need to present social connections to the world (Sun & Wu, 2012, p. 422), and to trust one's own digital literacy skills in order to manage privacy on platforms like Facebook (Sun & Wu, 2012, p. 423). According to Sun and Wu (2012, p. 429), the need to belong is an important factor in managing Facebook self-presentation but is dependent on the extent to which one trusts the Internet, and one's digital skills, to manage and keep secure a digital version of oneself.

Marwick and boyd (2011) highlight how writers "imagine" particular audiences in their work. The process of shaping identity and writing status updates on social media constructs the audience:

> While Facebook or Twitter users don't know exactly who comprises their audience addressed, they have a mental picture of who they're writing or speaking to—the audience invoked. Much like writers, social media participants imagine an audience and tailor their online writing to match.
> (Marwick & boyd, 2011, p. 128)

For Marwick and boyd (2011), the management of one's online identity is akin to a form of "micro-celebrity" (drawing on Senft, 2008) in which "individuals learn how to manage tensions between public and private, insider and outsider, and frontstage and backstage performances" (Marwick & boyd, 2011, p. 130). The "backstage" space is explored and problematized by Hogan (2010), who argues that although "some individuals draw open the stage's curtain to let the world see their tastes" (p. 380), it is simplistic to argue that this offers a glimpse into private lives. Instead, these "tastes are not a backstage but rather are a front." Sherry Turkle's (2011) analysis of "presentation anxiety" among US college students' use of Facebook highlights how the self-presentation issues experienced by young people now play out online, whereby their "likes" and interests are tortuously considered in order to shape others' perception of them (Turkle, 2011, p. 184). By contrast, Cheung's (2000) relatively early study (in Internet terms) of personal web homepages made the point that although a degree of self-censorship is inevitable, the active curation of oneself allowed "people to present their 'selves' to the public . . . beyond [the] crude images circulated in popular media" (p. 51). To some extent we might see the active 'liking' of particular pages or the stating of interests or cultural consumption on Facebook as attempts to usurp established norms of what young people might be presumed to be interested in.

Although much primary research indicated here is with young people of student age, Livingstone (2008) notes some distinctions in presentational practices between younger and older teenagers. The latter group, she claims, express "a notion of identity lived through authentic relationships with others" (Livingstone, 2008, p. 407). Lewis and West (2009) are also interested in young people's behaviors on Facebook, university students in particular, and the process of "friending" and its facilitation in the development of online social capital. Their study of UK undergraduate students found that Facebook "enabled broad, low pressure and low commitment communication with acquaintances" (p. 1223). Although it seemed to facilitate the "weak ties" that Granovetter (1973) speaks of, the researchers found the platform did little for building "bridges" between different friendship groups (Lewis & West, 2009, p. 1223).

The case studies we present here should be seen in the context of these discussions of online identity creation and management as we explore the ways in which students articulate their use of Facebook in terms of both self-presentation and the raising of their social capital.

Case Study 1—We Level Up: Bridging and Bonding through Social Media, Transition Mentoring and Peer Support

The first case study examines how Facebook was used to support students through their pre-entry induction into student life within the Birmingham School of Media and to support their enrollment and induction into the School experience upon their arrival. In response to advice encouraging UK academic institutions to "nurture a culture of belonging" from within "the academic sphere" (Thomas, 2012, p. 6), the school launched its online transition mentoring program, "Level Up," in the summer of 2012. With the desire to create a strong sense of student engagement and belonging, measures were established to facilitate the pre-entry induction of students, to enable their successful integration through the creation of an online student community prior to arrival. In fostering the pre-entry management of student relationships, Facebook played a significant, yet relatively unplanned-for, role in the transition of new students into the school and in developing their awareness of the demands of academic study.

The project had at its heart a series of online activities managed across the summer period culminating in the school's formal induction period in September 2012. The project's ambition was to assist in the practical introduction to university and the social life of students, as well as to provide an insight into the rigours of academic study. Materials were presented from the students' perspective, with the Level Up content being written, designed and managed by students and staff. These activities were designed across two sites: a stand-alone website (http://bcumedia.com/welcome/), comprising an introduction to student life within the school, and the dynamic learning and teaching activities that were planned for delivery across our Virtual Learning Environment (VLE). Featuring a series of short weekly activities aligned around the analysis of the media, these were designed to give a flavor of the activities available to students of the Birmingham School of Media while simultaneously creating opportunities to socialize online with current students already studying the course and their peers who would be arriving in September 2012. On their arrival, the online experience was extended with opportunities for offline interaction as the Transition Mentors acted as aides for the new student cohort throughout induction week and into the academic calendar.

Despite the provision of 'official' online spaces, the study found that the pre-entry cohort (of 188) were happy to socialize and chat on Facebook (which is reflected in the accumulation of 141 Facebook "likes" during the pre-entry induction period). Resistance to engaging with the taught online learning environment was evident. Research conducted into the take-up and the reach of Level Up's activities demonstrated that although 32% of users said they looked at the learning materials, it was not until the Level Up mentors moved these activities over from the VLE onto Facebook and Twitter that students began to *engage* with the content.

Focus group discussion among the twelve Level Up Transition Mentors was conducted at three key points across the pre-induction period. These focus groups consisted of between four and six mentors and were used to steer future activities. Research conducted after the induction period took the form of a questionnaire administered to the 188 strong first-year 2012/13 cohort. The survey response rate was 87%, with 45% of respondents reporting use and engagement with the Facebook page as their preferred mode of pre-entry discussion with the school. Additionally, individual follow-up interviews were conducted with ten first-year undergraduates, selected based on their participation and nonparticipation.

Whereas Level Up steering group discussions were used to direct live activities and to troubleshoot as problems arose, follow-up research amongst the 2012/13 first-year cohort was used to assess the success of the project as a means of inducting new students. During the early stages of the Level Up program we were experiencing some password-orientated difficulties in driving the students to engage with the online learning environment, and as a result one Level Up mentor made the comment,

> If you want to get the students excited about doing work in their holidays, you need to make it attractive. Why don't we meet them on their own turf and do it on Facebook? Perhaps something on Twitter too, but they all seem to be using Facebook . . . Excited might be a bit too strong, but if it's there under their noses, they are bound to be a little bit interested, surely?
>
> (Focus Group Participant 1A)

After much consideration (and undermining months of careful planning for delivery of the learning materials within the VLE) it was decided to follow the above sentiment and move the learning activities into the "social" space of Facebook. This reactive approach resulted in more pre-entry students choosing to engage with the learning activities. One first-year undergraduate student commented on the differences in perception between Facebook and the VLE. She describes how, as a new student coming into the school, she felt that

> Facebook is a safe space. It's the place we know, and we're familiar with it. Moodle's not. We had to learn that and it felt a bit too much like work to be honest. I personally couldn't remember my log-ons, but I liked reading the Facebook comments. I am still learning how to use Moodle now.
>
> (Focus Group Participant 1B)

This is rather ironic considering that part of the ambition of the project was to raise the incoming students' awareness of how the VLE works. Although a minority of students did make use of the VLE, students more readily aligned themselves with Facebook as a result of their preexisting immersion in the format. Consequently, Facebook offered valuable opportunities for peer mentoring, as identified by Flint and Roden (2013).

In this specific context of pre-entry induction, Facebook acted as an important means of bridging the gap between school life and the university experience. Facilitating that transition, the site also allowed for the continued strengthening of those student relationships into the academic year as the Level Up Transition Mentors and new students exchanged personalized friend requests and migrated away from the official Level Up page into their own private space. For the students who used it, the Facebook page offered not only a place to meet prior to their arrival at Birmingham City University but also the opportunity to befriend current students within the School of Media. As one student commented,

> It was great to have the official School of Media pages as a place to ask questions and meet people, but once I had found people on the course that were my kind of people, I would send them a friend request and post on their wall instead.
>
> (Focus Group Participant 1C)

In some sense we might see this reference to "my kind of people" as a validation of Sun and Wu's (2012) observation of the need to belong among Facebook users but also, to a degree, we can see how students shape an "imagined audience" (Marwick & boyd, 2011) in very much their own image.

Although the Facebook group proved invaluable during the induction of new students into the School, the second of our case studies moves on to examine how student Facebook use shifts from a pre-entry peer mentoring induction tool and means of confidence building, to the learning environment and beyond, examining Facebook's use as an academic organizing tool and means of professional engagement.

Case Study 2—Social Media and Employability

A concern of many UK universities' courses with a vocational edge is to ensure that students have sufficient employability competences by graduation. Such skills may be 'soft' in nature and cover everything from communication skills to effective curriculum vitae writing. At Birmingham City University's School of Media there is increasing emphasis on the role that social media may play in supporting students to develop professional networks. In examining students' attitude to the use of social media in a professional context, a relatively complex picture emerges of potentially conflicting uses of professional and personal online social spaces.

Focus groups of between four and six students each were created with three groups comprising active users of social media sites and another group of more tentative users. Many focus group participants expressed a preference for separating their personal and professional profiles, usually, but not exclusively, keeping Facebook for personal socializing while employing Twitter and blogs for more professional interaction. However, it was noted that several students had established separate Facebook pages for micro-business use. Through this they created a business network of "friends," posting examples of their video or photographic work, and in return received small-scale commissions for similar projects. One student was carrying out this kind of activity from his personal Facebook account, but was aware of a tension between personal and professional activity:

> I've had just quite casual business, so it's been okay, but I wouldn't want like quite big companies to know me as a person, but as a professional, and that's why I've realized now that I'm getting a bit more popularity, that I want an actual website, that's professional.
> (Focus Group Participant 2A)

Although the students tended to perceive Facebook as a social rather than professional space it seemed to provide a cost-effective and convenient platform on which to launch their micro-businesses, allowing students the opportunity to experiment with establishing their business personas in a relatively risk-free environment, both financially and personally. This demonstrates a pragmatic utilization of the site; as implied in the preceding comment, however, the focus group participants were uncomfortable when professionals impinged on their personal world. One television student describes receiving an offer of work via a Facebook inbox message, from someone who wasn't a "friend":

> She was a producer at MTV and she just started talking to me about something I could have worked on, and she had my email, but she chose to go on FB to message me, which was weird.
>
> (Focus Group Participant 2B)

The students seemed to impose unwritten etiquette about the rules of engagement on social media sites and questioned the professionalism of industry workers if they didn't abide by them. A postgraduate student in the focus groups explained the context, as she understood it:

> I think on Facebook there is very much a social etiquette, like I was always told from opening my account and starting to make professional friends; that it's ok to add them, and that it's ok to talk to them if they are genuinely friends, but if there's an opportunity for a placement or a job, that you do that formally through email or writing in to them, that you don't send an inbox message and say, 'Hi, do you remember me and can I have that placement' or whatever, because that isn't considered the done thing.
>
> (Focus Group Participant 2C)

Obviously, not all students are so circumspect, and several focus group students mentioned unguarded, sometimes drunken posts on Facebook, which they later regretted. This was partially behind the rationale of separating their professional and personal profiles: they were still experimenting with the tensions between independence and responsibility. Some of the students did as the postgraduate in the preceding quote suggests and added professional contacts while on work placements who then became friends. This enabled continued contact and enlarged their networks. It also paid dividends in generating further placements, usually instigated by the professional.

The students used Facebook as an extension of their offline activity but differentiated between the real and the virtual, often demonstrating a maturity of approach and the desire to build genuine, rather than opportunistic allegiances: "In both social media and real life, not that social media isn't real life, but you know what I mean, it's all about making conversation, it's not about saying, I do this, can I have a placement please" (Focus Group Participant 2D). The students showed an awareness of the differences between their professional and personal profiles, understanding that they were constructing an identity, a version of themselves, presenting an almost entirely positive image. As one student put it, "everything in social media you select, you're picking the highlights . . . and you can create this online persona of who you are. I think it's mad sometimes" (Focus Group Participant 2E). They were conscious of appealing to an "imagined audience" (Marwick & boyd, 2011) and of being judged by their profile and the photographs on their pages:

> You've got to be conscious of who's going to be looking at it. If you're creating a profile for yourself, you're creating an online presence, and if you want professionals to see it, and think, yes, they'll be good for a job, you've got to be conscious of what you're putting on there, of what they're actually going to read. If you're on Facebook and you've got pictures of you going out and getting wasted, then they're going to think, oh well, they're doing that all the time.
>
> (Focus Group Participant 2E)

The majority of students in the focus groups described checking Facebook first thing in the morning and often the last thing at night, habitual and recurrent usage that corresponds with the findings of other studies (Ellison, Steinfield, & Lampe, 2007; Grosseck, Bran, & Tiru, 2011). Alongside this desire to interact socially, they used Facebook as an academic networking tool. In group-work projects, they described creating private Facebook groups, finding them more useful as a communication tool than e-mail for ensuring everyone knew the logistics of a project and for sharing documents. Because they knew each team member checks Facebook regularly, they were reassured that everything would have been seen by everyone. Some students also used it creatively for revision workshop sessions, with someone in the group posing a question and others seeing if they could answer it. These applications demonstrate the flexibility of Facebook as a social networking tool, in both academic and project work, but also reveal how students find inventive uses for the platforms without necessarily needing an institutional helping-hand. As Roblyer et al. (2010) note, "Students seem much more open to the idea of using Facebook instructionally than do faculty" (p. 138).

The research suggests that students have a strong sense of the pliability of a platform such as Facebook and adapt it to their needs. What we might presume to be a personal space is utilized in a flexible way. As van Dijck (2013) points out, "users have come to understand the art of online self-presentation and the importance of [social networking sites] as tools for (professional) self-promotion" (p. 200). In this way they are sensitive to the platform's status and actively "curate" in the manner described by Cheung (2000).

Conclusion

Our case studies offer insights into the ways in which students manage identity and the development of online social capital through the use of Facebook. In the first case study, students seem to "lure" the institution into recognizing and acknowledging the platform's legitimacy. Students specifically cited Facebook's "bonding" potential, using it as part of a strategy to develop a sense of belonging to the institution and fellow students. There's little evidence of presentation anxiety (Turkle 2011, p. 184) among this cohort. However, in the second case study, there are tensions. Facebook use is more carefully managed with online social capital as a recognized resource and a balancing between "frontstage" and "backstage" performances. In addressing specific issues around identity and social capital, we would argue that the student is "an agent in control, mastering social media for information, social relationships and self-expression in everyday life" (Bechmann & Lomborg, 2012, p. 7). Students recognize the tensions that exist in utilizing Facebook but are increasingly savvy about managing their online presence, recognizing how they create personal and professional capital from the ways in which they put the platform to use. Given this, tertiary-level educators should be wary of giving overly simplistic advice about use of this and other social networking sites.

One unexpected finding from our research is the degree to which the University's carefully considered choice of VLE is rejected by students in favor of commercial online spaces. Valenzuela et al. (2009, p. 893) find that Facebook's invitation to online participation is key: "certain specific features of Facebook enable users to engage in behaviors that contribute to their social capital." At both ends of their university experience, in 'bonding' with other students or 'bridging' to potential employers, students sense that whatever the shortcomings of Facebook (not least its purpose to serve up "the active user [as] a 'tool' for the companies to exploit in economic value creation" [Bechmann & Lomborg, 2012, p. 9]), there remains much to be gained in the short-term by immersing themselves in its social spaces.

References

Bechmann, A., & Lomborg, S. (2012). Mapping actor roles in social media: Different perspectives on value creation in theories of user participation. *New Media & Society, 15*(5), 765–781.

Cheung, C. (2000). A Home on the web: Presentations of self on personal homepages. In D. Gauntlett (Ed.), *Web studies* (pp. 43–51). London: Arnold.

Ellison, N. B., Steinfield, C., & Lampe, C. (2007). The benefits of Facebook "friends:" Social capital and college students' use of online social network sites. *Journal of Computer-Mediated Communication, 12*, 1143–1168.

Flint, E. & Roden. J. (2013). Social media: An effective way to build a community and develop partnerships to promote student engagement? In C. Nygaard, S. Brand, P. Bartholomew, & L. Millard (Eds.), *Student engagement: Identity, motivation and community* (pp. 213–234). Farringdon, England: Libri Publishing.

Goffman, E. (1959). *The presentation of self in everyday life*. New York: Doubleday.

Granovetter, M. S. (1973). The strength of weak ties. *American Journal of Sociology, 78*(6), 1360–1380.

Grosseck, G., Bran, R., & Tiru, L. (2011). Dear teacher, what should I write on my wall? A case study on academic uses of Facebook. *Procedia-Social and Behavioral Sciences, 15*, 1425–1430.

Hogan, B. (2010). The presentation of self in the age of social media: Distinguishing performances and exhibitions online. *Bulletin of Science, Technology & Society, 30*(6), 377–386.

Lewis, J., & West, A. (2009). "Friending": London-based undergraduates' experience of Facebook. *New Media & Society, 11*(7), 1209–1229.

Livingstone, S. (2008). Taking risky opportunities in youthful content creation: teenagers' use of social networking sites for intimacy, privacy and self-expression. *New Media & Society, 10*(3), 393–411.

Marwick, A. E., & boyd, d. (2011). I tweet honestly, I tweet passionately: Twitter users, context collapse, and the imagined audience. *New Media & Society, 13*(1), 114–133.

Roblyer, M. D., McDaniel, M., Webb, M., Herman, J., & Witty, J. V. (2010). Findings on Facebook in higher education: A comparison of college faculty and student uses and perceptions of social networking sites. *The Internet and Higher Education, 13*(3), 134–140.

Senft, T. M. (2008). *Camgirls: Celebrity & community in the age of social networks.* New York and Oxford, England: Peter Lang.

Sun, T., & Wu, G. (2012). Traits, predictors, and consequences of Facebook self-presentation. *Social Science Computer Review, 30*(4), 419–433.

Thomas, T. (2012). *Building student engagement and belonging in higher education at a time of change: Final report from the What Works? Student Retention and Success programme.* London: Paul Hamlyn Foundation.

Turkle, S. (2011). *Alone together: why we expect more from technology and less from each other.* New York: Basic Books.

Valenzuela, S., Park, N., & Kee, K. F. (2009). Is there social capital in a social network site? Facebook use and college students' life satisfaction, trust, and participation. *Journal of Computer-Mediated Communication, 14*, 875–901.

van Dijck, J. (2013). "You have one identity": Performing the self on Facebook and LinkedIn. *Media, Culture & Society, 35*(2), 199–215.

15

Should We Be Friends? The Question of Facebook in Academic Libraries

ZARA T. WILKINSON

Rutgers, The State University of New Jersey

Librarians, on the whole, are preoccupied by the predominance of technology in daily life. This is especially true for academic librarians, because today's universities are filled with young men and women who have the Internet on their cell phones and a paper-thin tablet in their backpacks. Ismail (2010, p. 11) describes this "net generation" as "technologically savvy and wanting results instantly and easily—products of growing up in a highly wired environment." For them, she says, "Life . . . would be incomplete without daily interaction via IM, Google, and social networking on MySpace and Facebook" (Ismail, 2010, p. 10–11). In order to keep up with their patrons, and to continue providing top-rate information services at the point of need, librarians are implementing mobile sites, Facebook pages, and Twitter accounts.

In particular, the social networking website Facebook has become increasingly popular among the general population and increasingly present in the college and university environment. Responding to this popularity, many librarians at two- and four-year institutions have cultivated presences for their libraries on Facebook and other social media sites. Many librarians see Facebook as an opportunity to engage with students on their own terms and in their own social environment: "If librarians truly wish to be where their students are, Facebook is an effective way to reach them" (Mack et al., 2007). Library Facebook pages have been used for many different purposes and have garnered various degrees of success. Now that Facebook is not so new, and is in fact an accepted part of everyday life for a large part of the Western world, librarians continue to ask how they can use it most effectively. This chapter considers the many ways academic libraries can use Facebook, including reference and research help, marketing and promotion, library branding, and user interaction and feedback.

Libraries on Facebook: An Uncertain Path

Early articles written by librarians such as Mathews (2006) and Miller and Jensen (2007) offered useful how-to tips for librarians who were interested in harnessing the Facebook craze in their libraries. In 2007, Mack et al. observed that most of the library literature about Facebook "focused on giving background information on Facebook, and explaining to librarians why we should care about it." In the same year, Charnigo and Barnett-Ellis (2007, p. 26) observed that few scholarly articles examined Facebook's role in the provision of library services. Although Facebook was working its way into the public consciousness and was being discussed on library electronic mailing lists and blogs, it was not yet being examined critically. To correct this perceived lack, Charnigo and Barnett-Ellis surveyed 126 academic librarians regarding their knowledge of Facebook and its use.

Some of these librarians felt that Facebook was "most beneficial as a virtual extension of the campus" and that it "had a positive influence on fostering collegiate bonds and school spirit" (Charnigo and Barnett-Ellis, 2007, p. 30), but many seemed to believe that Facebook was a part of a nonacademic, social sphere populated only by students and their social circle. Whereas some librarians in the study felt that Facebook was an effective marketing tool, most felt that Facebook should remain a student-only space with no involvement from librarians, professors, or administrators. In a 2009 study at Valparaiso University, students exhibited a similar division of opinion. Although some were accepting and even encouraging, describing libraries on Facebook as "a really good idea" and "appreciated," others were more doubtful: "Facebook is to stay in touch with friends or teachers from the past. E-mail is for announcements. Stick with that!!!" (Connell, 2009, p. 33).

Despite the hesitance of some librarians and students, the majority of academic libraries now maintain Facebook pages. In 2011, Gary Wan set out to study the Facebook pages of university libraries that were members of the Association of Research Libraries (ARL). He found that 90% of the 115 ARL libraries had at least one Facebook page. Two had official Facebook groups instead, but Wan determined that those groups functioned as pages. Of the libraries with Facebook pages, approximately 95% had been created in 2007 or 2008. Slightly fewer than half of the Facebook pages were created in 2007, slightly more than one year after Facebook registration was opened to the public and around the time that the "pages" functionality was introduced. As evidenced by Miller and Jensen (2007), Mack et al. (2007), and Charnigo and Barnett-Ellis (2007), in 2007 Facebook began to appear more frequently and feature more prominently in the library literature. Along with Facebook's rise in popularity among the general population, such exposure likely encouraged many librarians to create Facebook pages around the same time.

Even now that many libraries maintain Facebook pages as a matter of course, librarians continue to struggle with how to encourage students to interact with the library account. Many librarians report that library Facebook pages receive minimal use by students, and researchers such as Gerolimos (2011) and Wan (2011) have found that library Facebook presences, by various metrics, are perhaps not as successful as librarians hope them to be. In an illuminating example, Baggett and Williams (2012) describe the social media habits of a small group of students at Shenandoah University. The Shenandoah undergraduates were very familiar with social media; they accessed Facebook every day, some also used Google+ and Tumblr, and all had used Skype at least once (Baggett & Williams, 2012, p. 20). However, despite the experience these students had with social media in general and Facebook more specifically, none were aware that the library had a Facebook page (Baggett & Williams, 2012, p. 21).

Gerolimos (2011, para. 28) claims that "library pages on Facebook are not among the most popular or at least the most known pages on Facebook." He examined the Facebook wall posts of 20 U.S. academic libraries, chosen for their robust Facebook presences and a certain specified number of wall posts. More than 90% of the Facebook posts he examined received no comments. Although some of those had been "liked," indicating some degree of user interaction, 63% of posts received no comments and no "likes." Whereas Gerolimos focused on the amount of feedback received by individual Facebook posts or status updates, Wan (2011) defines the success of a library's Facebook page by the number of fans:

> The number of Fans is used to measure the success of a specific page. For all pages in the study, this number varies from 6 to 2280, with a median of 136. Overall, the numbers of Fans are not impressive: 35.8% of pages have fewer than 100 Fans, and 31.4% of them attract between 100 and 200 Fans.
>
> (p. 314)

More than 60% of the academic libraries in Wan's (2011) study had fewer than 200 fans, which does at first glance seem "not impressive." However, although fans and feedback may be the easiest metric by which to judge Facebook pages, they may not be the most effective: most libraries, for example, are not judged solely by their door count figures. In fact, Bodnar and Doshi (2011) question whether number of fans or friends is an appropriate measure of a Facebook page's value at all. As they suggest, perhaps other measures should be explored in future research (pp. 108–109).

Reference Services on Facebook

With in-person reference desk statistics down across the board, librarians are becoming increasingly likely to embrace online interactions with their constituents. Many academic libraries have begun to offer "real-time" chat and text message reference services in addition to the more traditional services found at the reference desk. As Facebook and other social media technologies are nearly ubiquitous on college campuses, they offer librarians an opportunity to bring the brick and mortar library into the social online spaces that undergraduate and graduate students already inhabit. This indicates that Facebook deserves more attention as a venue for what might be called "legitimate" library services, in addition to outreach and other more social uses of Facebook. Twitter also carries a lot of potential for librarians who want to be available to students who are, more often than not, "connected" on a 24/7 basis. However, Facebook's considerably more static interface better supports a coherent reference interview. Answering reference questions on the library's wall creates a public archive of library-related information that future users can consult, either for answers to individual questions or simply for reassurance that they too will receive a reply that is both quick and of good quality. In addition to the use of the wall for reference services, Facebook private messages provide an opportunity for students to reach out privately, should they be embarrassed to ask their question for all to see.

But do students ask reference questions on Facebook? In 2007, Mack et al. reported on off-desk reference statistics logged by one librarian over the fall 2006 semester at the Pennsylvania State University. They found that almost 29% of off-desk reference questions answered that semester were received on Facebook. The number of reference questions received via Facebook (126 of 441) was higher than, individually, the number of reference questions received over e-mail, phone, instant message (IM), and in-person. The researchers note that all of the Facebook reference questions were asked by undergraduate students, leading them to suggest that a shift in educational and societal norms was in process. However, other librarians have not replicated these findings. In a survey a couple years later, Ismail (2010) found that students were not interested in seeking research help through various nontraditional online platforms. Students at Marywood University rated possible research help using Facebook and MySpace lower than all the other options in the study (IM, Moodle/Course Management System, and e-mail). In both of these studies, e-mail was rated very highly—it was highest in Ismail's study and second highest in the research completed by Mack et al.

A number of factors might have contributed to these differences in results. Mack et al. (2007), for example, tracked actual usage, whereas Ismail's (2009) survey documented students' perceived or desired usage. Students may not necessarily want to use Facebook for reference interactions, but they may still find it to be convenient in the moment, especially if the library is closed. Additionally, the lead librarian in the Mack et al. study explicitly encouraged students to contact him using Facebook, a factor that cannot be overlooked. Part of the reason why students in studies such as Ismail's report a reluctance to use Facebook to ask reference questions may simply be that no one has ever told them they *can* use Facebook for that purpose. Perhaps the librarian who specifically invites undergraduates to become his or her Facebook friends and to contact him or her if they need help *naturally* receives more Facebook reference questions than do others who do not make explicit invitations. It should also be mentioned that the librarian described by Mack et al. was advertising an individual Facebook page, not a Facebook page that represented that entire library. At the time of the study, Facebook did not yet allow organizations to create Facebook accounts, so a personal Facebook page would have been the only option. This may have had an effect on the outcome as well: rather than connecting to a library account with an unknown person at the helm, the students were reaching out to a specific person who they had previously met, and had presumably found helpful, offline.

Overall, the success of using Facebook for reference in academic libraries is unclear. Facebook and other social media platforms certainly possess a great deal of potential; they can help make librarians available to students who do not see the value in visiting the physical library space or who cannot, for whatever reason, easily take advantage of traditional research support services. However, libraries have not reported overwhelming amounts of success in this respect, and the true reasons for this are unknown. Perhaps students have not been encouraged to use Facebook for such a purpose, perhaps librarians have not truly bought into the social media reference interview, and perhaps students are simply not interested in interacting with the *library* as opposed to a *librarian*. Although the available data might support an argument that students are not interested in interacting with librarians on Facebook, it is also possible that research assistance isn't the right *kind* of interaction for a platform such as Facebook. Academic libraries also embrace Facebook for purposes other than reference: they also use it to market the library and its services, to promote specific programs or resources, to brand themselves as a part of their campus community, or to encourage feedback and comments from users.

Additional Library Uses for Facebook

In addition to expanding non-traditional reference services such as e-mail, IM, and text message to include Facebook, librarians and libraries can use Facebook for purposes that do not involve research assistance at all. Greenwell and Kraemer (2006) emphasize that social media platforms invite the participation of students as well as librarians: "Institutional users—such as libraries—can use the sites to facilitate two-way communication with users rather than the traditional one-sided web presence. User comments can enhance the site, making it more personally appealing to this audience and more timely" (Greenwell & Kraemer, 2006, p. 13). Greenwell and Kraemer liken the use of Facebook to other, more traditional forms of outreach: open houses, flyers, and tables at campus fairs (2006, p. 15). Mathews (2006) similarly places Facebook in the same category as "posters, flyers, campus emails, workshops, and subject guides" (p. 306).

Marketing, promotion, and outreach are some other very important uses of academic library Facebook pages. Like flyers and e-mail lists, Facebook is often used to distribute information to the library's user community. Wan (2011) found that the majority of posts on academic library Facebook pages were event announcements or information about library collections and resources (p. 316). In a survey of health science libraries, Hendrix et al. (2009) came to a similar conclusion: Facebook pages were primarily used to market the library and promote services or resources. Respondents reported that the most popular uses of Facebook included making announcements, posting photos, and simply establishing a presence on Facebook (Hendrix et al., 2009, p. 46). Facebook has also been examined as a way to disseminate individual resources. For example, Foster et al. (2010) used Facebook to market LibGuides. Librarians involved in the study used their own personal Facebook accounts to promote LibGuides to the general university Facebook group and to interest groups such as individual academic departments.

Facebook can also be used to market or promote the library as a whole. As a social medium that is "fundamentally about relationships" (Phillips, 2011, p. 512), Facebook is very useful in determining or strengthening the relationship between students and the university library. Phillips (2011) found that libraries were using Facebook in order to present themselves as "approachable" and to "develop a rapport with students" (p. 520). She observed that libraries were using Facebook socially, in order to establish themselves as a part of a community and to brand themselves as friendly rather than stuffy or intimidating. Instead of merely using Facebook as a tool to advertise library services and answer questions, academic librarians can embrace it as a way to create stronger working and support relationships with students: "if Facebook can help cultivate a brand that expands beyond books, students may discover that the library is more relevant and approachable than they previously perceived, and a valuable part of their personal networks" (Phillips, 2011, p. 512). Library branding is one of the most promising uses of Facebook. Facebook offers a way to manage the public face of an academic library in an accessible, up-to-date, and easy-to-curate forum.

Facebook may also have untapped potential as a place to collect informal feedback from patrons. Petit (2011) discusses several examples of how patrons request library materials using social media. The frustration patrons feel when they cannot find the books or other materials they need can cause them to reach out in the most convenient and least uncomfortable fashion: on the Internet. Gerolimos (2011) also documented a small number of patrons (7% of the comments in his sample) using library Facebook pages in order to make suggestions, although the specific suggestions cited in that study were related to facilities or policies rather than to library collections. In contrast to Petit, Gerolimos and others have found that patrons are relatively reluctant to use library Facebook accounts for such communication. For example, Jacobson (2011) observes that library Facebook pages may be used more efficiently to distribute information *to* patrons rather than to collect information *from* them:

> However, uses for communication from patrons or "fans," communicating
> library needs, and as a forum/discussion space for users may not be an

ideal use. Most pages observed in this study did not have any "fan" posts or user discussion even when the space was provided for them.

(p. 87)

Despite the fact that library Facebook pages seem to be ideal locations for patrons to present their own ideas and comment on the library, similar to a community whiteboard or suggestion box, the library literature documents very few students turning to Facebook for such uses. As with reference, the true reason for this reluctance is unknown.

Facebook can be used to communicate and connect with other campus communities and the public, not just with students. Gerolimos (2011) found that students were not always the target population for a library's Facebook page: "Also, . . . it was apparent that libraries' Facebook pages have become, in several cases, a 'family' place for colleagues where they can chat with each other, rather than a professional outreach tool or even an efficient marketing tool" (para. 50). Although Gerolimos interpreted staff use as a failure of the library's presence on Facebook, it is important to note that students are not the only users of an academic library and that student engagement may not be the only goal of a library Facebook group. According to Gerolimos, 70% of feedback on library Facebook pages came from people who were or used to be employed by the library or from former students and employees of the university. Although perhaps not the core users of an academic library, these groups can be important participants in the development of an academic institution or library's brand. Perhaps future research will investigate the potential of Facebook as an outreach tool geared toward alumni, former (or prospective) employees, and the community at large. An academic library's Facebook page can also be "friends" with the pages of other organizations on campus, such as the Alumni Association, Residence Life, the School of Arts and Sciences, or the Honors College. These Facebook connections, as well as the ability to "share" the status updates made by these other organizations, creates opportunities for building campus relationships and sharing information about the library with faculty and staff.

Facebook and Academic Libraries: A Look Ahead

For all the questions and concerns about whether or how academic libraries should be using it, Facebook continues to be an important presence in the lives of university students. For that reason, if for no other, libraries should continue to maintain their pages. Although student interest and involvement may vary, a relatively small effort is needed to maintain a Facebook page, and so even a small usage may justify an active page. Furthermore, the ease with which Facebook can be integrated with other social media, such as Twitter, Tumblr, Pinterest, and Instagram, means that a similarly small amount of effort is required to maintain an active and robust library presence on multiple platforms. That said, although a Facebook account can be maintained with a small time commitment, the maintainers of library Facebook accounts need to consider that a Facebook page is more effective if it remains consistently active, projects a cohesive library brand, and responds to contact initiated by users (by "liking" wall posts or responding to private messages).

Some librarians have ethical concerns about the increased use of Facebook by academic libraries. First and foremost, some scholars and practitioners are hesitant to tie the delivery of library services to a noneducational commercial enterprise:

> We should, however, view [Facebook's] widespread use with some skepticism, not only because its popularity might change but mostly because Facebook is above all a commercial company and its goals, means, expectations, and, ultimately, economic gains are different from the ones that academics and students should serve or aim toward.
>
> (Gerolimos, 2011, para. 3)

Some librarians are also worried about Facebook and privacy. As far back as Charningo and Barnett-Ellis's (2007) survey, almost 20% of librarian respondents were concerned about the privacy implications of using the site. Few people who have used Facebook with any degree of regularity would disagree that the site's popularity has caused people to become more comfortable about sharing personal information and thoughts online. Although Facebook does allow users to control what information their friends can access, numerous changes have been made to these controls since Facebook's inception, and those changes were not always well advertised to Facebook users. These ethical and privacy concerns have validity and should continue to be considered as Facebook and other social media platforms grow in size and popularity.

Ethical issues aside, a social media site is only as valuable as its users, and Gerolimos is not the only one reminding librarians that Facebook may not last. Jacobson (2011) cautions librarians with similar sentiments:

> librarians should not get too attached to Facebook, as there is always the next tool or social networking site that people are using. Web 2.0 applications move quickly and the Internet is constantly changing; librarians should be prepared to leave their hard work behind to jump to the next tool.
>
> (p. 88)

The repeated mentions of MySpace in the library literature on social media in general and Facebook more specifically are a testament to the transience of even the most popular social media platforms. It is true that Facebook may not be forever, and Twitter and Tumblr, as well as social image-sharing platforms such as Pinterest and Instagram, are gaining popularity among university student populations. Perhaps, next year or in five or ten years, eighteen-year-olds will no longer have Facebook accounts, and perhaps many a library profile will sit unused. However, even then, perhaps the successes and failures of academic library Facebook pages will continue to inform the adoption and use of new social media platforms and other emerging technologies.

References

Baggett, S. B., & Williams, M. (2012). Student behaviors and opinions regarding the use of social media, mobile technologies, and library research. *Virginia Libraries, 58*(1), 19–22. Retrieved from http://search.ebscohost.com/login.aspx?direct=true&db=llf&AN=74026953&site=ehost-live

Bodnar, J., & Doshi, A. (2011). Asking the right questions: A critique of Facebook, social media, and libraries. *Public Services Quarterly, 7*(3–4), 102–110. doi:10.1080/15228959.2011.623594

Charnigo, L., & Barnett-Ellis, P. (2007). Checking out Facebook.com: The impact of a digital trend on academic libraries. *Information Technology & Libraries, 26*(1), 23–34. Retrieved from http://search.ebscohost.com/login.aspx?direct=true&db=llf&AN=502910220&site=ehost-live

Connell, R. S. (2009). Academic libraries, Facebook and MySpace, and student outreach: A survey of student opinion. *Portal: Libraries & the Academy, 9*(1), 25–36. Retrieved from http://search.ebscohost.com/login.aspx?direct=true&db=llf&AN=502966191&site=ehost-live

Foster, M., Wilson, H., Allensworth, N., & Sands, D. T. (2010). Marketing research guides: An online experiment with LibGuides. *Journal of Library Administration, 50*(5), 602–616. doi:10.1080/01930826.2010.488922

Gerolimos, M. (2011). Academic libraries on Facebook: An analysis of users' comments. *D-Lib Magazine, 17*(11), 5–5. doi:10.1045/november2011

Greenwell, S., & Kraemer, B. (2006). Internet reviews: Social networking software: Facebook and MySpace. *Kentucky Libraries, 70*(4), 12–16.

Hendrix, D., Chiarella, D., Hasman, L., Murphy, S., & Zafron, M. L. (2009). Use of Facebook in academic health sciences libraries. *Journal of the Medical Library Association, 97*(1), 44–47. doi:10.3163/1536-5050.97.1.008

Ismail, L. (2010). What net generation students really want: Determining library help-seeking preferences of undergraduates. *Reference Services Review, 38*(1), 10–27. doi:10.1108/00907321011020699

Jacobson, T. B. (2011). Facebook as a library tool: Perceived vs. actual use. *College & Research Libraries, 72*(1), 79–90.

Mack, D., Behler, A., Roberts, B., & Rimland, E. (2007). Reaching students with Facebook: Data and best practices. *Electronic Journal of Academic & Special Librarianship, 8*(2). Retrieved from http://search.ebscohost.com/login.aspx?direct=true&db=llf&AN=502920442&site=ehost-live

Mathews, B. S. (2006). Do you Facebook? Networking with students online. *College & Research Libraries News, 67*(5), 306–307. Retrieved from http://search.ebscohost.com/login.aspx?direct=true&db=llf&AN=502983380&site=ehost-live

Miller, S. E., & Jensen, L. A. (2007). Connecting and Communicating with Students on Facebook. *Computers in Libraries, 27*(8), 18–22. Retrieved from http://search.ebscohost.com/login.aspx?direct=true&db=llf&AN=502922334&site=ehost-live

Phillips, N. K. (2011). Academic library use of Facebook: Building relationships with students. *The Journal of Academic Librarianship, 37*(6), 512–522. doi:10.1016/j.acalib.2011.07.008

Petit, J. (2011). Twitter and Facebook for user collection requests. *Collection Management, 36*(4), 253–258. doi:10.1080/01462679.2011.605830

Wan, G. (2011). How academic libraries reach users on Facebook. *College & Undergraduate Libraries, 18*(4), 307–318. doi:10.1080/10691316.2011.624944

Part 5
Boundaries and Privacy

16

Unfriending Facebook? Challenges From an Educator's Perspective

KATE RAYNES-GOLDIE AND CLARE LLOYD

Curtin University

Although Facebook catered exclusively to university students until 2006, it was not designed for educational use. Yet, the use of Facebook as a pedagogical tool is increasing. For example, recent research has shown that the use of Facebook in teaching can provide valuable opportunities for informal learning (Leaver, 2012). Although Facebook may improve learning outcomes, the architecture and policies of Facebook create a number of significant privacy and boundary management issues for students and educators alike. Despite these concerns, research thus far has largely centered on the experience of students (Huijser, 2008; Karl & Peluchette, 2011; Madge, Meek, Wellens, & Hooley, 2009; Mazer, Murphy, & Simonds, 2007; Teclehaimanot & Hickman, 2011). Moreover, these studies focus on social challenges, such as embarrassment or identity management, while ignoring the problems caused by Facebook itself—for example, confusing and continually changing privacy settings, or the commodification of user data. The result is that risks to educators are overlooked—risks that become even more pressing as the use of Facebook in educational contexts becomes less of a choice as students, for example, increasingly abandon more formal learning management systems (LMS) in favor of Facebook (Allen, 2012; Bosch, 2009). To address this gap in the literature, we draw on autoethnographic data triangulated with existing research to summarize the challenges of using Facebook for education, from an educator's perspective, with a particular focus on challenges arising as a result of Facebook's policies and design. Overall, these issues can be understood in terms of control, with Facebook challenging the ability for educators to maintain control of their professional identity, workload and intellectual property and of their freedom from surveillance and commodification.

Professionalism

As with most occupations, educators are expected to behave in a professional manner. In education, an important element of professionalism is the maintenance of appropriate relationships and boundaries with students. At a tertiary level, universities mandate that their staff maintain "appropriate relation-ships" with students in order to provide unbiased assessments and avoid other conflicts of interest (Curtin University, 2013). The architecture of Facebook, however, complicates the management and regulation of professional relation-ships, especially between teachers and students. Facebook's design creates a phenomenon called *context collapse*, which is "the flattening and merging of all life's social boundaries in terms of contexts, identities and relationships— such as personal and professional identities and contacts—into one larger context" (Raynes-Goldie, 2012, p. 196). This flattening is most apparent in Facebook's Friendship feature, which defines all relationships in terms of the binary "Friend/Not-Friend," thereby conflating all manner of relationships and their associated hierarchical power structures, into one, singular relationship descriptor. Here we use Friendship to distinguish Facebook Friendship from friendship in its conventional sense. Facebook's choice of *Friend* implicates the values and expectations of the word, for example, closeness and familiar-ity (Fono & Raynes-Goldie, 2006), thereby potentially sending students who are Friends with their teachers the wrong message. In an interview with the *Chronicle of Higher Education* in 2007, US academic Nancy Baym provided a telling example of how these problems can manifest:

> A few weeks ago, a young man she did not know tried to friend her, says Ms. Baym [*sic*], an associate professor of communication studies at the University of Kansas. The same student e-mailed her the next day, ask-ing to get into a class that had a waiting list. He must have thought, "If she's my friend, then she'll let me into the class," she says. Young, female faculty members already struggle to be seen as authority figures, says Ms. Baym [*sic*]. It was easy to imagine what might happen: "But how could you have given me a D? You're my friend on Facebook!"
>
> (Lipka, 2007, p. A1)

Educators may decide that they can avoid these issues by simply not sending students Friend requests. In the courses we teach, Facebook groups are used, thereby allowing interaction between staff and students without requiring that everyone be Friends. However, this does not resolve the issue of unsolicited Friend requests from students, which educators receive regardless of how/if Facebook is being used, as Baym's example shows. The appropriate way to pro-fessionally handle these requests, such as the meaning of *friendship* itself, is a vague, gray area for educators. Indeed, while university policies are generally more accepting—or perhaps more vague—with respect to students and teach-ers being Friends, the rules in a secondary level school vary even more greatly, in some cases Friendship is allowed, whereas in others it is banned entirely (Akiti, 2013).

Similar concerns have been echoed by our colleagues in universities in Canada, the United Kingdom and Australia. These concerns included "When is being Friends with my students appropriate (if ever)?", "If one student is Friended, do I then have to accept all requests from students to avoid upsetting them or appearing to play favorites?", "What if I don't like the student?" and "How will our Friendship be viewed by other students, staff or my university?"

As these concerns point to, the maintenance of appropriate relationships and boundaries relies on both parties having a shared expectations and understandings, which can be a challenge considering that understandings of what online Friendship means can vary widely between individuals, and indeed, even between two Friends (Fono & Raynes-Goldie, 2006). Facebook Friendship creates the same situation for educators and students, thereby challenging the ability for educators to regulate and maintain professional boundaries and expectations with students or, indeed, even knowing what the appropriate boundaries are.

Complicating matters further, Friendship is not only a relationship descriptor, but it is also a privacy control. When individuals become Friends, they mutually grant each other access to their profiles, likes, photos, relationships, comments, status updates and so on—information that is added both by the individual as well as the individual's Friends. The result is that teachers gain access to the personal activities of their students—activities that teachers would not otherwise know about—for example, as a colleague shared with us, finding out that a student went out drinking the night before a major assignment was due. This creates yet another challenge for educators with respect to professionalism—in this case remaining as neutral as possible with respect to student assessment. As one professor described, "it can be a case of '[too much information]' where I am learning things about my students that I did not want to know" (Wright & Bollman, 2008).

Just as teachers gain access to their students, the reverse is also true. Friendship potentially grants students access to personal information that inadvertently reflects negatively on a professor in the context of their work. This information can include photos or activities acceptable in a personal context but not necessarily a professional one. As a 2013 study suggests, students form expectations of their professors' competence based on their Facebook profiles (Sleigh, Smith, & Laboe, 2013). Specifically, respondents ranked a fictional Facebook profile that contained a photo of a professor holding a beer as less respected and less competent than a similar profile that contained a photo of a professor and his son (Sleigh et al., 2013).

As these examples highlight, the maintenance of professionalism requires the knowledge and ability to appropriately manage one's identity, or what Goffman (1959) terms "impression management." However, that control is largely taken away from users on Facebook, both through Friendship as well as longer term policy and feature changes, such as continually altering the visibility, context and display of the personal information of its users. For example, Facebook has been gradually shifting its default settings, so that today, most information that was once private by default in 2004 is now public by default (McKeon, 2010). Similarly, the introduction of the newsfeed in 2006 took information shared in one context (an individual's profile), and pushed it out to all Friends, making information which had degree of privacy by virtue of its obscurity, suddenly much accessible and thus less private (boyd, 2008a).

As educators, we recognize the need to share certain aspects of ourselves with students as a part of the educational process; for example, it helps for students to feel more connected and supported. However, a critical difference exists between sharing this information in the physical classroom versus online. Unlike the physical world, Facebook is a mediated environment, and thus everything shared on the site is persistent, transferable, aggregateable, scalable, searchable and cross-indexible (boyd, 2008b; Tufekci, 2008). The result is that the information educators decide to share on Facebook is much harder to control in terms of who sees information, when that information is seen and in what context. Thus, there is a significant difference in choosing to reveal bits of information in a classroom setting and having Facebook reveal information for you without giving you an idea of who is seeing what, or when, and even sometimes, as has been the case, revealing information that was previously private (Lindlar, 2011). These issues become even more pressing for educators with less technological literacy or simply little time to stay aware and responsive to Facebook's latest changes.

Workload

The second way that Facebook poses a challenge for educators is the management of workload, an issue that has largely been unexamined by research thus far. As noted, Facebook was not designed as an educational platform; rather, it is a social utility. As such, its features are designed to facilitate social interaction—a goal that, in many ways, is not in line with the needs of educators. In particular, Facebook's communication features are designed to create persistent contact and ambient awareness, which is, as Thompson (2008) describes, "very much like being physically near someone and picking up on his mood through the little things he does—body language, sighs, stray comments—out of the corner of your eye." In practice, ambient awareness on Facebook occurs primarily through the newsfeed and customized notifications, which continually push activities, comments, status updates, photos and so forth to a user's e-mail or mobile phone, as well as to his or her account on Facebook itself. The culture of Facebook has co-evolved with these features enabling persistent, constant contact, with users updating and checking their Facebook profiles throughout the day and night on their phones and computers (Allen, 2012). Accordingly, there is an expectation of continual updates and instantaneous replies. It is an expectation that also extends to educational uses of Facebook. In some situations, educators can find themselves on call during most evenings and weekends, with students asking questions at all hours. Similarly, unlike the telephone, there is no time of day when it is considered inappropriate to send a message on Facebook. Accordingly, when an educator logs into Facebook to talk to her friends outside of work hours, she might be being inundated with questions from students, or worse, have her phone constantly buzz because a student had tagged her in a post with another pressing question. The consequence for educators is a collapse in work/life boundaries, which challenges their ability to manage their workload and protect their personal time.

The expectation of educators who are always accessible is also increasingly common in courses delivered online, an expectation perhaps exacerbated (or even partially created) by students having their online experiences informed by Facebook's instantaneous culture. As one professor observed in a large scale study looking at online education, changing expectations and the impact on workload, "When you work online, you're available—they expect you to be available 24/7" (Tynan, Ryan, Hinton, & Lamont Mills, 2012, p. 101). One approach to help manage this collapse in work/life boundaries is for an educator to set up a separate Facebook account specifically for teaching, which is an approach we have used. Although this helps to reduce unwanted communications and requests outside of work hours, clear expectations must also be set with students about staff working hours. Unfortunately, however, this approach did not do much to address another issue that we observed in our teaching: if questions were left unanswered for long, a sort of echo chamber/broken telephone effect would occur, by which students would increase each other's concerns or accidentally create and spread misinformation, such as a misunderstood assignment requirement or due date.

Surveillance, Commodification and Intellectual Property

As noted, examinations of Facebook in education tend to focus on challenges that ultimately arise because of the way people use Facebook, rather than because of Facebook itself. The first two issues we examined—professionalism and workload management—can, to some extent, be managed by setting consistent policies that create shared understandings and expectations between students and educators. In this section, however, we examine issues that cannot easily be mitigated by educators because they occur at the level of Facebook's architecture and policies—that is, Facebook's status as a highly commodified, highly surveilled environment.

Facebook meticulously tracks, records and analyzes the activities of all its users. Facebook's databases are composed both of information overtly shared by users, as well as their online activities, such as profile views or likes. Facebook further augments this database by gathering information from other sources, creating what are called "shadow profiles" (Morris, 2013). Consider that in 2014, Facebook will have been operating for ten years, meaning that

Facebook will have an unprecedented ten years' worth of information on some of its earliest adopters.

According to the Facebook IPO documents, 85% of Facebook's revenue in 2011 came from advertising (Frommer, 2012), advertising that leverages Facebook's massive database of user information to give marketers new and questionable ways to track and target consumers. For example, Facebook cross-references the personal information it collects with its "retail partners" (Facebook, 2013). These partners are then able connect the online activities of users with their actions in the physical world, thereby revealing if a given user buys a product after being shown an advertisement for it on Facebook. Thus, the very use of Facebook exposes educators and students to data collection, data mining, marketing and a loss of control of intellectual property. Put simply, on Facebook, users are not the customer; rather, they are the product (Rushkoff, 2011). While educators in industrialized nations may assume they must be protected by their country's privacy laws, the reality is not so straightforward. Facebook is an American-based company, a country that has a relatively ineffective mishmash of privacy laws with no independent body to enforce them (Stanley, 2009). The result is that Facebook has much more freedom with respect to the use of the data it collects about its U.S. and Canadian users who enter into an agreement with Facebook Inc., whereas the rest of the world enters an agreement with Facebook Ireland Ltd. (Facebook, 2012). While users from the rest of the world are protected by European Union (EU) privacy law, Facebook's Terms of Service require that users agree to have their "personal data transferred to and processed in the United States" (Facebook, 2012), which potentially exposes all users to governmental surveillance given the U.S. government's direct access to Facebook's servers as a result of PRISM (Verge Staff, 2013).

In light of these concerns, a number of privacy strategies can be deployed, such as using a fake account with an alias, installing Ghostery or using a VPN (virtual privacy network). Although these tools provide some degree of protection for students and teachers, it is not the same as simply not using Facebook, which is not a realistic option for many individuals, given the social and educational costs of opting out (Marwick, 2011). Indeed, many educators do not even have this choice, especially if they are contract staff. This raises some yet unanswered questions about duty of care. Western Australian law states that employers must provide workplaces "where employees are not exposed to hazards" (Government of Western Australia, 2005, p. 6). In this case, these hazards are physical. Yet, Facebook's questionable actives do beg the question, does (or should) Facebook's highly surveilled, highly commodified environment count as a hazard, even if the hazard is non-physical?

Finally, there is the issue of intellectual property. In Australia, universities hold copyright of teaching materials (Australian Vice-Chancellors' Committee, 2002), whereas in the United States the situation is a bit more vague, with educators sometimes maintaining ownership over their teaching materials (Crews, 2006). However, Facebook retains a license for any uploaded material, a license that grants the company the ability to use the material in any way they see fit, including sub-licensing it to another company. This license does not expire even after a user deletes uploaded content or deactivates their account (Facebook, 2012; Smith, 2013). Because using Facebook for educational purposes is still a relatively new phenomenon, these laws and policies have not yet been tested, but there is the potential for educators or universities to lose control of their teaching materials.

In conclusion, we have briefly explored the challenges faced by educators who use Facebook to teach. Although we acknowledge that Facebook does create valuable informal and authentic learning experiences, we have also shown that there are significant risks for both educators and students. Although many of the issues raised can be addressed by creating shared understandings and expectations between staff, students and universities, our concerns arising because of Facebook's revenue model and intellectual property claims are out of the hands of educators, and indeed users more broadly. Unless (or until) privacy legislation provides reasonable protection for social media users, educators wishing to use Facebook to teach will be essentially be making the choice between privacy and pedagogy.

References

Akiti, L. (2013). Facebook off Limits? Protecting Teachers' Private Speech on Social Networking Sites. *Valparaiso University Law Review, 47*(1), 119–167. Retrieved from http://scholar.valpo. edu/cgi/viewcontent.cgi?article=2257&context=vulr

Allen, M. (2012). An Education in Facebook. *Digital Culture and Education, 4,* 213–225. Retrieved from www.digitalcultureandeducation.com/volume-4/dce1077_allen_2012_html/

Australian Vice-Chancellors' Committee. (2002). *Ownership of Intellectual Property in Universities: Policy and Good Practice Guide.* Retrieved from www.universitiesaustralia.edu.au/ resources/324/302

Bosch, T. E. (2009). Using Online Social Networking for Teaching and Learning: Facebook Use at the University of Cape Town. *Communicatio: South African Journal for Communication Theory and Research, 35*(2), 185–200. Retrieved from www.tandfonline.com/doi/full/10. 1080/02500160903250648

boyd, d. (2008a). Facebook's Privacy Trainwreck: Exposure, Invasion, and Social Convergence. *Convergence: The International Journal into New Media Technologies, 14*(13), 13–20. Retrieved from http://con.sagepub.com/cgi/content/abstract/14/1/13

boyd, d. (2008b). *Taken Out of Context: American Teen Sociality in Networked Publics* (Doctoral dissertation). University of California, Berkeley.

Crews, K. (2006). Instructional Materials and "Works Made for Hire" at Universities: Policies and Strategic Management of Copyright Ownership. In K. M. Bonner (Ed.), *The Center for Intellectual Property Handbook* (pp. 15–38). New York: Neal-Schuman Publishers. Retrieved from http://papers.ssrn.com/sol3/papers.cfm?abstract_id=1540811

Curtin University. (2013). Code of Conduct. Retrieved May 30, 2013, from http://complaints.curtin. edu.au/conduct/index.cfm

Facebook. (2012). Statement of Rights and Responsibilities. Retrieved May 30, 2013, from www. facebook.com/legal/terms

Facebook. (2013). Help Centre: Interacting with Ads. Retrieved June 2, 2013, from www.facebook. com/help/499864970040521/

Fono, D., & Raynes-Goldie, K. (2006). Hyperfriends and Beyond: Friendship and Social Norms on LiveJournal. In M. a. C. H. Consalvo (Ed.), *Internet Research Annual Volume 4: Selected*

Papers from the Association of Internet Researchers Conference. New York: Peter Lang. Retrieved from http://k4t3.org/publications/hyperfriendship.pdf

Frommer, D. (2012). How Does Facebook Make Money? Retrieved May 30, 2013, from www.splatf. com/2012/02/facebook-revenue/

Goffman, E. (1959). *The Presentation of Self in Everyday Life.* New York: Anchor Books.

Government of Western Australia. (2005). *General Duty of Care in Western Australian Workplaces.* Retrieved from www.commerce.wa.gov.au/worksafe/PDF/Guidance_notes/general_duty_ of_care.pdf

Huijser, H. (2008). Exploring the Educational Potential of Social Networking Sites: The Fine Line Between Exploiting Opportunities and Unwelcome Imposition. *Studies in Learning, Evaluation, Innovation and Development,* 5(3), 45–54. Retrieved from http://eprints.usq.edu.au/ 4426/2/Huijser_2008_Sleid.pdf

Karl, K. A., & Peluchette, J. V. (2011). "Friending" Professors, parents and Bosses: A Facebook Connection Conundrum. *Journal of Education for Business,* 86(4), 214–222. Retrieved from www.tandfonline.com/doi/abs/10.1080/08832323.2010.507638

Leaver, T. (2012, October). *Facebook, Student Engagement and the "Uni Coffee Shop" Group.* Paper presented at the Proceedings from Internet Research 13, Salford, England.

Lindlar, C. (2011, January 12). Facebook 'Deceived' Users By Sharing Private Information. *Huffington Post UK.* Retrieved from http://www.huffingtonpost.co.uk/2011/12/01/facebook-guilty-of-privacy-breach_n_1122749.html

Lipka, S. (2007). For Professors, "Friending" Can Be Fraught. *Chronicle of Higher Education,* 54(15), A1. Retrieved from www.csun.edu/pubrels/clips/Dec07/12–05–07A.pdf

Madge, C., Meek, J., Wellens, J., & Hooley, T. (2009). Facebook, Social Integration and Informal Learning at University: "It Is More for Socialising and Talking to Friends About Work Than for Actually Doing Work." *Learning, Media and Technology,* 34(2), 141–155. Retrieved from www.tandfonline.com/doi/abs/10.1080/17439880902923606

Marwick, A. (2011). "If You Don't Like It, Don't Use It. It's That Simple." ORLY? [Blog entry]. Retrieved September 19, 2011, from http://socialmediacollective.org/2011/08/11/if-you-dont-like-it-dont-use-it-its-that-simple-orly/

Mazer, J. P., Murphy, R. E., & Simonds, C. J. (2007). I'll See You on "Facebook": The Effects of Computer-Mediated Teacher Self-Disclosure on Student Motivation, Affective Learning, and Classroom Climate. *Communication Education,* 56(1), 1–17. Retrieved from http:// s3.boomrrang.com/dev_files/files/COMM201_Behrenshausen_See_You_on_Facebook.pdf

McKeon, M. (2010). The Evolution of Privacy on Facebook. Retrieved from http://mattmckeon. com/facebook-privacy/

Morris, K. (2013, June 26). Facebook Shadow Profiles: What You Need to Know. *Mashable.* Retrieved from http://mashable.com/2013/06/26/facebook-shadow-profiles/

Raynes-Goldie, K. (2012). *Privacy in the Age of Facebook: Discourse, Architecture, Consequences* (Doctoral dissertation). Curtin University, Perth, Australia.

Rushkoff, D. (2011). You Are Not Facebook's Customer [Blog entry]. Retrieved from www.rushkoff. com/blog/2011/9/26/you-are-not-facebooks-customer.html

Sleigh, M. J., Smith, A. W., & Laboe, J. (2013). Professors' Facebook Content Affects Students' Perceptions and Expectations. *Cyberpsychology, Behavior, and Social Networking,* 16(7), 489–496. Retrieved from http://online.liebertpub.com/doi/abs/10.1089/cyber.2012.0561

Smith, O. (2013, January 4). Facebook Terms and Conditions: Why You Don't Own Your Online Life. *The Telegraph.* Retrieved from www.telegraph.co.uk/technology/social-media/9780565/ Facebook-terms-and-conditions-why-you-dont-own-your-online-life.html

Stanley, J. (2009). *Enforcing Privacy: Building American Institutions to Protect Privacy in the Face of New Technology and Government Powers.* New York: American Civil Liberties Union. Retrieved from www.aclu.org/files/assets/ACLU_Report_-_Enforcing_Privacy_2009.pdf

Teclehaimanot, B., & Hickman, T. (2011). Student-Teacher Interaction on Facebook: What Students Find Appropriate. *TechTrends,* 55(3), 19–30. Retrieved from www.editlib.org/p/32942/ proceeding_32942.pdf

Thompson, C. (2008, September 7). Brave New World of Digital Intimacy. *New York Times Magazine.* Retrieved from www.nytimes.com/2008/09/07/magazine/07awareness-t.html

Tufekci, Z. (2008). Can You See Me Now? Audience and Disclosure Regulation in Online Social Network Sites. *Bulletin of Science, Technology & Society,* 28(1), 20–36.

Tynan, B., Ryan, Y., Hinton, L., & Lamont Mills, A. (2012). *Out of Hours: Final Report of the Project e-Teaching Leadership: Planning and Implementing a Benefits-Oriented Costs Model for*

Technology Enhanced Learning. Australian teaching and Learning Council. Retrieved from http://eprints.usq.edu.au/21319/2/Tynan_Ryan_Hinton_Mills_LRTC_2012_PV.pdf

Verge Staff (2013, July 17). Everything You Need to Know About PRISM. *The Verge*. Retrieved from www.theverge.com/2013/7/17/4517480/nsa-spying-prism-surveillance-cheat-sheet

Wright, J., & Bollman, M. (2008). Professors and Students Come Facebook to Facebook. *Lee Clarion Online*. Retrieved from http://leeclarion.com/life/2008/09/17/professors-and-students-come-facebook-to-facebook/

17
Role Confusion in Facebook Groups

PERNILLA JOSEFSSON

School of Computer Science and Communication,
KTH Royal Institute of Technology, Sweden

FREDRIK HANELL

Division of ALM and Book History, Lund University, Sweden

During recent years communication between teachers and students in the context of higher education has become increasingly visible. One explanation is the use of parallel educational venues, such as learning platforms and the broad admittance of social networking services (SNSs). The use of SNSs such as Facebook—that are public by default—leads to changed conditions for teaching, providing by design others the ability to view any individual's *performance* and, depending on the individual's privacy settings, to follow their digital traces. This increased visibility has great impact on how teachers carry out their profession, and there is an imminent risk of confusion between the professional and private role. To better understand how student and teacher roles are managed and performed today we will here investigate how the increased visibility affects the performance of these actors in higher education, and to what Goffman (1959) refers to as *roles*.

In this chapter we discuss how student and teacher roles are performed and negotiated in two Facebook groups used by both teacher trainees and teacher trainers (in the following referred to as students and teachers, respectively) at two Swedish universities. We use a dramaturgical metaphor to analyze the results of two ethnographic studies. Ultimately, the aim of the investigation is to answer how the visibility inherent of Facebook affects the presentation of self in teacher-led Facebook groups.

Performance of an Individual

Erving Goffman (1959) takes a social theory perspective in his book *The Presentation of Self*, where he gives a dramaturgical metaphor on face-to-face interaction, and argues that society is not homogeneous and therefore we must act differently in different settings. Comparing how people act in their daily life with theatrical performance Goffman suggests the concept of a front region or front stage, where the individual is exposed to her peers, and the back region or backstage which represents the private or unexposed performance of the individual. By performance he refers to "all the activity of a given participant on a given occasion which serves to influence in any way of the other participants" (Goffman 1959, p 15). The others who are involved in the performance are seen as audience, observers, or co-participants.

The metaphor suggests that an individual's role, acted consciously or not, will lead her to design the impression of self. When an individual projects a definition on the situation, she implicitly or explicitly claims to be a particular kind of person. As a consequence of this comes an understanding that obliges others to value and treat her in the manner that persons of her kind have a right to expect.

Hogan (2010) uses Goffman's metaphor to argue that the *review-ability* and *search-ability* in social media are reminiscent of the feeling you can get from an art exhibition. According to Hogan, digital traces of performance are left behind and create spaces that can be characterized as of long-term identity exhibitions. Hogan's metaphor calls attention to these past data and emphasizes that "performance" is also connected to other factors such as temporal, spatial, and identity-related (the "time-space-identity" locus).

Zhao et al. (2013) expand on both Goffman and Hogan's metaphors, suggesting that we are moving into a world where individuals' digital traces express much of who we are. Their findings suggest that the Facebook platform consists of three different functional regions: a performance region, an exhibition region and a personal region. By region, Zhao refers to a set of goals, concerns, contexts, and corresponding system features, emphasizing that these regions have both spatial and temporal aspects. The performance region is considered to be consistent with Goffman's metaphor and is described as the place where individuals can make decisions about creating and managing contents according to their needs for self-presentation. In the exhibition region, modeled on Hogan's metaphor, the focus is on past data and long-term needs concerning identity construction. The personal region is presented as the place where users manage their Facebook data around perceived personal values.

Drawing on Goffman's dramaturgical metaphor, Hogan's exhibition metaphor and Zhao et al.'s functional regions, we argue that both students and teachers can assume a professional role as well as a private role. These roles come with different expectations, such as having different levels of authority. By using SNSs, the roles have become more and more intertwined. When we refer to roles in this chapter we choose to use the definition established by Goffman (1959, p. 16): "Defining social role as the enactment of rights and duties attached to a given status, we can say that a social role will involve one or more parts and that each of these different parts may be presented by the performer on a series of occasions to the same kinds of audience or to an audience of the same persons."

Facebook in Educational Settings

Two opposing views can be identified in the growing body of research on Facebook in educational settings: one that is approving Facebook and one more reluctant. The latter emphasizes that students have less use of Facebook for academic purposes. Madge et al. (2009), for example, claim that students perceive SNSs as a social and recreational space and do not want it spoiled by academic discussions. Selwyn (2009) explored students' education-related uses of Facebook and found that this use was based on criticizing learning experiences and events, exchanging logistical or factual information about teaching and assessing requirements, on instances of supplication and moral support with regards to assessment or learning, or on promoting oneself as academically incompetent or disengaged. Hew (2011) reviewed three current findings of Facebook studies and shows that there is little empirical evidence to support the effectiveness of Facebook in educational settings. None of the three studies included could confirm any statistically significant effects regarding, for example, the impact of teachers' self-disclosure on Facebook, nor were significant effects on students' online discussions and social presence presented.

The approving view sees the potential of Facebook in educational settings in terms of possibilities to support new forms of communication between students and teachers (Bosch, 2009; Lampe et al., 2011), as well as promoting well-being and the accumulation of social capital (Ellison et al., 2007). Although not explicitly connected to educational use, these factors are arguably of importance when establishing a constructive learning environment. Similarly, Mazer, Murphy and Simonds (2007) show that Facebook can nurture student–teacher relationship and show that it can have positive effects on students' motivation if teachers reveal personal information through Facebook. The new ways of nurturing relationships between students and teachers inevitably lead to a redrawing of social borders (c.f., Bosch, 2009), and also challenge traditional roles.

boyd and Ellison (2013) define an SNS as a networked communication platform on which its users generate the contents and have unique profiles with publicly visible connections. The visualization of a individual's social network is achieved through a so-called *user profile*. Therefore, it is not surprising that the first comprehensive review on Facebook in the social sciences found that the main focus of identity research is on user profiles (Wilson, Gosling, & Graham, 2012). The Facebook user profile is an interesting starting point for research on identity and presentation of self, but much information regarding management and performance of student and teacher roles is to be found in communication between individuals.

Two Ethnographic Studies

To explore the role performance of students and teachers, we conducted the same study at two universities. The data include online observations in two different Facebook groups and interviews with the participants in these groups,

Table 17.1 Overview of participants and data collection

	University A	*University B*
Group	Group A	Group B
Teachers	Teacher A1, A2	Teacher B
Students	Student A1, A2, A3	Student B1, B2, B3
Students in group	208 (185 female, 23 male)	23 (16 female, 7 male)
Number of posts	201	119
Group character	Open (public)	Closed
Data collection	April–May 2012	February–March 2013

both teachers and students; see Table 17.1. We studied teachers and students from teacher training courses in order to gain a meta-perspective of movements between the professional and private roles. These particular subjects are interesting as the students experience Facebook in the educational context in both roles, and from two perspectives.

We adopted an ethnographic approach inspired by Markham and Baym (2009) with the aim not to disturb the communication that occurred in the online settings. Influenced by Jeffrey and Troman (2004) we used a selective intermittent time mode; that is, the amount of time spent on fieldwork was determined by the development of the research. The main material for the presented study was gathered from two universities in Sweden (University A and University B) and consists of nine semi-structured interviews (with three teachers and six students) as well as communication data, both visual and textual, collected from two Facebook groups (Group A and B). Observation notes complemented the data collected from the groups, and the posts were read and reread together with ethnographic observation notes (see Davies, 2008).

A *Facebook Group* is a feature that allows users to communicate with a selection of people. One *post* is here defined as an individual entry in the group, including subsequent comments. The interviews were conducted to explain the findings from the Facebook groups (Davies, 2008; Kvale & Brinkmann, 2009). We included all the teachers who were members of the groups and chose student participants based on their level of activity, with the assumption that a higher activity level corresponds with more user experience.

University A has 25,000 students and is characterized by cross-disciplinary programs and an international environment. Group A was open (public) and consisted of two teachers and 208 students. The group administrator was Teacher A, who experienced that the activity among the students in the group he initiated was unevenly distributed. A handful of students were very active and made posts or comments almost every day, about twenty students wrote something to the group at least once every month, while the majority of the students acted only as "lurkers" who do not contribute (Wang & Yu, 2012). The data collection in Group A was done during April and May 2012 and included 201 posts and subsequent comments to these.

University B enrolls 12,000 students and has a profile of work-integrated learning. The participants in the study were all part of the teacher training program and were members of Group B. This group was closed and included one teacher and 23 students. The activity in this group was more evenly distributed among the students than compared to Group A. However, there were also several students acting as lurkers. All the course's learning resources were available in the Facebook group; these included notes about the lectures and slides, which were, in turn, uploaded by the teacher as documents. The data collection in Group B was done during February and March 2013 and included 119 posts and subsequent comments to these.

General Findings

At University A, Teachers A1 and A2 observed that most of the students use Facebook routinely, through laptops and smartphones. They also expressed frustration with the difficulties in having discussions using the university's official learning management system (LMS). With the desire to engage the students and increase efficiency in communication, Teacher A1 initiated and created a Facebook group.

At University B, Teacher B was inspired by the pedagogical concept of *flipped classrooms* (Lage et al., 2000) and regarded the use of a Facebook group as a new way for him to explore that concept. He expressed a wish to give lectures more relevant to students based on their interests and on the intended learning outcomes of the course. The teacher emphasized that students should learn for their profession rather than for passing an examination.

The experience reflected by both students and teachers about their participation in the Facebook groups confirmed that the groups were used for discussions and that the discussions maintained a focus on topics relevant for the courses. The students also expressed that using the groups was important to them in supporting their educational needs.

Reflections on Authority

All teachers discussed issues regarding what we in this chapter consider to be elements of authority. Both Teacher A1 and A2 mention the problematic aspect of being both teacher and examiner—being both a partner in learning but also the formal examiner of the student. Because all the teachers in the study at times have formal responsibilities as examiners, the authority associated with this role is partly transferred to the teacher role in general, contributing to a perceived high level of authority. This issue was emphasized by Teacher A2, who wanted to keep his roles as examiner and teacher separated. The desire to separate the two made him point out for the students that they would only be assessed during examination. The role of the examiner in terms of authority was discussed both by teachers and students, and also both in the use of the groups and outside of that context.

We found clear differences in perspectives among the students. For instance, Student B1 explained how the presence of the teacher in Group B had had an impact on how posts were formulated. Students avoided private matters, kept the language more strict, and the contents relevant to the topic of the group. The teacher presence also increased the willingness to "show off." Another perspective given by students in Group A was that the conversations in the Facebook group made them feel more equal to the teachers in the discussions. They compared this to being in the classroom where they experienced "a different hierarchy of power." Student A2 discussed authority from the perspective of being a teacher trainee and explained that he felt a need to uphold and present the expected image of "an authoritarian role" when he performed as a teacher. He feared that the use of Facebook might contribute to causing a loss of confidence in him in his role as a teacher.

Reflections on Roles

All three teachers found that their teacher role changed over time when using Facebook groups. Teacher B argued that he distanced himself from the act of *teaching* and instead ended up approaching *learning*. Using the Facebook group, he felt that the students assumed more responsibility in relation to their education: "I tell myself that these students are truly amazing. I miss them [. . .] Their interpretation was unrestricted by authority."

Both Teacher A1 and A2 emphasized that it is important to be the same person everywhere, regardless of the situation or place, whether it is on Facebook, at the university campus, or in town. Teacher A2 described himself as "a unified person that sometimes performs certain tasks and certain duties." Both teachers found it difficult to separate the *teacher-self* from the *private-self*. Rather than considering this a problem, Teacher A1 saw it as positive and "interesting, if you can let it spill over." When Teacher B described his use of the Facebook group, he explained that he tried to distinguish the private role from the professional role by differentiating his use and that he would "strive for a professional touch." He distinguished between his role as a teacher and his private role: "I try to separate the private and the professional."

According to Student A1, a large number of the participants perceived the Facebook group just to be another LMS. She explained that some of her fellow students considered the teachers who participated in the group to be representatives of the university. This was contrary to her own opinion, as she believed the teachers to be "two dedicated teachers [. . .] who are interested in developing communication with teacher trainees." The student described them as acting more in the role as teachers than examiners assessing student performance. Student A2 explained that the teachers are participating in the Facebook group in their private roles: "students have a hard time realizing that [Teacher A1] and [Teacher A2] are there as persons. When they are talking, it has nothing to do with the university." The same student explained that many of his fellows avoid visiting the Facebook group. According to him, this was the result of an uncertainty regarding the use of the group and the nature of teacher participation. From Student A2's perspective, most students perceive that the teachers have less authority in the Facebook group, and therefore, teachers should act differently in the Facebook group than they do on campus.

Reflections on Performance

Teacher A provided an illustrative example of the students' ideas of what it means to be a teacher in a Facebook group, and how these ideas can be challenged: One student posted an April Fool's joke to Group A, suggesting that the university was about to close down the program. In the early stages of the conversation that followed, Teacher A1 joined in on the joke and confirmed that this was "unfortunately true." Teacher A1 also systematically erased comments suggesting that this post was a joke. A number of students believed the April Fool's joke to be true, and one of them made a formal complaint to the head of the department. As a result, Teacher A1 posted a formal apology to the group.

Overall, Teacher B felt that conversations in Group B allowed openness, which meant that it was acceptable to post messages of emotional character. However, this was not the case from the start. Teacher B recalled the students' reactions asking "Are you allowed to do that?" the first time he published a post of a more provocative character. The teacher interpreted the comments as expressions of confusion towards what is considered to be appropriate for him as a teacher to discuss, because he is an authority figure assessing their performance. After settling this initial confusion he found that it became more legitimate to post different things to the group and that the use of the Facebook group "became more like the use of the regular Facebook."

Discussion and Conclusion

With the aim to understand how students and teachers roles are performed in social networking services, we investigated their activity in two different Facebook groups. Drawing on Goffman's dramaturgical metaphor (1959), Hogan's exhibition metaphor (2010), and Zhao et al.'s functional regions (2013), we argue that students and teachers alike can assume a professional role as well as a private role.

Along with the use of Facebook, social roles have become more intertwined than before and the negotiation of the professional role as a teacher and the private role becomes important to understand. Our findings illustrate how confusion can arise within the two different groups. For example, differences concerning the level of authority for a certain role were reflected. Some students interpreted that the teacher's presence suggested that an assessment of their performance could take place. Other students understood the teacher's presence as being of a more private character with less authority.

When the teachers' performances in the groups diverged from the students' expectation of their presence, confusion arose and negotiation took place. In our case, the teachers anticipated the students considering them as individuals by adjusting the threshold for what is "proper" action from teachers in their professional role. This could be compared with Goffman's metaphor and the approach to performance in which teachers project a definition of each situation and claim treatment accordingly. Attempts to blend front region performance in the group with more private, back region performance could be seen in both our examples: first, when discussing with personal engagement and then when taking part of a joke. The discussions that occurred about "proper behavior" strongly relate to levels of authority. However, it should be added that students found that the teacher's presence in the groups included less authority as compared to the same teacher's presence in the classroom. This would suggest that being a teacher involves several other social roles, for instance the role of the examiner, the mentor, or the partner in learning. The notion that digital traces express much of who we are emphasizes the importance of understanding perceived personal value of the performance.

The preceding examples illustrate the risks of performing a role that not everyone in the audience expects or sympathizes with. It was shown that it is easier to move between roles when you communicate in a Facebook group, but the risk of misunderstanding is also greater. Based on this, we would like to stress the *importance of clarifying the purpose of implementation and use of SNS in higher education.* We also stress the *importance of clarifying the role in which one act,* and to *communicate what is expected when performing a social role* in order to widen the acceptance of the performed roles and to avoid confusion.

Our findings confirm previous research showing that traditional social borders between students and teachers are partly redrawn due to the use of Facebook. The findings are also important in understanding how SNSs have an impact on communication between students and teachers. We see that a negotiation of behavior takes place in the Facebook groups, which is dependent on the individuals' specific performances. Implementations of SNS in higher education offer a change of scenery, blending the more private and the professional roles and inviting new interpretations of expected behaviors in the professional teacher role. To investigate long-term effects on these student-teacher relationships, longitudinal studies are needed.

References

Bosch, T. E. (2009). Using online social networking for teaching and learning: Facebook use at the University of Cape Town. *South African Journal for Communication Theory and Research,* 35(2), 185–200.

boyd, d. m., & Ellison, N. B. (2013). Sociality through social network sites. In W. H. Dutton (Ed.), *The Oxford handbook of Internet studies* (pp. 151–172). Oxford: Oxford University Press.

Davies, C. A. (2008). *Reflexive ethnography: A guide to researching selves and others*. London: Routledge.

Ellison, N. B., Steinfield, C., & Lampe, C. (2007). The benefits of Facebook "friends:" Social capital and college students' use of online social network sites. *Journal of Computer-Mediated Communication, 12*(4), 1143–1168. doi:10.1111/j.1083–6101.2007.00367.x

Goffman, E. (1959). *The presentation of self in everyday life*. New York: Doubleday.

Hew, K. F. (2011). Students' and teachers' use of Facebook. *Computers in Human Behavior, 27*(2), 662–676. doi:10.1016/j.chb.2010.11.020

Hogan, B. (2010). The presentation of self in the age of social media: distinguishing performances and exhibitions online. *Bulletin of Science, Technology & Society, 30*(6), 377–386.

Jeffrey, B., & Troman, G. (2004). Time for ethnography. *British Educational Research Journal, 30*(4), 535–548.

Kvale, S., & Brinkmann, S. (2009). *Den kvalitativa forskningsintervjun* (2a upplagan). [The qualitative research interview]. Lund, Sweden: Studentlitteratur.

Lage, M. J., Platt, G. J., & Treglia, M. (2000). Inverting the classroom: A gateway to creating an inclusive learning environment. *The Journal of Economic Education, 31*(1), 30–43.

Lampe, C., Wohn, D. Y., Vitak, J., Ellison, N. B., & Wash, R. (2011). Student use of Facebook for organizing collaborative classroom activities. *International Journal of Computer-Supported Collaborative Learning, 6*(3), 329–347. doi:10.1007/s11412–011–9115-y

Madge, C., Meek, J., Wellens, J., & Hooley, T. (2009). Facebook, social integration and informal learning at university: "It is more for socializing and talking to friends about work than for actually doing work." *Learning, Media and Technology, 34*(2), 141–155.

Markham, A. N., & Baym, N. K. (2009). *Internet inquiry: Conversations about method*. Los Angeles: Sage.

Mazer, J. P., Murphy, R. E., & Simonds, C. J. (2007). I'll see you on "Facebook": The effects of computer-mediated teacher self-disclosure on student motivation, affective learning, and classroom climate. *Communication Education, 56*(1), 1–17.

Selwyn, N. (2009). Faceworking: exploring students' education-related use of Facebook. *Learning, Media and Technology, 34*(2), 157–174. doi:10.1080/17439880902923622

Wang, X., & Yu, Y. (2012). Classify participants in online communities. *arXiv*. Advanced online publication. arXiv:1203.1995

Wilson, R., Gosling. S., & Graham, L. (2012). A review of Facebook research in the social sciences. *Perspectives on Psychological Science, 7*, 203–220.

Zhao, X., Salehi, N., Naranjit, S., Alwaalan, S., Voida, S., & Cosley, D. (2013). The many faces of Facebook: Experiencing social media as performance, exhibition, and personal archive. In *CHI '13 proceedings of the SIGCHI conference on human factors in computing systems* (pp. 1–10). New York: ACM.

18

Varying Cultural Conceptions of the Private Sphere and Their Impact on the Use of Social Media Networks as Educational Tools: A German and Chinese Comparison

XUN LUO AND FERGAL LENEHAN

Friedrich Schiller University of Jena (Germany)

This chapter examines the interface between culture and social media network usage. In order to do this three diverse elements are brought together: (1) The recent discourse surrounding the topic of privacy within Internet ethics, (2) the cultural specifics of the teacher–student relationship in China and Germany and (3) an empirical study of Chinese and German university teachers and students in relation to their social media network usage. It argues, ultimately, that cultural differences in relation to the teacher–student relationship and notions of privacy still exist and have an impact on the wider use of Facebook for educational purposes.

Internet Ethics and Notions of Privacy

The philosophical engagement with the ethics of computer usage has its roots in the early 1980s, while from the mid-1990s rival orientations, Cyber Ethics, Computer Ethics and Media Ethics, gained currency (Capurro, 2004). By the early 2000s this academic orientation took what may be termed an "intercultural turn" and began to engage with the ethics of computer technologies and especially the Internet in relation to their global reach beyond narrow spatial and cultural boundaries. The culturally complex notion of privacy also acquired a central place within this more recent debate, with some authors (Miller & Weckert, 2000) seeing the supposed erosion of the private sphere as the central challenge to engage with in relation to new technologies. Three rival terms have been used within this internationalized English-language discussion that examines the ethics of Internet usage in a transnational context. Luciano Floridi (2006) has labeled this specific ethical perspective broadly as the Philosophy of Information or simply Information Ethics; Rafael Capurro (2008) has used the term Intercultural Information Ethics, whereas Charles Ess (2008) writes of Global Information and Computing Ethics. These authors have also engaged differently with the notion of privacy.

Luciano Floridi (2006) has attempted to provide what he has termed an ontological interpretation of informational privacy. What he calls the "infosphere" retains certain ontological features, that is, specific agents, a specific environment and specific interactions implementable in that environment. "Ontological friction" in Floridi's theory refers to forces that oppose the information flow within an area of the infosphere, the work of a certain type of agent to obtain, filter and block information. Informational privacy is, thus, in his view, a function of the ontological friction within the infosphere, whereas a breach of one's informational privacy represents a breach of one's personal identity, as each individual is, he believes, constituted by his or her information (Floridi, 2006). Inherent to Floridi's (2006) theory is a somewhat problematic non-fragmented idea of the self, although the very notion of privacy remains a slippery and culturally dependent concept, which he, indeed, freely admits.

Rafael Capurro's approach has been one of comparative philosophy in which he has dealt with contrasting cultural notions of privacy. He has repeatedly undertaken this by using a somewhat simplistic West/East dichotomy, and the narrative thread of his texts frequently deviates haphazardly between various micro and macro levels. Indeed he has often tended towards extreme generalizations that even superficially embrace other vast global regions beyond his West/East dichotomy. Leading from a comparative discussion of concepts of the self, he writes, for example, that "in a very general way we can say that the concept of privacy in the West is oriented towards the individual, while Eastern countries—and also other cultures like the African ones, for instance—stress the concept of community and give privacy at least partly a negative connotation" (Capurro, 2005, p. 46). In more recent texts he has argued that Internet ethics thinkers must move away from examining privacy and should engage with more diverse topics such as online communities, governmentality, mobile phones and the digital divide (Capurro, 2008).

Charles Ess, on the other hand, sees an interconnection in Aristotelian and Confucian thought, which, he believes, constitutes a "meta-pluralism" because each tradition recognizes the possibility of an "interpretive pluralism that applies and interprets central ethical standards in different ways," while each tradition also makes use of metaphors of harmony and resonance (Ess, 2006, pp. 219–220). While admitting that vast West/East differences in relation to human nature and, thus, in relation to traditional conceptions of privacy, exist, he does ultimately argue that emerging data protection laws in China, Hong Kong, Thailand and Japan point toward an evolving cultural intersection in the praxis of privacy. He sees privacy now, thus, as a "shared value"—even if it takes "different manifestations in diverse cultural contexts" (Ess, 2006, p. 224).

In Germany, for example, he believes that privacy is justified in terms of the rights of autonomous citizens of democratic societies, whereas in China informational privacy is, in his view, seen as critical for electronic commerce and any intersection in the praxis of privacy comes from capitalist intersections (Ess, 2006). Ess's text again shifts uneasily between various micro and macro cultural levels, while the idea that something enshrined in law may in fact have very little effect in terms of everyday culture is something he fails to consider. Lü (2005), in a text that Ess actually draws on extensively for his Chinese context, also argues similarly to Ess believing that "Western-like" notions of individual privacy have gained increased currency in China within the last three decades. Privacy is also central to educational processes and may be seen as a notion that greatly influences the teacher–student relationship. How this has been perceived in a German and a Chinese context is presently examined.

Privacy and the Student–Teacher Relationship

The student–teacher relationship within Chinese cultural history is usually seen as greatly influenced by Confucian moral teaching and is often couched in the terms of a father–son relationship (Clark & Gieve, 2006). Thus, Xun Luo and Sebastian Kück (2011) have argued that the teacher not only plays the role of a transmitter of knowledge but also that of a quasi-parent figure, in which he or she, in line with student expectations, takes care that the students do equally well in their lives outside of formal education. Students, on the other hand, often see it as their duty to respect and obey their teachers and lecturers. Thus, a harmonious relationship is generally constructed, which, Sally Chan (1999) argues, essentially takes on familial characteristics. In accordance with this understanding of roles, Vathsala Sagayadevan and Senthu Jeyaraj (2012) argue that Chinese students converse with university teachers concerning matters relating to their lives outside of college, whereas lecturers are responsive to this. Thus, although some of the mentioned authors may perhaps argue in a somewhat problematic culturally static manner that may not give due appreciation to the dynamic nature of culture, scholars view the student–teacher relationship in China as still marked by familial characteristics.

In contrast to the traditional relationship-oriented teacher–student association in China, Judith Ricken (2011) perceives student and lecturer interaction at German third-level colleges as distant and focused solely on work issues, with university matters remaining central to lecturer–student conversations, whereas contact outside of the university context remains, she believes, an infrequent occurrence. This orientation is characterized by the separation of professional and private lives (Schroll-Machl, 2003). According to Sylvia Schroll-Machl (2003, p. 158) this feature originates historically from Lutheran Protestantism; perhaps a somewhat problematic religiously based contention given that Germany has had an extensive history of secularization, while of course the

German-speaking world has also, historically, been evenly divided between Lutherans and Catholics. Lutheranism, Schroll-Machl (2003, pp. 161–162) believes, traditionally distinguishes between two worlds: the private, religious inner world and the public, societal outside world, which remain inherently separate from one another. Thus, although some of the literature on the subject perhaps argues in a somewhat problematic manner, the German student–teacher relationship is usually characterized by the idea that a clear separation of professional and private lives still very much exists.

These culturally and historically based depictions of the student-teacher relationship within German and Chinese higher education were fused with the privacy discussion from Internet Ethics to form the theoretical and cultural assumptions underpinning an empirical study. Lü's (2005) and Ess's (2006) contention that an emerging intersection in the notions of privacy within these wider cultural contexts is to be viewed was tested via a study of the university teacher–student relationship at specific German and Chinese universities. Our intention, however, is not to engage in wide-ranging generalizations concerning masses of people inhabiting global spaces conveniently called the "West" and the "East." The wider question we concentrate upon is thus: May a residue of German and Chinese cultural and ideational history still be seen within the relationship of university teachers and students from these universities? The more direct research question guiding the study was: To what extent does a notion of privacy play a role in teacher–student interaction on social media networks?

Empirical Study

Methodology

Participants

Altogether 41 students (both graduates and undergraduates, with 21 from Germany) and 21 lecturers (11 from Germany) based at departments of English, German and intercultural communication in China and Germany, who live permanently in these nation-states and who use social media networks, participated in the survey. The sample German lecturers and students all came from the University of Jena, whereas the Chinese test persons came from five different third-level colleges in Beijing, Shanghai, Tianjin, Nanjing and Chengdu. Because Facebook (with more than 750 million active users) is not officially available in China, registration with a functionally very similar platform, Renren, was concentrated upon instead. Formerly known as Xiaonei, Renren, which can be translated into English as "people," has more than 160 million users and retains a user interface that is almost identical to Facebook (Marshall, 2008). Lin Qiu, Han Lin and Angela K.-y. Leung (2013) have, however, already shown that some differences also exist in relation to knowledge sharing between Facebook and Renren.

Procedure

The survey questionnaire was developed and then pilot tested with six partici-pants. A final draft was revised based on the feedback acquired in the pilot study. The survey questionnaire contained structured and open-ended questions. It consisted of two parts: Part 1 included three questions that probe participants' usage behavior on Facebook and Renren. Part 2 included three questions that address implicitly the issue of how cultural conceptions of the private sphere affect teacher–student interaction on social media. The questionnaires were conducted and completed in German and Chinese, respectively, and the results have been translated into English by the authors.

Data Analysis

The data analysis relates to two distinct thematic areas: Usage behavior and the role of privacy in social media networks. The usage behavior of the test persons is depicted according to the frequency of their logging in, as well as their most common activity on the social media network. In relation to the concept of privacy the situation regarding the establishment of contact between lecturers and students, and their general position and opinion relating to this, was exam-ined. As open and closed questions were asked, the analytical methodology encompasses both descriptive statistics as well as qualitative content analysis and frequency analysis. In the qualitative content analysis categories arising from test persons' answers to the open questions were constructed, in which text sections from each category were counted. Via frequency analysis the indi-vidual categories were prioritized. In order to acquire a succinct overview the results of the four subgroupings (German lecturers and students, Chinese lec-turers and students) are placed alongside each other in table form.

Results

Facebook/Renren Usage

The usage behavior of test persons on Facebook/Renren was investigated via two questions: How often do you log onto Facebook/Renren? and What do you use Facebook/Renren for? The reason for registering with the social media network was also asked.

In Figure 18.1 the log in frequency is depicted via six categories. Those who log onto Facebook/Renren more often than once every three days are seen here as active users. According to this definition the percentage of active Facebook/Renren usage for the four test-person groups is as follows: 65% for Chinese stu-dents, 100% for German students, 50% for Chinese lecturers and 90% for German lecturers. Fifty percent of Chinese lecturers tested and 25% of Chinese students only used Renren once a month. The reason for this in relation to the Chinese lecturers tested is, we suggest, probably due to their relative unfamiliarity with

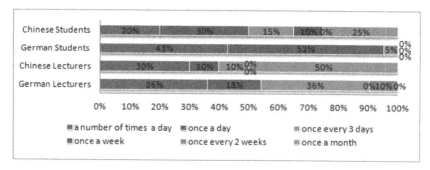

Figure 18.1 Login frequency

social media. Chinese students, on the other hand, also simultaneously avail of other programs and instruments (e.g., QQ, Wechat), whose functions in relation to communication may be seen as partly more favorable.

Sixteen Facebook/Renren activities were given, and respondents had to list the three to five they undertake most frequently. The percentage displayed in Figure 18.2 represents the frequency of an activity undertaken by each subgroup. Based on this, the six most frequent activities of each subgroup were listed. Despite similarities regarding some basic activities such as writing and answering messages, following and commenting on friends' updates, differences between the German and Chinese respondents are noticeable here also. Whereas Chinese test persons chiefly engage in reading comments about updates, the German test persons utilize instead functions such as messaging and chatting. This suggests again that the Chinese test persons probably use other programs for messaging and chatting.

There are also two favored activities only named by the German respondents: "arranging meetings with friends" and "following my group updates." This would definitely suggest that Facebook retains great potential for communication not simply between two individuals but also within a group or community, something that could undoubtedly be used for learning purposes. Three respondents described also how they registered initially with Facebook in order to register for classes during a semester spent at a university abroad. The majority of test persons stated that they use Facebook/Renren in order to maintain contact with friends who live in other places, often abroad (named 56 times). It was suggested 11 times that respondents would like to get to know new people via Facebook/Renren, whereas it was stated 7 times that they came to Facebook simply out of curiosity.

Privacy and Lecturer/Student Contact
The respondents were asked whether they have either students or lecturers among their list of friends on Facebook/Renren and how open they would be to establishing with their students or lecturers social media network contact. They were also then asked to provide reasons for their answer.

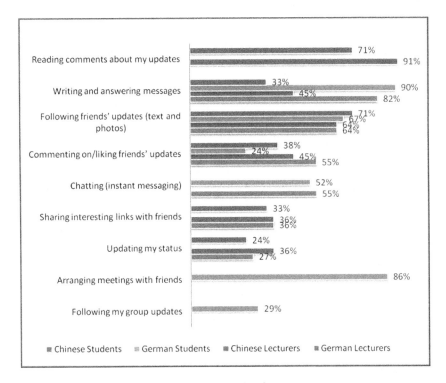

Figure 18.2 Most common activities on Facebook/Renren

In Figure 18.3 one may notice stark differences between the test persons from German and Chinese universities. Whereas only 45% of the German lecturers surveyed had students within their list of friends, all of the Chinese lecturers questioned had many or some students within their contact list. Whereas 35% of the Chinese student test persons had no lecturers within their list of friends, a substantially higher 90% of surveyed German-based students did not have any lecturers within their list of Facebook friends.

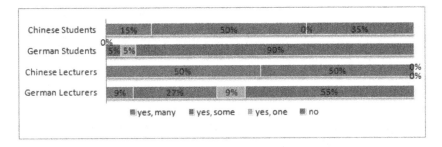

Figure 18.3 Students/lecturers in list of friends on Facebook/Renren

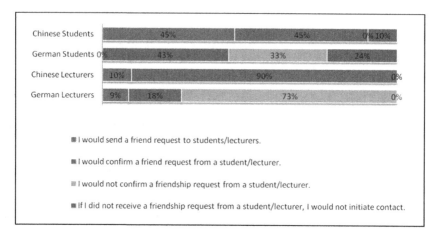

Figure 18.4 Participants' willingness to establish contact

Figure 18.4 shows that 73% of the surveyed German lecturers would not confirm friend requests from students, whereas 100% of the Chinese lecturers questioned would be willing to include students in their list of friends. Although no German student tested would send a friend request to a college lecturer, 45% of the Chinese test persons would. As well as this, 33% of German students would be willing to decline a friend request from one of their lecturers, which none of the Chinese students surveyed could countenance.

We used content and frequency analysis to examine the answers received; Table 18.1 summarizes in categories the reasons given for the positive or negative response to the respective questions. The frequency with which these categories appear is displayed.

In comparison to the Chinese test persons, who were largely positive in relation to establishing contact between the two subgroupings, the German lecturers and students sampled found this a lot more problematic as they consciously and explicitly stated that they wanted to protect the private sphere of their lives by clearly separating their personal life and professional life. Despite this some German lecturers surveyed would not completely exclude the notion of establishing Facebook contact with students, as long as a conflict of interests did not ensue. This, they write, relates especially to former students and students with part-time departmental jobs. In order to utilize Facebook as a communicational instrument for learning purposes, yet without entering into the private sphere of lecturers and students, one German lecturer stated that he would instigate a thematic grouping on Facebook within which he could then become active with students. This is undoubtedly a convincing statement and points toward the way in which Facebook may be successfully integrated into university life for learning purposes.

Table 18.1 Participants' reasons for positive/negative reactions

	Chinese Students	German Students	Chinese Lecturers	German Lecturers
Reasons for positive reaction: yes	1. lecturers can also be friends (3) 2. to build a closer relationship to the lecturers (2) 3. no reason not to (2) 4. to respect lecturers (1) 5. when I know the lecturers (1)	1. no reason not to (2) 2. out of politeness (1)	1. communication with students after class is possible (3) 2. out of politeness (3) 3. to build a closer relationship to the students (2) 4. good availability (2)	1. only if no conflict of interests (2) 2. but it depends on the students (1)
Reasons for negative reaction: no	1. to protect the private sphere (1) 2. there are other learning platforms (1) 3. Renren is not an instrument for learning (1)	1. to protect the private sphere (only share with friends, clear separation of private life and college) (12) 2. there are other possibilities for contact (e-mail, university learning platforms) (1)	(0)	1. to protect the private sphere (separation of private life and work) (7) 2. there are other learning platforms (1)

The answers emanating from the sampled Chinese lecturers suggest that they are fundamentally open to establishing close relationships with their students. They also would confirm a friend request from a student out of politeness. For Chinese lecturers Renren constitutes a new way of maintaining contact with students after class. Especially advantageous is the fact that students are easily reached at any time via Renren. Despite this, one Chinese lecturer stated that he would not use Renren to comment on his private life. For this reason he would also not make students feel obliged to be "friends" with their lecturers on social media networks.

Even if approximately half of the German students sampled (43%) as well as almost half of the Chinese students surveyed (45%) stated that they would confirm their lecturers' potential friend request, the Chinese students' reasoning for this displays decidedly more desire to establish a closer relationship with their university teachers. From their perspective, lecturers may indeed really become friends. Once they know the lecturers, they would not generally have a problem adding them to their list of contacts. In comparison more of the German student test persons gave concrete reasons why they would not confirm a friendship request from a lecturer. Most explicitly stated that they would prefer to separate their private life from their university life; a sentiment voiced by only one of the Chinese students surveyed. Indeed, the German students viewed other forms of contact, such as e-mail and university learning platforms, as more suitable for communicating with lecturers.

Conclusion

One may not, of course, make simplified generalizations regarding vast amounts of people from the results of a small qualitative study as conducted here. Such a study may, however, point towards certain trends from which one may make tentative conclusions. Although traces of an evolving global cultural commonality may indeed be seen among the German and Chinese groupings, in that all of the surveyed test persons engage with very similar social media network technologies, differences are also evident in relation to the test person's more exact usage behavior and attitude to privacy. As communicational technologies develop and become fashionable at such rapid speed this behavior will probably, indeed, always be evolving and never really retain a quality that one could term uniform. Regarding the test persons' social media network usage, it is clear that a very substantial residue of the respective historical, sociocultural conception of the teacher–student relationship remains evident: The Chinese test persons often viewed this relationship in a quasi-familial manner, whereas the German test persons emphasized the separation of university and non-university life. Indeed, a large number of the German test persons surveyed perceived this explicitly using the language of privacy, a signifier with extensive cultural significance for the teacher–student relationship in Germany, not explicitly mentioned in any of the survey questions. Although a small number of the Chinese test persons also utilized the language of privacy, this was not significant enough to suggest anything resembling a cultural intersection in relation to the praxis of privacy. Indeed, this study suggests that the notion of the private still retains culturally very particular characteristics and that Lü (2005) and Ess (2006) are mistaken in their suggestion of an emerging cultural intersection in relation to the private sphere. If Facebook is to be widely utilized in an educational context then this should be done, it is clear from this study, via the creation of a separate group identity; many still identify Facebook as a leisure tool and are uncomfortable using it in a more formal context.

References

Capurro, Rafael. (2004). Informationsethik—Eine Standortbeschreibung. *International Journal of Information Ethics, 1,* 5–10.

Capurro, Rafael. (2005). Privacy. An intercultural perspective. *Ethics and Information Technology, 7,* 37–47.

Capurro, Rafael. (2008). Intercultural information ethics: foundations and applications. *Journal of Information, Communication and Ethics in Society, 6*(2), 116–125.

Chan, Sally. (1999). The Chinese learner—a question of style. *Education + Training, 41*(6/7), 294–305.

Clark, Rose, & Gieve, S. N. (2006). On the discursive construction of "The Chinese learner." *Language, Culture and Curriculum, 19*(1), 54–73.

Ess, Charles. (2006). Ethical pluralism and global information ethics. *Ethics and Information Technology, 8*(4), 215–226.

Ess, Charles. (2008). Luciano Floridi's philosophy of information and information ethics: Critical reflections and the state of the art. *Ethics and Information Technology, 10*(2), 89–96.

Floridi, Luciano. (2006). Four challenges for a theory of informational privacy. *Ethics and Information Technology, 8*(3), 109–119.

Lü, Yao-Huai. (2005). Privacy and data privacy issues in contemporary China. *Ethics and Information Technology, 7*(1), 7–15.

Luo, Xun, & Kück, Sebastian. (2011). Gibt es Lernstile, die kulturspezifisch sind? Eine interkulturelle Annäherung an das Lernstilkonzept anhand einer vergleichenden Untersuchung am Beispiel deutscher und chinesischer Studenten. *Interculture Journal, 15,* 37–62.

Marshall, Matt. (2008, April 30). *Xiaonei, the Facebook of China, raises $430M—better funded than Facebook.* Retrieved July 2, 2013, from http://venturebeat.com/2008/04/30/xiaonei-the-facebook-of-china-raises-430m-better-funded-than-facebook/

Miller, Seamus, & Weckert, John. (2000). Privacy, the workplace and the Internet. *Journal of Business Ethics, 28*(3), 255–265.

Qiu, Lin, Lin, Han, & Leung, Angela K.-y. (2013). Cultural differences and switching of in-group sharing behavior between an American (Facebook) and a Chinese (Renren) social networking site. *Journal of Cross-Cultural Psychology, 44*(1), 106–121.

Ricken, Judith. (2011). *Universitäre Lernkultur. Fallstudien aus Deutschland und Schweden.* Wiesbaden, Germany: VS Verlag für Sozialwissenschaften.

Sagayadevan, Vathsala, & Jeyaraj, Senthu. (2012). The role of emotional engagement in lecturer-student interaction and the impact on academic outcomes of student achievement and learning. *Journal of the Scholarship of Teaching and Learning, 12*(3), 1–30.

Schroll-Machl, Sylvia. (2003). *Die Deutschen—Wir Deutsche. Fremdwahrnehmung und Selbstsicht im Berufsleben.* Göttingen, Germany: Vandenhoeck & Ruprecht.

Part 6
(Re)Configuring Facebook

19
Changing Facebook's Architecture

SKY CROESER

Curtin University

There are increasing pressures on tertiary-level educators to adopt Facebook in their teaching, or at the very least to acknowledge its role in informal learning. At the same time, commentators are expressing concerns about Facebook's use, many of which focus on issues relating to social privacy, our ability to limit access to personal information to specific groups of people (Raynes-Goldie, 2010). This chapter argues that in addition to considering potential violations of social privacy, educators need to be aware of risks associated with institutional privacy: threats to Facebook users posed by institutions, including Facebook itself, other commercial organizations, and government agencies. As a corollary to this, educators should be addressing the ethical implications of using a platform that sells users' data and that sells users themselves as an audience to advertisers.

In considering these issues, it is important to consider Facebook's architecture—the user interface and affordances of the platform—as well as Facebook's statements of policy. For example, although it is technically possible for users to have fine-grained control over their privacy settings, in practice the location of these settings in a menu structure separated from content discourages users from doing so. Similarly, although users are able to limit the amount of information they share with Facebook, many aspects of the platform's design encourage users to share information about others, as well as about themselves. Educators' responses to Facebook therefore need to consider ways to engage with—and disrupt—the platform's architecture directly. Browser extensions offer one avenue for doing this, as they allow users to disrupt Facebook's mechanisms for gathering information, and Facebook's targeted advertising.

Facebook's Use in Tertiary Education: Benefits and Concerns

Facebook has become an increasingly popular service, with over ninety percent of students at some universities reporting that they have accounts (Hew, 2011, p. 633). The service now holds a unique position in the online information ecology, offering an all-encompassing experience which incorporates an increasing range of services, such as online chat, e-mail-like messaging, groups, and the sharing of content (Allen, 2012, p. 214). These features and Facebook's popularity are prompting a number of educators to suggest that teachers explore ways to use the service for tertiary education (see Bosch, 2009; Munoz & Towner, 2009; Roblyer, McDaniel, Webb, Herman, & Witty, 2010). However, clear frameworks for Facebook use at university have not yet been developed, and many educators are unsure of how to approach the platform.

To date, there is very little work exploring the formal incorporation of Facebook into tertiary education, barring the chapters in this volume, with more work focusing on informal use. Although some scholars have taken the dearth of literature on formal use of Facebook to mean that Facebook has limited educational value (Hew, 2011, p. 668), others have argued that it is precisely Facebook's ability to blend formal and informal learning that gives it its value. Allen (2012, p. 218) argues that concerns about the ways in which Facebook weakens boundaries between formal and informal behaviors are misplaced: pedagogical research tends to suggest that blurring formal and informal learning strengthens, rather than undermines, learning. At the very least, Roblyer et al. (2010) suggest that Facebook can serve as a practical way for teachers to contact students (p. 135). Even when teachers do not actively engage with Facebook, students may create their own groups to support their learning (particularly for online study). Ties formed through these groups "can last far longer than any single unit, and seeing online students self-organise social and support opportunities that persist is highly significant in them helping each other enjoy learning online with the same opportunities as campus based face to face students" (Leaver, 2012, p. 107). Not only does Facebook offer new possibilities for supporting students' learning, but students are also likely to use Facebook as an informal support structure for their studies whether teachers encourage its use.

Educational use of Facebook necessarily raises concerns, many of which relate to the ways in which Facebook's architecture undermines the boundaries and hierarchies traditionally taken for granted in the classroom. As Baran's (2010) research suggests, students are unlikely to make a clear distinction between their informal, social communication on Facebook and more formal learning and communications on the platform. Furthermore, Facebook's attempts to encourage the use of real names and significant sharing of personal content mean that

> *any* use of Facebook will necessarily confront both teachers and students with the fact that, in an online environment which is so closely entwined with real identities, real places and persistent communication, they are always explicitly negotiating the boundaries between formal and informal.
> (Allen, 2012, p. 223, emphasis in original)

This overlap between offline and online space, and between in-class and external identities, may have educational benefits, but it also leads to uneasiness about privacy for both teachers and students.

On the whole, privacy concerns among users relate to social privacy, rather than institutional privacy: threats to privacy from Facebook itself. Social privacy has also been the primary concern of educational scholars writing about Facebook, who worry that students may share information on Facebook that is inappropriate for other students, teachers, or future employers to see or that teachers may expose more of their lives to students than is desirable. Acquisiti and Gross (2006, p. 16), for example, worry that a significant proportion of users do not know whether privacy controls exist on Facebook, or how to use them, whereas Hew (2011) notes that students' concerns about "unwanted Facebook audiences (e.g., current or future employers, university administrators, and corporations) showed no relationship with information revelation" (p. 666), and Grimmelman (2009, p. 1165) discusses the potential consequences of authority figures having access to students' Facebook profiles. Concern about teachers' privacy is often linked to the idea of maintaining distance between teachers and students in order to reinforce teachers' authority. Some scholars recommend that teachers limit self-disclosure online in order to "maintain a level of professionalism that does not cross the boundary of the teaching-student relationship" (Munoz & Towner, 2009, p. 8). These issues are important. Students have faced serious penalties when information shared on Facebook reached unintended audiences (Johnson, 2010; Jones, 2012; Mytelka, 2013), and even teachers who wish to challenge the traditional role of teacher-as-authority-figure will need to navigate Facebook carefully. However, more attention needs to be paid to the institutional aspects of privacy on Facebook.

Concerns about the volume of information shared with Facebook and the ways in which this information may be used need to be put in the context of Facebook's architecture. As Peterson (2010, p. 22) notes, Facebook makes its money from users' data, and it is in the company's interests to build an architecture that enables and facilitates sharing. Facebook provides people with powerful privacy settings that allow users to divide their Friends into groups, and control access to particular statuses or content, but this happens within the context of an environment which does not privilege privacy or facilitate the use of these settings (Peterson, 2010, p. 29). Whereas Peterson (2010) considers this to be "strange" and against the interests of Facebook itself (p. 36), Raynes-Goldie (2012) has demonstrated that a persistent pressure towards increased disclosure is both in the financial interests of the company and is an ideological goal of Mark Zuckerberg, the founder and CEO of Facebook, who still plays a significant role within the company.

Insofar as privacy settings exist on Facebook, they are there precisely to facilitate sharing. As Raynes-Goldie (2012) notes, the "feeling of safety and closedness" (p. 161) initially provided by e-mail verification combined with school networks helped early users to feel safe sharing their information, and this (false) sense of boundedness has continued to support the sharing of users' content on the platform. Facebook's architecture consistently provides people with "signals suggesting an intimate, confidential, and safe setting" (Grimmelmann, 2009, p. 1160), encouraging a systematic misunderstanding of privacy risks. Privacy settings, although finely grained, are mostly located separately to content, making it difficult to easily adjust who can see a particular photo, for example (boyd, 2008). In addition to this, Facebook's architecture is constantly changing in ways that cause sudden privacy lurches: sudden shifts in the audience that can access users' content, or in the audience's likelihood of being 'pushed' content that previously required concerted effort to find (Grimmelmann, 2009, p. 1169; Peterson, 2010, p. 20). Although this is, in part, inspired by Zuckerberg's conviction that more openness and sharing will lead to a better world (Raynes-Goldie, 2012, pp. 148–152), it is also linked to the Facebook business model.

Facebook's immense success as a company is reliant on the data shared by users, as well as by the time users spend on the site. Data are sold to marketing services, whereas Facebook sells advertisers a customized audience, which will allow them to "reach the right audience for your business and turn them into customers" (Facebook, 2013a). Facebook's architecture and defaults encourage users to share large amounts of information about their interests and lives, while

> the structure of the pages even facilitates this self-categorising by providing a preset selection of categories. The value of this pre-categorised data for marketing analysis is obvious, and Facebook allows marketers to access much of it so they can create "SocialAds" targeted to the individual user.
> (Hendry & Goodall, 2010, p. 6)

None of the privacy settings control Facebook's access to one's content (Hendry & Goodall, 2010, p. 7; Raynes-Goldie, 2012, p. 105), although some of the settings listed under "Adverts" do limit the ways in which Facebook can share that content. This means that even if a person is careful about his or her social privacy on Facebook, successfully navigating the complicated privacy settings in order to limit content to intended groups, one is still sharing all his or her data—including information on Friends and on how one communicates with them—with Facebook.

A user is also, by extension, sharing his or her information with third parties. In 2013, Facebook announced that it would be building partnerships with data brokers in order to help marketers "reach their current customers with relevant ads on Facebook" (Facebook, 2013c). Data brokers match non-Facebook data (such as marketing data based on a user's purchases) with Facebook data in ways that may be unsettling for users:

> While Facebook may be taking steps to limit identifiable data flowing back to the data brokers, the result for users could be eerie. Users might find themselves seeing advertisements that are based on actions they took in the real world as well as personal facts about their life and circumstances that they have been careful not to put on Facebook.
> (Opshal & Reitman, 2013)

In other cases, Facebook data will be matched with information gathered from online tracking services so that "websites you visited when you were not logged into Facebook will be used as the basis for showing you advertisements on Facebook. This will happen whether you are logged in to Facebook or not, and regardless of whether you consent to tracking or not" (Opshal & Reitman, 2013). The links being made between online and offline data have important implications for privacy, especially as it becomes increasingly likely that this data is also being shared with government agencies in the United States and elsewhere (Opshal & Reitman, 2013; Rushe, 2013). These issues play a remarkably small role in the academic literature on Facebook's potential role in tertiary education.

Although some attention is being paid to the potential problems with using cloud services and other commercial platforms in schools (see SafeGov.org & Ponemon Institute, 2013), there is no work directly addressing the serious ethical questions surrounding encouraging, or even requiring, university students to use a service that enables the sharing of personal information (and is structured to undermine informed consent for that sharing) and that packages that information for reselling, and then creates targeted advertising for users. Targeted advertising may not only unsettle users by demonstrating the extent to which our information is accessed by marketers; it may also cause problems for the ways in which it pinpoints our insecurities. One popular article discussed the psychological toll of repeatedly seeing weight-loss advertisements and hinted at the stress that couples trying to get pregnant could feel when subject to advertisements suggesting they might be infertile (Beckman, 2008). Similarly, whereas the place of advertising more generally, including online advertising, in schools has received some attention (see Molnar, Boninger, Harris, Libby, & Fogarty, 2013; Molnar, Boninger, Wilkinson, & Fogarty, 2009), there seems to be very little concern about advertising within tertiary education spaces. Specific commercial relationships (Liptak, 2013) and kinds of advertising, such as advertisements for payday loans (Kennedy, 2013), have been questioned or banned, but there are few, if any, pushes for "commercial-free" campuses in the same way that some schools have been declared "commercial-free" (Molnar et al., 2009, p. 18). The focus among educators on social privacy issues involved in Facebook use has completely overshadowed attention to institutional privacy and to the ethics of turning our students' data into a product for Facebook's commercial gain. Even when writing on Facebook's use in tertiary education directly gives advice to educators or raises questions about the use of Facebook (Greenhow, Robelia, & Hughes, 2009, p. 253; Munoz & Towner, 2009; Roblyer et al., 2010, p. 138), advertising and institutional privacy receive no mention.

Responding to Facebook: Tactics and Strategies for Educators

Discussions about how to use Facebook in tertiary education have tended to focus on how to manage personal privacy, or on other issues such as pedagogical approaches to informal learning on the platform. While this work is valuable, it predominantly fits within the scope of what de Certeau (1984) called "tactics": hidden, "clever tricks, knowing how to get away with things" (p. xix). Tactical responses do not change Facebook's architecture, rather they respond to it, attempting to "cheat" by not following the Terms of Service, or by using the platform in ways discouraged by the architecture. One of the most common tactics advocated is for teachers to limit the amount of information shared on the platform, and recommend that students do the same. This draws on existing "subversive privacy practices," which Raynes-Goldie (2010) describes some users as engaging in, such as "wall cleaning" (periodic deletion of content). The most extreme form of this is the suggestion made by some university administrations that students delete Facebook profiles entirely before applying for jobs (Peterson, 2010, p. 8). More moderate advice from Munoz and Towner (2009, pp. 8–9) recommends that teachers cultivate a "professional" Facebook profile, both for pedagogical purposes and to set an example for students, which implicitly suggests limiting which kinds of information are shared on the site. Much of the advice suggesting that both students and teachers pay careful attention to information shared with Facebook is useful, particularly for addressing concerns over social privacy. However, it is important to remember that the architecture of Facebook continually encourages more sharing, and that Facebook's agreements with data brokers mean that privacy threats related to the site do not only originate with content shared on Facebook.

Another tactic suggested by the literature is for teachers and/or students to take steps to separate their offline identities from their Facebook profiles. Raynes-Goldie (2010) discusses the use of aliases on Facebook as a subversive privacy practice which potentially allows users of the platform to remain "invisible" to unwanted observation: teachers may prevent students from being able to see their personal profiles; students may prevent university authorities, employers, classmates, or other unwanted audiences from being able to access potentially damaging information (such as photographs that suggest heavy drinking). Related to this, Munoz and Towner's suggestion that teachers create a completely separate professional profile implies using an alias to "hide" their personal profile. Presumably, students could also create a personal profile that is hidden by use of an alias or privacy settings and could use a different profile for educational purposes. Anecdotally, there are already many teachers and students using aliases and/or multiple accounts to hide their Facebook profile from an education setting or to separate out educational and personal profiles. There are, however, several problems with these tactics. First, they are contingent on Facebook's unwillingness or inability to enforce its terms of service, which prohibit both the use of aliases (Facebook, 2013b) and the creation of multiple accounts (Facebook Help Centre, 2012). Second, they may be ineffective. The huge amount of data which Facebook is able to access and analyze, in combination from the data available through data brokers, means that Facebook identities are often verified through e-mail addresses, phone numbers, and networks of Friends, rather than merely through the profile name. Facebook's recent acquisition of a facial recognition start-up (Van Grove, 2012) creates further potential for our "real" identities to be matched with aliases. As well as the implications for institutional privacy, Facebook's ability to create links between our profiles and other aspects of our identity can create important breaches of social privacy. Even with an alias, it is quite possible that Facebook will suggest a person to unintended audiences in the "people you may know" selections.

The most common tactic educators advocate when it comes to Facebook is, unsurprisingly, education. Acquisti and Gross's (2006) comparison of visible user profiles on Facebook before and after a survey was administered on privacy issues notes that even without specific instructions, the survey itself motivated some users to change their privacy settings (p. 20), suggesting that even minimal interventions can be meaningful. Some authors advocate specific instructions to students about privacy settings (Munoz & Towner, 2009, p. 9), whereas others suggest a form of education about potential harms of Facebook, and responses that make fuller use of privacy settings, that is, based on discussion and rooted in the experiences of students' Facebook use (Greenhow, Robelia, & Hughes, 2009, p. 253; Grimmelmann, 2009, p. 1204). Although these tactics are useful, they are necessarily limited. As noted earlier, privacy settings relate only to social privacy and do not allow users to limit Facebook's access to their information. Additionally, education about privacy on Facebook must contend with the fact that the platform's entire architecture is geared toward sharing, and frequent 'privacy lurches' make it difficult even for informed users to keep track of their privacy settings.

The limitations to tactical responses to privacy issues on Facebook suggest that it makes sense to complement these with more strategic responses. de Certeau (1984) distinguishes tactics from strategies: whereas tactics respond to existing architectures, strategies relate to the structure of systems and totalizing discourses, the way in which spaces are organised and controlled (p. 38). Although de Certeau sees strategies as primarily deployed by those in power and as relating to physical spaces, the configurability of software means that even those who do not control Facebook as an institution have some freedom to engage in strategies that reconfigure their experience of its architecture. Browser extensions provide one way to do this, as they can help to create significant changes to users' experience of the web.

Educators who are concerned about the ethics of requiring or encouraging students to expose themselves to targeted advertising in the course of their education may suggest the use of Adblock Plus or other extensions that stop advertisements from appearing within the browser. Some extensions, such as Flashblock, NoScript, and Better Pop Up Blocker, target particular scripts or software types, such as all JavaScript or Flash objects. Adblock Plus relies on a combination of techniques, including subscription lists and manual blocking of objects, to block advertisements. This can radically change users' experience of the web, including Facebook: switching between ad-blocked and normal browsing of Facebook should demonstrate this. However, the creator of Adblock Plus has explicitly stated that he hopes the extension will go beyond changing individual's browsing experience, eventually making the use of intrusive online advertising economically inefficient (Palant, n.d.). This is unlikely to come about at current usage levels: Adblock Plus, the "most popular extension for Chrome" (Gundlach, 2012), is only installed by approximately 10 percent of Chrome users, and only around 9 percent of users across browsers have some sort of ad-blocking extension, although this is higher for visitors to technology-related content (ClarityRay, 2012). Nevertheless, using extensions that block advertising goes beyond a tactical response to Facebook's architecture, fundamentally undermining one of the central pillars of the platform's design and purpose.

A number of browser extensions also address some of the privacy concerns related to Facebook's partnership with data brokers. Educators who are currently opening discussion with students around social privacy may wish to complement this by including mention of anti-tracking browser extensions that help to protect institutional privacy, such as Disconnect, Ghostery, DoNotTrackMe, and Priv3. These browser extensions block cookies, scripts, widgets, and other means of gathering users' data and have a less noticeable effect on users' experience of the Web, although they may cause problems by blocking features of some sites. Many of these extensions also display a list of the tracking services that access particular websites, which can be useful in building students' understanding of the extent of online data gathering by marketing organizations. As in the case of ad-blocking extensions, anti-tracking extensions challenge the underlying architecture of Facebook and its reliance on gathering and selling large amounts of user data to advertisers.

Other browser extensions may also help to deal with educators' concerns about the use of Facebook or other platforms. Leechblock, for example, can be used by students to limit their use of Facebook and other social media or to create clearer demarcations between study-related and recreational Internet use. HTTPS Everywhere is also strongly recommended for more secure browsing. The extensions mentioned here can also be useful in dealing with threats to institutional privacy by other corporations: many concerns have been raised about the myriad of Google services many people use every day and the extent to which this may affect our privacy. There are also other strategies and tactics educators may explore, such as disabling cookies (Auerbach, 2012), to deal with the commodification of users' data and the extensive advertising on platforms which we use.

Conclusion

We should remain aware that none of the strategies or tactics here, alone or in combination, wholly address concerns about use of the platform in an educational setting. It is worrying that so little of the writing about Facebook's use in education, tertiary or otherwise, has addressed the ethical issues involved in the commodification of users' data and attention on the platform. Concerns about social privacy need to be matched by an understanding of the challenges to institutional privacy that Facebook's architecture and business strategy pose. This is particularly pertinent as more information emerges about the extent of Facebook and other social networks' collusion with the US National Security Agency. Tactical responses that urge students to be careful with their Facebook use can, in this vein, usefully be complemented by strategic use of browser extensions that create radical shifts in users' experience of and relationship to Facebook. This is likely to raise questions about the ethics of using a service while simultaneously undermining the fundamentals of its business model. Unfortunately, it is not possible for educators to remain neutral: if we wish to either actively or tacitly use Facebook in our teaching, we need to grapple with the complex power relations involved in using a commercial service.

References

Acquisti, A., & Gross, R. (2006). Imagined Communities: Awareness, Information Sharing, and Privacy on the Facebook. In G. Danezis & P. Golle (Eds.), *Privacy Enhancing Technologies* (pp. 36–58). Berlin and Heidelberg: Springer. Retrieved from http://link.springer.com/chapter/10.1007/11957454_3

Allen, M. (2012). An Education in Facebook. *Digital Culture & Education*, 4(3), 213–225. Retrieved from www.digitalcultureandeducation.com/cms/wp-content/uploads/2012/12/dce1077_allen_2012.pdf

Auerbach, D. (2012, October 25). 4 Simple Changes to Stop Online Tracking. *Electronic Frontier Foundation*. Retrieved May 22, 2013, from www.eff.org/deeplinks/2012/04/4-simple-changes-protect-your-privacy-online

Baran, B. (2010). Facebook as a formal instructional environment. *British Journal of Education Technology*, 41(6), 146–149. doi:10.1111/j.1467-8535.2010.01115.x

Beckman, R. (2008, September 3). Facebook Ads Target You Where It Hurts. *Washington Post*. Retrieved from http://articles.washingtonpost.com/2008-09-03/news/36877581_1_facebook-ads-facebook-page-facebook-targets

Bosch, T. E. (2009). Using Online Social Networking for Teaching and Learning: Facebook Use at the University of Cape Town. *Communicatio*, 35(2), 185–200. doi:10.1080/02500160903250648

boyd, d. (2008, October 22). Putting Privacy Settings in the Context of Use (in Facebook and Elsewhere). *apophenia*. Retrieved from www.zephoria.org/thoughts/archives/2008/10/22/putting_privacy.html

ClarityRay. (2012, May). Ad-Blocking, Measured. Retrieved from www.clarityray.com/

de Certeau, M. (1984). *The Practice of Everyday Life: Michel de Certeau*. (S. F. Rendall, Trans.). Berkeley: University of California Press.

Facebook. (2013a). Advertising on Facebook. *Facebook*. Retrieved May 30, 2013, from https://www.facebook.com/about/ads/

Facebook. (2013b). Facebook Terms. Retrieved June 2, 2013, from www.facebook.com/legal/terms

Facebook. (2013c, February 27). Facebook Studio: New Ways to Reach the Right Audience. *Facebook Studio*. Retrieved from www.facebook-studio.com/news/item/new-ways-to-reach-the-right-audience

Facebook Help Centre. (2012). Disabled—Multiple Accounts. *Facebook*. Retrieved January 9, 2013, from www.facebook.com/help/149623348508517/

Greenhow, C., Robelia, B., & Hughes, J. E. (2009). Learning, Teaching, and Scholarship in a Digital Age Web 2.0 and Classroom Research: What Path Should We Take Now? *Educational Researcher, 38*(4), 246–259. doi:10.3102/0013189X09336671

Grimmelmann, J. (2009). Saving Facebook. *Iowa Law Review, 94*, 1137–1206.

Gundlach, M. (2012). AdBlock. Retrieved January 9, 2013, from https://chrome.google.com/webstore/detail/adblock/gighmmpiobklfepjocnamgkkbiglidom?hl=en

Hendry, J., & Goodall, K. (2010). *Facebook and the Commercialisation of Personal Information: Some Questions of Provider-to-User Privacy*. Retrieved from http://papers.ssrn.com/abstract=1550821

Hew, K. F. (2011). Students' and Teachers' Use of Facebook. *Computers in Human Behavior, 27*(2), 662–676. doi:10.1016/j.chb.2010.11.020

Johnson, C. (2010, January 28). Facebook post gets student-athlete expelled. *news10.net*. Retrieved from www.news10.net/news/article/74202/0/Facebook-post-gets-student-athlete-expelled

Jones, P. (2012, April 25). 3 Students Expelled Over Facebook Posts About Killing Classmates—CBS Chicago. Retrieved from http://chicago.cbslocal.com/2012/04/25/3-students-expelled-over-facebook-conversation-about-killing-classmates/

Kennedy, K. (2013, March 6). University Bans Payday Loan Companies from Advertising on Campus. *MoveHut*. Retrieved from www.movehut.co.uk/news/university-bans-payday-loan-companies-from-advertising-on-campus-12460/

Leaver, T. (2012). Twittering Informal Learning and Student Engagement in First-Year Units. In A. Herrington, J. Schrape, & K. Singh (Eds.), *Engaging Students With Learning Technologies* (pp. 97–110). Perth, Australia: Curtin University.

Liptak, A. (2013, February 6). Sotomayor Plans for Pepsi Event Stirs an Outcry. *The New York Times*. Retrieved from https://www.nytimes.com/2013/02/07/us/politics/sotomayor-plans-for-pepsi-event-stirs-an-outcry.html

Molnar, A., Boninger, F., Harris, M. D., Libby, K., & Fogarty, J. (2013). *Promoting Consumption at School: Health Threats Associated with Schoolhouse Commercialism*. Retrieved from http://nepc.colorado.edu/publication/schoolhouse-commercialism-2012

Molnar, A., Boninger, F., Wilkinson, G., & Fogarty, J. (2009). *Click: The Twelfth Annual Report on Schoolhouse Commercialism Trends*. National Education Policy Centre. Retrieved from http://nepc.colorado.edu/publication/schoolhouse-commercialism-2009

Munoz, C., & Towner, T. (2009). Opening Facebook: How to Use Facebook in the College Classroom. *Society for Information Technology & Teacher Education International Conference 2009, 2009*(1), 2623–2627.

Mytelka, A. (2013, February 18). Student Expelled for Facebook Posts Sues 2-Year College in Minnesota. *The Ticker*. Retrieved from https://chronicle.com/blogs/ticker/student-expelled-for-facebook-posts-sues-2-year-college-in-minnesota/55805

Opshal, K., & Reitman, R. (2013, April 22). The Disconcerting Details: How Facebook Teams Up With Data Brokers to Show You Targeted Ads. *Electronic Frontier Foundation*. Retrieved from www.eff.org/deeplinks/2013/04/disconcerting-details-how-facebook-teams-data-brokers-show-you-targeted-ads

Palant, W. (n.d.). Adblock Plus: Frequently Asked Questions. *Adblock Plus project*. Retrieved July 22, 2009, from http://adblockplus.org/en/faq_project#contribute

Peterson, C. (2010). Losing Face: An Environmental Analysis of Privacy on Facebook. Retrieved from http://works.bepress.com/cpeterson/2

Raynes-Goldie, K. (2010). Aliases, Creeping, and Wall Cleaning: Understanding Privacy in the Age of Facebook. *First Monday, 15*(1). Retrieved from http://firstmonday.org/htbin/cgiwrap/bin/ojs/index.php/fm/article/view/2775/2432

Raynes-Goldie, K. (2012). *Privacy in the Age of Facebook? Discourse, Architecture, Consequences* (Doctoral dissertation, Curtin University, Perth, Australia). Retrieved from www.k4t3.org/wp-content/uploads/2012/09/privacy_in_the_age_of_facebook_raynes-goldie.pdf

Roblyer, M. D., McDaniel, M., Webb, M., Herman, J., & Witty, J. V. (2010). Findings on Facebook in Higher Education: A Comparison of College Faculty and Student Uses and Perceptions of Social Networking Sites. *The Internet and Higher Education, 13*(3), 134–140. doi:10.1016/j.iheduc.2010.03.002

Rushe, D. (2013, June 9). Technology Giants Struggle to Maintain Credibility Over NSA Prism Surveillance. *The Guardian.* Retrieved from www.theguardian.com/world/2013/jun/09/technology-giants-nsa-prism-surveillance

SafeGov.org, & Ponemon Institute. (2013). *UK School Opinions of Cloud Services and Student Privacy.* Retrieved from www.ponemon.org/news-2/50

Van Grove, J. (2012, June 18). Facebook buys facial recognition startup Face.com. *Reuters.* Retrieved from www.reuters.com/article/2012/06/18/idUS404710296120120618

20

Facebook, Disability and Higher Education: Accessing the Digital Campus

KATIE ELLIS AND MIKE KENT

Curtin University

Universities have a digital shadow—an online campus with its own lecture theatres, tutorial rooms, libraries and cafes. With the majority of students using social networking sites as a preferred mode of communication (Cluett, 2009), Facebook is an increasingly important component of this digital campus and is being utilized as a way to connect students throughout their university studies. Facebook holds great potential for the inclusion of people with disabilities yet has a problematic history with accessibility (Ellis & Kent, 2010). Although universities and colleges generally take their responsibilities to make their physical, analogue campuses accessible for people with disabilities, this concern is not always translated into the digital campus and Facebook in particular. For example, Darrell Shandrow, a student with vision impairment studying at Arizona State University, was recently profiled by the *Chronicle of Higher Education* regarding his university's use of an inaccessible Facebook app (Parry, 2010). Shandrow is an interesting case study because he is tech savvy and makes highly effective use of digital technologies to successfully navigate what is an inaccessible world—he uses text-to-speech software to access the Internet, he navigates the built environment using Foursquare to identify nearby buildings and uses iPhone apps to identify money in his wallet. In addition, "he blogs, tweets, shoots video, and hosts an online radio show" (Parry, 2010). However, he was locked out of the university's Facebook Student Union in 2010. Although it is highly unlikely that any university would build a new building without wheelchair access, often their digital platforms are the equivalent of inaccessible Internet stairs for people with vision impairments.

Yet the Internet has provided a great opportunity for people with disabilities, who are currently under-underrepresented in the university environment (Sachs & Schreuer, 2011; Wentz, Jaeger, & Lazar, 2011) although growing in number with the increased use of e-learning serving to promote inclusion for this group of people (Fichten et al., 2009). Studying online can provide potential access for people who might otherwise have difficulty physically attending campus. Facebook provides a venue for learning and teaching, as well as a place to socialize with fellow students and to make networks of contacts that will serve students beyond the date of graduation. However this requires that this online platform is accessible to all.

This was the focus of *The Official Petition for a More Accessible Facebook* launched by a student, Andrew McKay, just four months after the network was launched beyond the university environment to the wider public in 2007. The petition specifically asked Facebook to address seven areas of concern including the webpage layout, dropdown menus, dropdown boxes, the ability to adjust text size, newsfeed preferences, gifts, and the use of CAPTCHA as part of the sign up process for the network (McKay, 2007). The group stated,

> While the new Facebook may look pretty to some, Facebook has repeatedly ignored accessibility. For the growing number of people with visual impairments as well as learning disabilities using screen readers, screen magnification software, or any other adaptive software or hardware many parts of Facebook are unusable or horrendous looking. It is time for Facebook to take a stand and make its website useable for all.
>
> (para. 1)

It took Facebook three months to respond, at which point it announced that the gift store was now accessible. More than two years later the petition discussion board was still active with users complaining about the need to use the inaccessible CAPTCHA verification system. Although Facebook was initially slow to address accessibility issues, over time the company's attitude evolved in a positive way. Following pressure from the disability community, Facebook approached the American Foundation for the Blind in 2008 to try to make the site more accessible. Together they worked to improve the site's accessibility, to the point where Cahill and Hollier in 2009 noted that "Facebook has made great efforts to include a wealth of accessibility features and is a good choice for people with disabilities" (p. 11). Hollier's 2012 follow up study notes that despite working with the American Foundation for the Blind throughout 2008 and 2009 to improve accessibility, a number of access issues remain on the primary Facebook site that exclude people with vision impairments. Significantly, however, Hollier (2012) outlines several accessibility workarounds including mobile apps that integrate well with screen reading technology to improve access. These three stories about Facebook, students, disability and accessibility illustrate that what is considered a disability changes over time and the advancement and emergence of technology impacts on, and intersects with, this and further, the importance of Facebook to student life, especially for students with disabilities.

Universities have a responsibility to make both their learning environments and their campuses accessible to all, particularly people with disabilities. This is not just a moral responsibility, but one backed by legislation in many countries including Australia, the United States and the United Kingdom (Roberts, Crittenden, & Crittenden, 2011; Wentz et al., 2011). Against this backdrop, our first aim in this chapter is to explore the often contentious and contested relationship between Facebook and people with disabilities, especially university students. This chapter examines how this relationship has developed over time and the implications for access to university, both for formal learning and teaching and to the benefits of the social contacts and interaction that a university education provides for both on campus students and those who study online or in a blended learning environment.

We take a cross-disability approach in this chapter, adopting the social model of disability. This model argues that disability exists in social practices rather than individual bodies. Disability is the impact of decisions made by society on an individual who has an impairment that prevents them playing a full role as members of that society (see Finkelstein, 1980; Oliver, 1996). Thus, Shandrow has a vision impairment but was *disabled* by his university's inaccessible Facebook engagement.

Finally, we are interested in the way disability is activated differently online and the implications this has for Facebook and higher education. While some people with impairments, such as those related to mobility, will be less disabled when accessing the Internet, others, such as those with print impairments, particularly visual impairments and cognitive impairments, such as dyslexia, will encounter more difficulties online. Disclosure and access to technology is a theme that runs throughout this chapter. Disclosure in this context refers to the ability of a person to choose to disclose to others that they have a disability. In an analogue context a person who is a wheelchair user will have limited choice about the disclosure of his or her particular impairment in a face-to-face meeting, whereas a person with dyslexia will have more options. In the context of an online text-based chat, this situation will be reversed.

Facebook and Communication in Higher Education

Facebook began its life as a digital social network for university students in the United States before it was made available to the wider public. It continues to play an important and active role in university student life. Students communicate with each other, staff and the institution through a variety of online mechanisms, with Facebook now prominent amongst these (Grey, Lucas, & Kennedy, 2010; McCarthy, 2010). Facebook provides a place where students can host and develop their own profile, share information and links with others, and make use of Facebook as a communications tool.

Specifically for people with disabilities, it can be used as a platform for learning and teaching, communication with the educational institution, and as an extended part of a university's digital campus where students socialize and develop the friends and networks associated with student life. In the context of the digital campus, "Facebook provides individuals with a way of maintaining and strengthening social ties which can be beneficial in both social and academic settings" (Bicen & Cavus, 2011, p. 493).

In addition to Facebook's prominent role in the university's community, it is increasingly being turned to as a place for both formal and informal learning and teaching. As other chapters in this book discuss in detail, Facebook can potentially play a number of different roles in an educational context: from having the potential to operate as a learning management system such as Blackboard or Moodle (Bateman & Willems, 2012), to supporting these systems for online and blended learning (Drigas, Vrettaros, Tagoulis, & Kouremenos, 2010; Grey, Lucas, & Kennedy, 2010), to a place where students can gather for informal learning outside of the official university environment (Haverback, 2009).

However, Facebook has a problematic history with accessibility and has been accused of excluding students with disabilities (Foley & Voithofer, 2008). There are a number of obstacles to access to web-based technologies such as Facebook including issues around the digital divide, the social construction of disability, and the legal discourse and the web accessibility discourse (Adam & Kreps, 2009). As Asakawa (2005) has observed, these problems with access tend to increase rather than improve as online platforms mature.

The Petition for a More Accessible Facebook's primary concerns were related to the inability of Facebook to work with adaptive technologies such as screen readers and the use of the inaccessible CAPTCHA verification system to create an account and use Facebook. Although many of these concerns have now been addressed, there are other accessibility issues for people with disabilities trying to use Facebook. Currently, people with vision impairments who are using a screen reader are advised to access the network through its mobile site because this presents a less cluttered screen to interpret. Although this is a useful adaption, it still limits the functionality and experience of the user. This is a potentially worrying trend to provide access, but to a less useful platform, as an alternative to existing online services (Wentz, Jaeger, & Lazar, 2011). There are also other current accessibility issues, such as video that is directly uploaded to Facebook not supporting captions (Hollier, 2012). This would be an obstacle for students with hearing impairments trying to access learning material presented in this way through Facebook. However, as Hollier (2012, p. 11) observes,

> despite the benefits, all of the popular social media tools remain inaccessible to some degree. Facebook, LinkedIn, Twitter, YouTube, blogging websites and the emerging Google+ all feature limited accessibly, denying many consumers with disabilities the opportunity to participate in social media. Fortunately, users have often found ways around the accessibility barriers such as alternative website portals, mobile apps, additional keyboard navigation shortcuts and online support groups. This is a rich

source of expertise, and social media users with disability continue to find creative ways to access the most popular platforms.

Although the resourcefulness and ability of people with disability to be active participants in making platforms such as Facebook more accessible is commendable (see Ellis & Kent, 2010), the moral and legal responsibility must lie with Facebook itself, and more directly with the higher education institutions. As Facebook delves further into the realm of higher education, it should take note of the student backlash against Amazon's Kindle when universities attempted to mandate student use of the eBook reader that was inaccessible to people with disabilities. When the Kindle was launched with controls that were inaccessible by people with vision impairments, the educational institutions were the subject of the lawsuit to stop them being used in formal learning and teaching. Similarly, a number of Facebook Apps, such as the student union App that excluded Darrell Shandrow, are inaccessible, independent of any accessibility issues with Facebook itself.

Accessibility and the digital campus is not just an issue for students. Lenartz (2012) notes the rising pressure on staff to use online social networking both inside and outside the classroom to connect with students. For university staff with disabilities this, as Liccardi et al. (2007) note, may also provide threats or opportunities depending on the nature of the individual staff member's impairment. Heijstra and Rafnsdottir (2010) have observed that e-learning makes it harder for academics to disengage from work and strike an appropriate work–life separation, and this problem is further exacerbated when the formerly private social network also becomes a place where students are expecting communications. For staff with impairments such as dyslexia, this use of more immediate communications can present additional challenges compared to more traditional and less immediate forms of online communications.

Legal Requirements for Access

Whereas Goggin and Newell (2003) noted the importance of legislation in the process of providing accessibility for people with digital technology, Wentz, Jaeger and Lazar (2011) find that laws that are supposed to prevent discrimination against people with disabilities differ from other civil rights laws. The person has to prove they are disabled and being discriminated against, and it is up to the discriminated individual to prosecute the law. As Jaeger (2012, p. 14) explains, "this difference means that disability rights laws are much harder to enforce, as people with disabilities must first prove that they have standing under the law, something no other population must do under civil rights laws."

Although this has resulted in only a limited number of cases being brought against higher education institutions over the accessibility of their digital footprint (Wentz, Jaeger, & Lazar, 2011), the increasing use of Facebook in higher education will mean that university administrators will need to be more mindful of their legal obligations to ensure that Facebook remains an accessible platform as it is increasingly integrated into university life. When Amazon's inaccessible Kindle eBook reader was proposed to be used by a number of higher education institutions in the United States for distributing electronic textbooks, the Foundation for the Blind and the American Council of the Blind joined to take legal action against the institutions to prevent it (Foley & Ferri, 2012). Following this case, the United States Department of Justice and Department of Education issued a joint statement noting that "[i]t is unacceptable for universities to use emerging technology without insisting that this technology be accessible to all students" (Perez & Assistant, 2010, para. 5). This legal caution should also equally apply to both Facebook and any apps it supports.

However, the developers of the Student Union app at Arizona State University argue that their app does not need to meet this accessibility requirement because "it's all just part of the social experience" (Parry, 2010). The app lacks a keyboard shortcut to launch, so if a person is only using a keyboard and no mouse, such as when using a screen reader to access the Internet, it cannot be accessed. It does not seem too onerous a requirement to include such a short cut in the app. This highlights the importance of making the whole of the digital campus as accessible as its analogue counterpart. No one would build a university café that deliberately excluded people in wheelchairs.

Disclosure

The way people communicate using Facebook also offers insight into the social construction of disability as it is activated differently on the Internet. Impairments that might be disabling in an analogue environment, such as a person being a wheelchair user, may find that this impairment has little impact on their access to online spaces such as Facebook. Other impairments that might be largely invisible in the analogue environment will have a greater impact online. People with a variety of print impairments, including those related to vision, dexterity and cognition, may also experience a disabling environment when accessing the Internet. Although people with a print impairment will be a significant group of those disadvantaged by disabling online design, increasingly, others such as those with hearing impairments will also be potentially disadvantaged.

The other aspect of the use of Facebook in higher education for people with disabilities is for those people for whom their impairment does not have impact on their ability to access the network. For this group of students, whose impairments in many cases will still be disabling in the context of visiting a university campus or attending lectures, the network provides a potential alternative and more readily accessible space to engage in social and learning activities. It also provides "the ability it affords the user to hide aspects of him—or herself. For people with disabilities, online communication may allow the removal of their disability from the forefront of the interaction" (Dobransky & Hargittai 2006, p. 316). As Liccardi et al. (2007, p. 230) observe,

> a student who is a wheelchair user can control the disclosure of their disability online, deciding when, where, and if, their disability is relevant to a social network discussion. For some disabled students controlling disclosure in this way can facilitate social presence with potentially positive learning outcomes. However, it should be noted that for other students print impairments, such as dyslexia, may represent uncontrollable disclosure, with negative impact on confidence and contributions. In these circumstances a student is disabled by the network, and both the student and network can suffer as a result.

This potential affordance, and threat, from the use of the network is mitigated by the literacy of the user in relation to the platform. A student who has not appropriately set their privacy settings on the network may find that their interactions result in a high level of unintended disclosure. Sachs and Schreuer (2011) cautioned that students with disabilities make less use of computers and information technology than do their peers. If Sachs and Schreuer's study is indicative of the broader student population, then issues of literacy with Facebook's operation are an area that universities need to address, if Facebook is intended both to be used as a learning and teaching platform and to be used by students to interact with both other students and the institution.

Whereas for the individual the ability to control his or her level of disclosure may be of great benefit, there are also broader issues associated with the visibility of students with disabilities in a higher education context. Many of the disabling impediments that people with disabilities encounter, both online and on campus, are the result not so much of deliberate discrimination, but rather lack of awareness. If students with disabilities were to all disappear behind their well-managed Facebook profiles, raising, or even maintaining, the current level of awareness becomes more problematic.

Conclusion and Future Avenues for Research

Students on campus increasingly access the universities' services and social life through the Internet (Cluett, 2010) and social networking in particular. As other chapters in this collection illustrate, Facebook offers great potential for both formal and informal communication in higher education. However, we are concerned that a growing group within the university setting, students with disabilities, will be left behind because neither universities nor Facebook see it as their responsibility to make the platform accessible.

Despite this, Facebook provides many opportunities for people with disabilities as a venue for socializing, communicating and learning. However, there are some notes of caution. Since its listing as a public company in 2012, Facebook has a greater obligation to its shareholders to increase revenues. One area the company is focused on is its mobile users (Team, 2013). This may threaten the current high level of accessibility the mobile site offers. This increased focus on a return on investment may also drive further change in the mainstream Facebook website that may also threaten user accessibility. As universities increasingly integrate this platform into their digital shadow, there is an increasing responsibility on these organizations to make sure that the platform and the apps they choose to deploy remain accessible.

References

Adam, A., & Kreps, D. (2009). Disability and disclosures of web accessibility. *Information, Communication & Society, 12*(7), 1041–1058.

Asakawa, C. (2005, May). *What's the web like if you can't see it.* Presented at Proceeding of the 2005 International Cross-Disciplinary Workshop on Web Accessibility (W4A), Chiba, Japan. Retrieved from www.ra.ethz.ch/cdstore/www2005-ws/workshop/wf01/1-asakawa.pdf

Bateman, D., & Willems, J. (2012). Chapter 5 facing off: Facebook and higher education. In L. A. Wankel & C. Wankel (Eds.), *Misbehavior online in higher education* (Cutting-Edge Technologies in Higher Education, Vol. 5, pp. 53–79). Bradford, UK: Emerald Group Publishing Limited.

Bicen, H., & Cavus, N. (2011). Social network sites usage habits of undergraduate students: case study of Facebook. *Proceedia—Social and Behavioral Sciences, 28*, 943–947.

Cahill, M., & Hollier, S. (2009). Social media accessibility review—version 1.0. *Media Access Australia.* Retrieved from http://mediaaccess.org.au/sites/default/files/files/Social%20Media%20Accessibility%20Review%20v1_0.pdf

Cluett, L. (2009). *How to survive networking in Facebook.* Retrieved from www.studentservices.uwa.edu.au/ss/smhub?f=289153

Cluett, L. (2010, January). *Online social networking for outreach, engagement and community: The UWA Student's Facebook page.* Paper presented at Educating for Sustainability. Proceedings of the 19th Annual Teaching Learning Forum, Edith Cowan University, Perth, Australia. Retrieved from http://otl.curtin.edu.au/tlf/tlf2010/refereed/cluett.html

Dobransky, K., & Hargittai, E. (2006). The disability divide in Internet access and use. *Information Communication and Society, 9*(3), 309–311.

Drigas, A., Vrettaros, J., Tagoulis A., & Kouremenos D. (2010). Teaching a Foreign Language to Deaf People via Vodcasting and Web 2.0 Tools. In M.D. Lytras et al. (Eds.) *WSKS 2010, Part II, CCIS 112* (pp. 514–521). Berlin Heidelberg: Springer-Verlag.

Ellis, K., & Kent, M. (2010). Community accessibility: Tweeters take responsibility an accessible Web 2.0. *Fast Capitalism, 7*(1). Retrieved from www.uta.edu/huma/agger/fastcapitalism/7_1/elliskent7_1.html

Fichten, C. S., Ferraro, V., Asuncion, J. V., Chwojka, C., Barile, M., Nguyen, M. N., Klomp, R., & Wolforth, J. (2009). Disabilities and e-learning problems and solutions: An exploratory study. *Educational Technology & Society, 12*(4), 241–256. Retrieved from www.adaptech.org/cfichten/abDisabilitiesAndE-LearningProblems.pdf

Finkelstein, V. (1980). *Attitudes and disabled people: Issues for discussion.* New York: International Exchange of Information in Rehabilitation.

Foley, A., & Ferri, B. A. (2012). Technology for people, not disabilities: ensuring access and inclusion. *Journal of Research in Special Education Needs, 12*(4), 192–200.

Foley, A., & Voithofer, R. (2008, March). *Social networking technology, NetGen learners, and emerging technology: Democratic claims and the mythology of equality.* Paper presented at the American Educational Research Association (AERA) national conference, New York. Retrieved from http://flynnfoley.typepad.com/FoleyVoithofer.pdf

Goggin, G., & Newell, C. (2003). *Digital disability: The social construction of disability in new media.* Lanham, MD: Rowman and Littlefield.

Grey, K., Lucas, A., & Kennedy, G. (2010). Medical students use of Facebook to support learning: Insights from four case studies. *Medical Teacher, 32*, 971–976.

Haverback, H. R. (2009). Facebook: Uncharted territory in a reading education classroom. *Reading Today, 27*(2), 34.

Heijstra, T. M., & Rafnsdottir, G. L. (2010). The Internet and academics' workload and work family balance. *Internet and Higher Education, 13*, 158–163.

Hollier, S. (2012). *Sociability: Social media for people with a disability.* Ultimo, New South Wales: Media Access Australia. Retrieved from http://mediaaccess.org.au/online-media/social-media

Jaeger, P. T. (2012). *Disability and the Internet.* Boulder, CO, and London: Lynne Rienner.

Lenartz, A. J. (2012). Chapter 16 establishing guidelines for the use of social media in higher education. In L. A. Wankel & C. Wankel (Eds.), *Misbehavior online in higher education* (Cutting-Edge Technologies in Higher Education, Vol. 5, pp. 333–353). Bradford, UK: Emerald Group Publishing Limited.

Liccardi, I., Ounnas, A., Pau, R., Massey, E., Kinnunen, P., Lewthwaite, S., Midy, M., & Sarker, C. (2007, December). The role of social networks in students' learning experience. *ACM SIGCSE Bulletin,* pp. 224–237.

McCarthy, J. (2010). Blended learning environments: Using social networking sites to enhance the first year experience. *Australasian Journal of Education Technology, 26*(6), 729–740.

McKay, A. (2007). The official petition for a more accessible Facebook. *Facebook.* Retrieved from www.facebook.com/groups/2384051749/

Oliver, M. (1996). *Understanding disability: From theory to practice.* Hampshire, England: Palgrave.

Parry, M. (2010, December 12). Colleges lock out blind students online. *The Chronicle of Higher Education.* Retrieved from http://chronicle.com/article/Blind-Students-Demand-Access/125695/

Perez, T. E., & Assistant, R. A. (2010, June 29). Joint statement from the US Departments of Justice and Education. Retrieved from www.ada.gov/kindle_ltr_eddoj.htm

Roberts, J., Crittenden, L. A., & Crittenden, J. C. (2011). Students with disabilities and online learning: A cross-institutional study of perceived satisfaction with accessibility compliances and services. *Internet and Higher Education, 14*, 242–250.

Sachs, D., & Schreuer, N. (2011). Inclusion of students with disabilities in higher education: Performance and participation in student experiences. *Disability Studies Quarterly, 31*(2).

Team, T. (2013, April 6). Facebook's gaining mobile traction but stock still needs a 15% haircut. *Forbes.* Retrieved from www.forbes.com/sites/greatspeculations/2013/05/06/facebooks-gaining-mobile-traction-but-stock-still-needs-a-15-haircut/

Wentz, B., Jaeger, P. T., & Lazar, J. (2011). Retrofitting accessibility: The legal inequality of after-the-fact online access for persons with disabilities in the United States. *First Monday, 16*(11). Retrieved from www.firstmonday.org/htbin/cgiwrap/bin/ojs/index.php/fm/article/view/3666/3077

Part 7

Conclusion—Beyond Facebook

21
Facebook Fatigue?
A University's Quest to
Build Lifelong Relationships
With Students and Alumni

MARIA L. GALLO

National University of Ireland, Galway

KEVIN F. ADLER

University of Cambridge

Is Facebook a revolutionary tool with immense higher education potential or a passing fad? Originally Facebook was a socializing space for college students that has expanded its reach and scope far beyond these humble beginnings. Facebook is a conduit for the proliferation of informal and formal uses by students, alumni, instructors and administrators. This chapter casts a critical eye on the literature discussing the use of Facebook in higher education, in particular on the site's ability to build relationships between and with students and alumni.

With the advent of "Facebook Fatigue" entering the public discourse, is it inevitable that this general Facebook malaise may also seep into higher education, leaving the lofty plans by institutions as the equivalent of a digital dinosaur? This chapter argues Facebook is not the forum for building student–, alumnus– or alumna–university relationships. Moreover, Facebook is not the panacea for other higher education ills: teacher–student disconnect, improving student engagement or increasing alumni activity with their alma mater.

By considering the Facebook literature through the lens of social capital, this chapter focuses on the superficiality of the relationships in this space. Although successful examples on the use of Facebook exist, these are not necessarily representative of wider Facebook uses. As the emergence of Facebook Fatigue looms, this could potentially alienate those relationships institutions wish to preserve and progress. The chapter concludes by presenting two case studies of the creative use of other online platforms by institutions to genuinely engage students and alumni with their alma mater.

Facebook Fatigue

"I took a break when it got boring" (Pew, 2013, in Van Grove, 2013, p. 1) is how one voice in a survey described their disillusionment with Facebook. Although Facebook has endured phenomenal global impact in a short time and a rapid increase in the number of individual accounts, a growing dissent within the Facebook community has emerged in the public discourse.

Headlines in the mainstream online media include "Facebook Fatigue Sets in for Six Million Americans: Users Bored With Site Deactivate Accounts Amid Privacy Fears" (Bates, 2011), "Facebook Loses Millions of Users as Biggest Markets Peak" (Garside, 2013) or "Study: Facebook Fatigue—It's Real" (Van Grove, 2013). Print media articles (Mills, 2013; Russell, 2013; Warner, 2013) along with online media sites and blogs (Allen, 2013; Merritt, 2013; Mitsuzuka, 2012; Peterson, 2013; Sawers, 2012) are also prevalent as Facebook itself gained momentum with the introduction of a public offering on the stock exchange. Often prompted by Internet surveys, this becomes a springboard for discussing Facebook Fatigue offering profiles of people who have elected to "log off" Facebook and feel the benefit of this Facebook freedom.

Common themes of boredom along with the overabundance and trivial nature of information shared on the site are outlined as reasons why Facebook is losing widespread appeal. The average Facebook user in 2012 had more than 300 friends, double the number of friends as 2009. The platform has become a place to amass acquaintances, noted as double the Dunbar number of key friendships an individual can manage (Shih, 2011), thus changing the dynamic of the information shared among these "friends" to become more shallow in nature (Chou & Edge, 2012). Despite the evidence of this Facebook Fatigue, there continues to be a belief in the longevity of the social media platform due to its allure in connecting you—however superficial—with others (Rainie, Smith, & Duggan, 2013). As Peterson (2013) writes, "So go ahead and quit Facebook for a while. You'll be back" (p. 1). The idea of logging off or closing down Facebook accounts seems to be a reaction to a counterculture movement.

The most alarming trend emerging from the Facebook Fatigue literature is the implications for higher education. A 2013 survey revealed that the Facebook demographic is getting older, which could be a concern for using Facebook to reach a younger undergraduate population and those prospective college students currently in secondary school (Rainie, Smith, & Duggan, 2013). Similarly, this survey points to a trend that the key undergraduate demographic—those between 18 and 29 years of age—intend on spending less time on Facebook and consider the platform to be less "cool" than in the past (Rainie, Smith, & Duggan, 2013).

Admittedly, there is little evidence to suggest that students and alumni are alienated from university connections by not engaging with Facebook. However, early articles on Facebook suggest that peer pressure was a factor for signing up for the social networking site in the first place (Ellison, Steinfield

& Lampe, 2007; Madge, Meek, Wellens, & Hooley, 2009), to fit into university life. There is potential that this same pressure may either force students to participate in the university-related content on the site to avoid the feeling they are 'missing out' or become disconnected with university content especially as universities increase their presence on Facebook and the pressure to be weary of Facebook increases among the key demographic.

Social Capital and Facebook

Putnam (2000) describes social capital as a public good and "the connections among individuals—social networks and the norms of reciprocity and trustworthiness that arise from them" (p. 19). The decline of this social capital is a lens through which to view Facebook Fatigue, applying the distinction between bridging and bonding social capital as a heuristic device. In bridging social capital, Putnam (2000) asserts that although some communities are composed of dozens or even hundreds of individuals and networks, connected by a common link, such as a social justice issue, towards creating more inclusive connections. Bonding social capital, on the other hand, is more exclusive, referring to the deepening of existing connections within a narrow network that exist around a shared experience.

Shih (2011) argues that sites like Facebook are influencing a change to social capital allowing people to maintain relationships regardless of geography, with little direct interaction, expense or effort. Facebook is also changing the social capital for students in a similar way (Ellison et al., 2007; Madge et al., 2009). Although students become members of various communities within their university, Facebook is a means to maintaining older friendships, especially with family and friends at home. Ellison et al. (2007) describe this as a form of maintenance social capital, that is, using Facebook to keep these, now peripheral, relationships alive.

Facebook provides a platform to enable universities and students to amass a base of weak ties, that is, casual relationships that would otherwise remain at a distance and with "interaction that is negligible" (Granovetter, 1973, p. 1361). It is the superficiality of these weak or absent ties, such as prospective students becoming "virtual friends" before attending university reported in Madge et al. (2009), that leads to a level of disengagement and disenchantment by the students using Facebook. Of course, Facebook Fatigue is context bound. Admitted students who are eager to soak up all aspects of their university (and future classmates) prior to the first day of class embrace Facebook as a wonderful tool to connect with each other and form the basis for a social life. However, this becomes less relevant when classes begin and students encounter ample opportunities to socialize with fellow classmates, club members and dorm mates, as noted in the literature (Chou & Edge, 2012; Madge et al., 2009). Over time, the mass broadcasting, superficial content and general noise leave students with the feeling of Facebook Fatigue. Chou and Edge (2012), for instance, discuss voyeurism by students who review the Facebook lives presented by these unknown "friends," creates disillusionment and a deeper disconnect among peers.

Facebook and Higher Education

There are several thorough literature reviews examining Facebook usage in higher education (Grosseck, Bran, & Tiru, 2011; Hew, 2011). First, universities consider the novel use of Facebook as a potential pedagogic tool. Several small-scale studies explore the use of social networking sites such as Facebook, to extend the traditional classroom online, with the university leading this online relationship (Bosch, 2009; Hung & Yuen, 2010). Institutions see promise in using Facebook as a supportive tool for academic learning, meriting extended research in this area (Bosch, 2009; Firth, 2010). Mazer, Murphy and Simonds (2007) report that some students value Facebook as another communication tool with their instructors, whereas Selwyn (2009) shows how students use Facebook as a peer-support tool to enable students to exchange information about their classes and assignments and to seek peer guidance on their studies. This literature on pedagogic use of Facebook focuses on the mechanics and the success of linking groups of students together as online communities, with little evidence on whether there is a deepening of the relationships in the process. If the aim is to create a wealth of social capital in the subject discipline or a student learning space, there is little evidence to suggest there is a deepening of these opportunities. Even with a moderator (instructor) ensuring regular and relevant subject content for learning purposes, simply joining the group (and bridging students together under this Facebook group) is not a guarantee that the information is processed or viewed, especially if the Facebook group is an information transmission forum. Learning activities and linking relevant news items to spark Facebook group discussion and comments, for example, need to be carefully designed and orchestrated to attract students to the group posts and need to begin to deepen the discipline learning.

Facebook also has the potential to act as a support mechanism to enhance the student experience, and, following graduation, there is also a suggestion that Facebook strengthens the alumni network and philanthropic giving (Farrow & Yuan, 2011; Shih, 2011). Some formal mechanisms of orchestrating this peer support include Madge et al. (2009), a study that highlights how universities encouraged prospective and new students to join the institution's Facebook page even before stepping on campus, with the hope students make friends and create a supportive network of peers early. Other studies examine Facebook as a more informal means for peer interaction and support (Selwyn, 2007, 2009). Although these connections may broaden a students' support network and friends on a common campus, there is little evidence to suggest these connections lead to a deep bond with these Facebook friends or a better student experience. In fact, the bridge of a new friendship built on nothing more than a shared start date for university collapses as the reality of real friendships are developed through campus experiences (Madge et al., 2009).

Students, on the other hand, generally perceive Facebook as a socializing site, with student-led informal learning purposes at best. Instead of a platform for creating new friendships, the literature suggests the site is used by students to maintain their existing offline relationships on campus (Ellison et al., 2007) and an instant connection with their peer group (Cheung, Chiu, & Lee, 2011; Lupsa, 2006). Universities choosing to engage in social media as a means to engage directly with students also recognize Facebook's ability to distract with peripheral "always online" updates, messages from friends and customized advertisements (Hung & Yuen, 2010) detracting from any academic purpose or official university support strategy. Moreover, students view Facebook as a site primarily for leisure purposes, not a professional or formal space (Cheung et al., 2011; Ellison et al., 2007).

Are universities invading the Facebook sanctuary of students? Is there a danger of another level of Facebook Fatigue emerging where students disengage with the novel attempts by the universities to use an informal space for formal purposes? Some of the limitations of using Facebook in higher education link with much of the Facebook Fatigue discourse: information getting "lost" due to an information excess, disengagement with others (and with studies) through overuse of the site and a general malaise for the platform. The bonding social capital that can emerge from narrowly focused peer-support networks demonstrate the value of Facebook for academic purposes; however, Hew (2011) in the review of literature asserts that there is a "scarcity of education-related Facebook use" (p. 665). These signs of Facebook Fatigue consequences have the potential to exasperate initial problems facing higher education instead of Facebook acting as part of the solution.

The university presence on Facebook can facilitate asymmetrical relationships, such as between student and faculty or between alumni and university administration. Many Facebook interventions described in higher education are university-led, not student-as-Facebook-user led; thus, the terms and type of relationship are controlled by the university. A university or class Facebook page may be a way to share information with students and alumni (Shih, 2011); however, the information shared and posted on the site tends to be limited to one-way information transmission by the institution outwards. The official posts by university administrators are a form of promotion, and although they may spark direct reaction through 'likes' or comments on Facebook, they are not, in the main, intended to initiate a university–student/alumnus/alumna discussion. In addition, this power relationship is tipped in favor of the university, holding the power in controlling any two-way interaction—if this interactive communication is initiated at all. McAllister (2012) outlines these power relations such as with a university's Facebook page created by university administrators to restrict the posting of comments or the sharing of photographs.

In another example, Herr and Dave (2012) describe a case in which a college offers new students (before they arrive on campus) a dedicated Facebook space as a platform for peer support, which is monitored by college administration in a 'hands-off manner' (Herr & Dave, 2012, p. 2). Although the purpose for monitoring is explained as a way to understand and then address queries that are discussed between these future classmates, there is a question about whether those new students are aware of the surveillance and whether this would change their comments on the site. In this case, although the Facebook app may provide a space for discussion between those in the midst of a shared experience of transitioning to college life, the other purpose for setting up the space by administration was in fact to understand the common student queries and to increase retention rates. Thus, these examples demonstrate that although a space for students and alumni to share a common experience of attending a university and potentially expanding bridging social capital opportunities for students or alumni, often through such formal university Facebook spaces, there is an absence of such a space to foster a deeper bond.

Reports that university administrators use Facebook to investigate students' on-campus behavior or online activity that may contravene university regulations (Bugeja, 2006) is another reason students may be wary of formal university uses of Facebook, as 'friends' with instructors may open up their profiles to scrutiny. Moreover, the potential to use this profile information for target program marketing (in the case of prospective students' "liking" a university's page) or fund-raising interests (in the case of alumni outlined in Shih, 2011) may cause a breakdown of trust by students to engage in a deeper relationship with their alma mater.

Although Facebook may provide an adequate tool for information sharing, announcements and events, even for academic purposes, the social network strips context away from connections. The richness of the initial ties connecting people is not the primary avenue by which people remain connected on Facebook. Therefore, an academic relationship in a Facebook space is competing with the clutter and attention of other non-academic materials on the site. Relationships formed around the university exist in a vacuum, rather than any reference to the common environment from which it emerged. The literature that supports the extension of social networking sites into the classroom also recognize its limits as a stand-alone medium of communication, outlining that Facebook works best to supplement or support pedagogy (Hung & Yuen, 2010). Facebook also widely reported in the literature as a source of distraction for students (Hew 2011; Hung & Yuen, 2010).

This chapter presents a caveat to universities against stretching what was the initial purpose of Facebook towards ambitions of wider pedagogic purposes and building meaningful lifelong alumni relationships. The structure and general usage of Facebook by the university has the potential of alienating instead of engaging students and alumni (Chou & Edge, 2012; McAllister, 2012). As an alternative, the next section presents various case study examples of the creative use of other online platforms by universities to genuinely engage students and alumni with each other opening the potential for a deeper connection with their alma mater.

Connecting Creatively Online

Koutropoulos (2010) outlines the development of a student and alumni networking site using Ning, and the challenges of the venture including combating a 'What's in it for me?' attitude by the students/alumni, which restricted widespread participation. Hung and Yuen (2010) also describe the merits of a customized site: "based on the researchers' belief that social networks for academic purposes created with Ning bring about more focused learning environments with less distraction" (p. 706). The article also argues that students and alumni were not self-sufficient on the site limiting the interactivity, thus increasing the institution's need to moderate the site, while also acknowledging general social network fatigue.

Moira Lists at Massachusetts Institute of Technology

In an interview conducted with a senior admissions counselor at Massachusetts Institute of Technology (MIT) in February 2013, "mailing lists are king." Moira Lists are subscription-based mailing lists with an '@mit.edu' address that can be created for any group or purpose by any student, and form an essential part of student and alumni life. This communication technique stands in stark contrast to the "official" Facebook pages, created by the institution's administrators and "are never very popular." For students, perhaps Moira Lists feel closer to hanging out with their friends, not being under surveillance, according to the MIT administrator, "which is one of the places where higher ed often gets it wrong in crossing the boundary." Students and many active alumni use the lists to communicate with others involved in their cause, club, residence hall, friend circle or research group. One alumni class president said that the lists are "mostly used as a tool for engaging with things on-campus . . . where alumni are still involved on Moira Lists is where alumni still want to be involved with things on-campus." Examples of active Moira Lists include "a list of awesome things for awesome people" (awesome.folks@mit.edu) and Bonfire Floor in Random Hall (sexyppl@mit.edu). As many alumni and students' lives become consumed by e-mail, these lists are simple to manage and use for event planning, information dissemination, class notes and general banter. The mailing lists are easily identifiable in a student's inbox with a clear subject line attributed to the Moira List (such as "[AwesomeAwesomePeople] Who's up for dinner in DC?"). Members can quickly scan e-mail subject lines to determine relevance in contrast to Facebook notifications from a myriad of pages, people, events, groups, birthday reminders and pokes. With many e-mail inboxes offering features such flagging, archiving and rules to move e-mails into folders, Moira list users find ways to organize the communications on their interested subject areas in a focused way. Additionally, given the ubiquity of online profiles elsewhere, mailing lists at MIT are able to remove the clutter of likes and unrelated content from a feed whilst maintaining clear context and unencumbered communication.

St. Mary's and Pinterest

In 2008, St. Mary's College of California (SMC) set up its own private social network. Like similar efforts at other institutions, the experiment was a failure. Following an alumni survey by SMC on their social media preferences, SMC revamped its active Facebook, Twitter and LinkedIn pages, while also using Pinterest to engage alumni and current students. Students can look through pictures of young barn owls, deer and "ubiquitous turkeys" in the "Wild Saint Mary's" Pinterest board or can peruse pictures of harpists, oil paintings and dancers in the "Artistic Expression" board. Other popular boards include "SMC Faculty in the News," "Field Guide to Student Life," "The Power of the Fan" and "What are you doing in Jan." According to an SMC administrator, Pinterest works best with "interesting stories and engaging content." Although SMC has yet to measure the relationship potential of this Pinterest work, the Alumni Office believes the platform currently tells a story in a medium that students and alumni enjoy. The interactions on Pinterest between students and alumni are context based; therefore, the motivation for initially visiting the site, continued interest and interaction is this content. SMC can create individualized profiles of student and alumni affinity, thus targeting other SMC activity—such as events—related to a specific interest, even using Pinterest itself as a means to promote the related activity.

These case studies demonstrate that social networking is not static and other media platforms are proving to be an effective means of communication and interactive space. The public popularity of certain social networking sites will also steer the direction of higher education engagement in the future, as instructors and administrators, along with students and alumni consider ways of engaging an educational experience with the interactivity of each platform.

Conclusion: Tread Carefully

The idea of "going where the students are" is a rationale for considering Facebook as a tool for engaging college students. However, the purpose of this chapter is to proceed with caution when considering the use of Facebook as a means of integration with the curriculum, improve student retention or to develop lifelong relationships. A "Facebook vacation" (Merritt, 2013) is increasingly a possibility with a level of disillusionment with the superficiality of the social networking site. Moreover, the Facebook Fatigue discourse underlines another cautionary tale: engagement for higher education purposes could be lost in a sea of information and wave of large numbers of inconsequential relationships. With an always-on generation and the use of social networking growing (Sawers, 2012), there is an expectation of an online relationship between university and students and lifelong relationship between university and alumni. To ensure the relationship is deepened and based on a concerted context, higher education should be strategic in articulating their purpose for using an online platform for engaging with their students and alumni. Facebook may prove to be the ideal space in which to capture this demographic with these university's goals firmly in mind, or another platform allowing for the university-related content to be central to creating context-driven interactions may prove to be a more effective choice. Given the case study examples and recent Facebook Fatigue movement that could infect campus users, those wishing to communicate with students and alumni may find it more effective to consider multiple social media channels to reach this on-campus and off-campus audience.

References

Allen, K. (2013) 'Facebook Fatigue: Do you need a break from the social network?' *Ragan's PR Daily*, March 11 [accessed March 30, 2013, www.prdaily.com/Main/Articles/Facebook_fatigue_Do_you_need_a_break_from_the_soci_14014.aspx].

Bates, D. (2011). 'Facebook Fatigue sets in for six million Americans: Users bored with site deactivate accounts amid privacy fears.' *Daily Mail Online*, June 14 [accessed on November 22, 2012, www.dailymail.co.uk/sciencetech/article-2003305/Facebook-fatigue-6m-US-bored-site-deactivate-accounts-amid-privacy-fears.html].

Bosch, T.E. (2009). 'Using online social networking for teaching and learning: Facebook use at the University of Cape Town.' *Communicatio: South African Journal for Communication Theory and Research*, 35:2, pp. 185–200.

Bugeja, M.J. (2006). 'Facing the Facebook.' *The Chronicle of Higher Education online*, January 23 [accessed on November 22, 2012, http://chronicle.com/article/Facing-the-Facebook/46904].

Cheung, C.M.K., Chiu, P.Y., and Lee, M.K.O. (2011). 'Online social networks: Why do students use Facebook?' *Computers in Human Behavior*, 27, pp. 1337–1343.

Chou, H-T.G., and Edge, N. (2012). '"They are happier and having better lives than I am": The impact of using Facebook on perceptions of others' lives.' *Cyberpsychology, Behavior and Social Networking*, 15:2, pp. 1–5.

Ellison, N.B., Steinfield, C., and Lampe, C. (2007). 'The benefits of Facebook "friends:" Social capital and college students' use of online social network sites.' *Journal of Computer-Mediated Communications*, 12, pp. 1143–1168.

Farrow, H., and Yuan, Y. C. (2011). 'Building Stronger Ties With Alumni Through Facebook to Increase Volunteerism and Charitable Giving.' *Journal of Computer-Mediated Communication*, 16, pp. 445–464.

Firth, M. (2010). 'Can Facebook engage students in critical analysis of academic theory?' *Asian Journal on Education and Learning*, 1:1, pp. 10–19.

Garside, J. (2013). 'Facebook loses millions of users as biggest markets peak.' *The Guardian online*, April 29 [accessed on August 11, 2013, www.theguardian.com/technology/2013/apr/28/facebook-loses-users-biggest-markets].

Granovetter, M. S. (1973). 'The strength of weak ties.' *American Journal of Sociology*, 78:6, pp. 1360–1380.

Grosseck, G., Bran, R., and Tiru, L. (2011). 'Dear teacher, what should I write on my wall? A case study on academic uses of Facebook.' *Procedia – Social and Behavioral Sciences*, 15, pp. 1425–1430.

Herr, E. and Dave, U. (2012). Social media in college recruitment and retention: Columbia College Chicago. In S. Whalen (Ed.), *Proceedings of the 8th National Symposium on Student Retention* (pp. 380–394). Norman: University of Oklahoma.

Hew, K.F. (2011). 'Students' and teachers' use of Facebook.' *Computers in Human Behavior*, 27, pp. 662–676.

Hung, H.T., and Yuen, S.C. (2010). 'Educational use of social networking technology in higher education.' *Teaching in Higher Education*, 15:6, pp. 703–714.

Koutropoulos, A. (2010). 'Creating Networking Communities Beyond the Classroom.' *Human Architecture: Journal of the Sociology of the Self-Knowledge*, 8:1, pp. 71–78.

Lupsa, C. (2006). 'Facebook: A campus fad becomes a campus fact.' *Christian Science Monitor*, December 13 [accessed on December 1, 2012, www.csmonitor.com/2006/1213/p13s01-legn.html].

Madge, C., Meek, J., Wellens, J., and Hooley, T. (2009). 'Facebook, social integration and informal learning at university: "It is more for socialising and talking to friends about work than for actually doing work."' *Learning, Media and Technology*, 34:2, pp. 141–155.

Mazer, J., Murphy, R., and Simonds, C. (2007). 'I'll see you on "*Facebook*": The effects of computer-mediated teacher self-disclosure on student motivation, affective learning, and classroom climate.' *Communication Education*, 56:1, pp. 1–17.

McAllister, S.M. (2012). 'How the world's top universities provide dialogic forums for marginalized voices.' *Public Relations Review*, 38, pp. 317–329.

Merritt, J. (2013). 'Facebook Fatigue.' *Online College Courses*, weblog post, February 25 [accessed March 30, 2013, www.onlinecollegecourses.com/facebook-fatigue].

Mills, C. (2013) 'Facebook Fatigue and the Aging Social Network.' *The Toronto Star*, April 5, [accessed on April 29, 2013, www.thestar.com/business/tech_news/2013/04/05/facebook_fatigue_and_the_aging_social_network.html].

Mitsuzuka, H. (2012). '8 signs of Facebook Fatigue.' *The First Echo*, weblog, April 27 [accessed on May 6, 2013, www.thefirstecho.com/2012/04/8-signs-of-facebook-fatigue.html].

Peterson, K. (2013). 'Facebook Fatigue: Users take time off.' *MSN Money*, February 6 [accessed on March 30, 2013, http://money.msn.com/now/post.aspx?post=bb66e250–195a-407f-a252-be4509be80ce].

Putnam, R. D. (2000). *Bowling Alone*. New York: Simon & Schuster.

Rainie, L., Smith, A., and Duggan, M. (2013). *Coming and going on Facebook: Pew Research Center Report* [accessed on March 30, 2013, http://pewinternet.org/Reports/2013/Coming-and-going-on-facebook/Key-Findings.aspx]

Russell, K. (2013). 'Logging on can make us feel left out.' *Irish Independent*, April 10, pp. 40–41.

Sawers, P. (2012). 'Facebook Fatigue is spreading but social media is on the rise, says Internet study.' *The New Web*, February 6 [accessed May 4, 2013, http://thenextweb.com/socialmedia/2012/02/06/facebook-fatigue-is-spreading-but-social-media-is-on-the-rise-says-internet-study/].

Selwyn, N. (2007). 'Screw Blackboard . . . do it on *Facebook!* An investigation of students' educational use of *Facebook*.' Paper presented to Pole 1.0—*Facebook* social research symposium, November 15 at University of London [accessed on November 22, 2012, www.scribd.com/doc/513958/Facebook-seminar-paper-Selwyn].

Selwyn, N. (2009). 'Faceworking: exploring students' education-related use of Facebook.' *Learning, Media and Technology*, 34:2, pp. 157–174.

Shih, C. (2011). *The Facebook era: Tapping online social networks to market, sell and innovate, 2nd edition*. Boston: Pearson Education.

Van Grove, J. (2013). 'Study: Facebook fatigue—it's real.' *CNET*, February 5 [accessed on March 29, 2013, http://news.cnet.com/8301-1023_3-57567745-93/study-facebook-fatigue-its-real/].

Warner, B. (2013). 'Facebook Fatigue among teens should freak out marketers.' *Bloomberg Business Week*, April 11 [accessed on April 29, 2013, www.businessweek.com/articles/2013-04-11/facebook-fatigue-among-teens-should-freak-out-marketers#_=1367064719031&id =twitter-widget-0&lang=en&screen_name=BW&show_count=false&show_screen_name=true&size=m>].

22

Understanding the Social Media Ecologies of Employees Within Higher Education Institutions: A UK-Based Case Study

CHRIS JAMES CARTER, LEE MARTIN AND CLAIRE O'MALLEY

University of Nottingham

Every once in a while, performing an audit of our digital lives can prove an educational experience. Like 1.11 billion other users worldwide, the chances are that you actively engage with Facebook on at least a monthly basis (Facebook, 2013). Furthermore, it is becoming increasingly unlikely that this will be the only form of social media with which you engage; perhaps like 288 million others you are transfixed with tweeting (GlobalWebIndex, 2013), or just maybe you are akin to the 238 million users who proclaim their professional credentials on LinkedIn (LinkedIn, 2013). Further reflection may even reveal something about how you prefer to manage your multifaceted digital life. Perhaps you elect to seamlessly blend the personal and professional spheres of your social world on just a smattering of sites. Or could it be that you compartmentalize the different facets of your life across numerous platforms, each serving its own distinct purpose? One thing is for sure: a plethora of choice facilitates numerous strategies for how we might undertake the management of our digital identities.

As an umbrella term used to encapsulate the online activities of social networking, content sharing, blogging and microblogging (Kaplan & Haenlein, 2010), 'social media' adopts many guises; from the battle-hardened, consistently familiar feel of Facebook and the staid hues of LinkedIn, to the youthful, aesthetic exuberance of Instagram and Pinterest. Although the well-documented demise of early social networking sites such as SixDegrees and Friendster (boyd and Ellison, 2007) serve as timely reminders that size of user-base is no guarantee of longevity, the ever-expanding range of social media to have blossomed around the fertile grounds of Facebook should provide impetus for social science researchers to broaden their focus out beyond the world's largest social networking site (see Wilson, Gosling and Graham, 2012).

As Kietzmann, Hermkens, McCarthy and Silvestre (2011: 242) state, "there currently exists a rich and diverse ecology of social media sites, which vary in terms of their scope and functionality." The ecological metaphor employed here forms an important foundation upon which much of the following discussion is constructed. Although Kietzmann and colleagues do not appear to explicitly attribute a definitive provenance to the term, the biological imagery appears to have much in common with media ecology theory, that is, "the study of media as environments" (Postman, 1970: 161). Although it is not the intention to frame the proceeding discussion specifically within the parameters of the theory, it seems meritorious to embrace the general notion that different forms of social media can constitute distinctive digital environments; discreetly fitting together to provide the user with a range of outlets for use within a professional context. To paraphrase McLuhan (2003: 271), social media ecologies are about interacting with the sites in ways that are complementary, rather than cancelling each other out.

A core aim of this chapter is to explore how employees within Higher Education Institutions (HEI) draw on different elements of their social media ecologies to support their interactions with students, colleagues and professional peers. HEIs are complex organizations, quite often with equally complex missions requiring the engagement of employees from across a distinct range of roles (Whitchurch, 2006). As reflected in a wider trend of organizations "going social" (Brown & Vaughn, 2011; KPMG, 2011), the increasing centrality of social media within the lives of the student population (Selwyn, 2009) provides a particularly compelling reason for Higher Education employees to take social media seriously, regardless of whether their role is primarily administrative or academic in focus. As the UK-based Joint Information Systems Committee (JISC) Information Strategy Guidelines emphasize, information is the "lifeblood" of HEIs (Orna, 2004; Pollock, 2000). As a form of communication technology, social media appear to excel precisely in supporting this endeavor.

Furthermore, in a digital society where reputation is becoming an increasingly prominent feature of the digital economy (Masum, Newmark, & Tovey, 2011), social media users employed within HEIs appear to be faced with an ongoing challenge of how to engage in authentic, open communication while attenuating the risk of reputational damage to either themselves or their employer. The following discussion draws on the qualitative findings of a case study to explore how employees of both administrative and academic roles within an HEI address this task while using Facebook and other elements of their social media ecologies to interact with students, colleagues and professional peers outside of their institution.

Middleton University: A Case Study

Middleton University (MU) is a pseudonymous HEI based in the United Kingdom. The university is attended by more than thirty-thousand students, employs several thousand members of staff and consistently ranks within an upper percentile of universities worldwide for its quality of research. Semi-structured interviews were conducted with fourteen full-time employees at MU, of which ten were in administrative positions and four in academic roles. Of these fourteen individuals, eight had managerial responsibilities and though nine could be classified as being within the maintenance stage of their careers (see Mount, 1984) with over ten years of professional experience, two were at the establishment stage of their careers, with less than two years of experience.

Questions in the semi-structured interviews addressed four core themes: background information, including their work role at the institution; how they used social media to support their professional activity; how they perceived their own digital identity and that of others; and, finally, how they managed the personal and professional aspects of their digital life. All interviews were transcribed, and thematic analysis subsequently conducted upon the content, following the process outlined by Braun and Clarke (2006).

Interactions With Students

Since its inception in 2004, Facebook has played a central role in supporting the social elements of student life; from its relationship with increased life satisfaction, social trust, civic engagement and political participation (Valenzuela, Park, & Kee, 2009) to improved self-esteem and the construction of different forms of social capital (Ellison, Steinfield, & Lampe, 2007). Commenting from an institutional perspective, Roger, a senior administrator at Middleton University (MU) indicated that social media were ideally placed "as a vehicle for engaging with students to enable [MU] to recruit more and better students." In comparing his perceptions of culture within HEIs to that of other corporate environments, Roger noted,

> The difference is I think we're much better placed to exploit the liberalism [of HEIs]; that freedom to actually use the benefits of social media to engage more meaningfully with students, who are part of this big learning community and, you know, to kind of test out boundaries.

The limits of these boundaries of engagement are not always easily defined, however. David is a professor within MU's Faculty of Social Sciences, wielding a prodigious publication record that is matched by an almost three thousand-strong Twitter followership and expanding swell of international visitors to his research-focused blog. David was acutely aware that many of these followers were students and while acknowledging the self-promotional utility of Twitter as a way of sharing ideas relating to his research ("It's a brilliant, brilliant exercise in forcing you to write."), he was initially reluctant to engage with Facebook. Eventually, he gave in to satisfy his curiosity about the traditionally clandestine conversations he felt his students were having online about his lectures:

> I joined Facebook because some students set up a group about me and the only way I could see what the little f***ers were saying was to join. I didn't want to join in my own name so I joined under a fake identity, which was fine and allowed me to see what they'd done. It wasn't too bad. In fact, it was sort of quite nice in some ways.

Although David's initial motivation for engaging with Facebook appeared to constitute a form of strategic reputation management, his colleague Peter, an associate professor based within the Faculty of Arts, was wary that using the site for monitoring extracurricular student debate introduced an element of risk to the student–teacher relationship that, for him, outweighed any potential benefits:

> Some misguided colleagues of mine search for their names and so forth and find discussions—sometimes very flattering, but nevertheless, discussions . . . The fact some of our students insist on putting drunken photos of themselves up and not using the privacy settings, prompted most of us—certainly myself—to talk explicitly to our third years about the use of Facebook and social media.

Not only does Facebook appear to present not only academic members of staff such as David and Peter with potentially awkward social situations to negotiate with their students, but also university administrators, such as Roger, are left with a fine line to traverse: litigious comments may fall neatly under the institution's existing disciplinary procedures, although viral trends such as "Confessions" pages on Facebook (e.g., Simon, 2013) present more complex challenges. Such pages can pose a significant threat to the institution's reputation, but equally, demanding their removal is an action accompanied with its own risks, not least the potential for it to be perceived as restricting freedom of speech throughout the student body. In this instance, "traditional" disciplinary strategies may not only be ineffective but, in fact, also serve to exacerbate situations further, a phenomenon referred to colloquially as "the Streisand effect" (see *The Economist*, 2013).

Conversely, although numerous studies have hinted at student reticence to interact with staff on Facebook (Hewitt & Forte, 2006; Madge, Meek, Wellens, & Hooley, 2009), a common challenge discussed by many of the interviewees was the management of friendship requests received from students within their institution. Without exception, all interviewees emphasized the importance of maintaining professional distance between themselves and students at MU by declining such requests. For most, the decision appeared a clear one to make, although for Jess, a student liaison officer whose role had become increasingly tied to communicating with students upon social media, the situation demanded greater consideration:

> The difficult thing I find is when you get requests from students. I kind of find that a little bit [pauses] I have these internal debates with myself. I've had about half a dozen, maybe even more, that have requested me as a friend on Facebook but I feel that I need to keep my personal Facebook account separate from my work life.

For Will, an early-career lecturer within the Faculty of Arts, Facebook represented a complex social space in which he communicated with nonwork friends, colleagues and professional peers. As such, the inevitability of talking informally about work simply emphasized further the pastoral responsibility he felt for not including students within his Facebook network. Like David, Will was aware of the increasing number of MU students following both his Twitter profile and blog. Perhaps one of the most prominent features of social media, and in particular Twitter, is the way in which for many users, it collapses multiple audiences into a singular context (Marwick & boyd, 2010).

Offering users relatively limited nuance in how privacy settings are managed, Will, like his fellow interviewees, appeared to be less concerned with controlling access to his Twitter profile than he was with regulating the content of his tweets. In particular, Will indicated feeling "very uncomfortable" with discussing anything that might be overtly political or controversial, primarily due to his concern with "isolating particular students." He was also wary of putting himself in situations where he may be "intellectually vulnerable" to his students; contrasting his own approach to that of a fellow early-stage academic with whom he was friends and whose "frank" tweets, he felt, would inevitably be discovered by her students and subsequently "seriously diminish her authority and her ability to control a class." However, as noted by Will,

> When you're trying to bear all these things in mind, you can actually end up coming across quite anodyne. One of my students joked the other day, "oh, you just post about work all the time on your Twitter feed" and I'm like [pauses] "yeah" [laughs] I do.

Thus, self-regulation appears to be an important aspect of interacting with the different elements of one's social media ecology. However, at the other extreme, excessive restriction and self-censorship is a concern with respect to how interesting subsequent content will actually be to students. Indeed, why use social media at all if one is to disavow its support for social interaction? One answer can be found through an exploration of how social media is used to support communication with coworkers and professional peers.

Interactions With Colleagues and Professional Peers

Frances is an associate professor within the social sciences and an active user of eight different social media platforms. The reason for engaging with such a diverse social media ecology appeared logical: "I guess at the moment there just isn't one site that does everything that I want. There's a bit of stuff on Academia. edu, there's a bit of stuff on Twitter and there's a bit on Facebook." Compartmentalizing and distributing these distinct facets (Farnham & Churchill, 2011) of her digital identity throughout her social media ecology appeared to provide Frances with a practical approach to fulfilling what Binder, Howes and Sutcliffe (2009) propose is a fundamental psychological need to maintain independent social spheres. Although largely succeeding in doing so, Frances admitted that with Facebook in particular, the boundary between her personal and professional life had become progressively blurred over time:

> I try to keep Facebook primarily for friends and family and Twitter primarily for academics, but the split never works out like that because, especially, there's quite a lot of academics who are on Facebook. So there are a bunch of academic people who I'm also friends with and that means I have to be more cautious about what I post there.

For most of the academic employees interviewed, their Facebook networks often contained work-related connections and, in particular, known colleagues at the university and professional peers they had previously met at conferences. As indicated in studies by Skeels and Grudin (2009) and Lampinen, Tamminen and Oulasvirta (2009), the social etiquette of handling Facebook friendship requests from more senior professional peers can also present HEI employees with a dilemma. As Frances remarked,

> You get a friend invitation from a very high profile academic in America and you think "you're a great academic, but I don't think I really want to be Facebook friends with you because I don't want to see your photos skiing and laying on beaches, and you don't want to see photos of my kids." But, you know, you sort of slightly feel as though it would be rude to say no with some of these things.

Conversely, almost all employees within administrative roles were unwilling to accept requests from current colleagues on Facebook; however, they were more comfortable doing so with former coworkers. For Abigail, an MU employee in a student support role, Facebook enabled her to keep in touch with former colleagues with whom she had remained close friends. However, Roger, a senior administrator with a relatively expansive social media ecology, emphasized that HEI employees need to be perceptive of the professional consequences that can arise from publicly sharing personal matters or strongly critical professional opinions amongst an audience of professional peers.

In particular, Roger warned that managing professional relationships could be especially problematic for those at the beginning of their career or for administrative employees who "don't enjoy the same protection [of freedom of speech as academic staff] and I'd say you've got to be more careful." However, few interviewees in academic roles appeared to place much faith in such protection, a point illustrated by the ubiquitous use of "my views are my own" disclaimers on their Twitter profiles, without truly believing in any legal protection that they might offer ("I don't know if it will make any blind bit of difference but I thought 'I might as well'. It's just a few words.").

In fact, for many of the interviewees, Facebook appeared to represent an element of their social media ecologies that supported relative freedom in what they felt able to share amongst friends and professional peers. For a number of academic employees in particular, the platform was referred to as providing a "safe audience"; a network that in comparison to the audiences of their Twitter profile or blog was largely known in an offline context and could be trusted to correctly interpret any potentially ambiguous content. Subsequently, some (e.g. Lewis, Kaufman and Christakis, 2008) have likened Facebook to the dramaturgical concept of a back stage or region; defined by Goffman (1959: 112) as "a place, relative to a given performance, where the impression fostered by the performance is knowingly contradicted as a matter of course".

However, in line with Hogan's (2010) critique of the analogy's application to Facebook, an interactional space that is considered to be private or "safe" is not necessarily the same as a 'back stage' region where individuals can "reliably expect that no member of the audience will intrude" (Goffman, 1959: 114) and engage in performances that might be inappropriate for the audience of the "front stage." Indeed, David's self-described conformity to the adage of "don't write anything that you wouldn't want to see on the front page of the Daily Mail" indicated that he still performed for a professional audience, despite his actual Facebook audience being largely homogenous in its composition of mostly nonwork friends.

In this sense, the perceived freedom in self-expression that Facebook appeared to provide HEI employees was merely relative to more publicly accessible elements of their social media ecologies, rather than "safe" in a more absolute sense. As noted by David, "Even if [others] have protected their stuff, people can get in. They can take screenshots. I mean, it's not that bloody safe." Indeed, rather than relying on the protection afforded by system privacy settings, the exclusion of certain behaviors on particular sites becomes a performance in itself, reflecting an active process of strategic reputation management that appeared to underpin the use of social media by many of the HEI employees interviewed.

Conclusion

As the case study of Middleton University hopefully illustrates, HEIs offer particularly fascinating social environments through which to explore the use of social media in a professional context. It seems likely that for as long as HEIs continue to embrace these social technologies to recruit, consult and educate students, both administrative and academic employees will need to think carefully about how they balance the needs of the organization against their own and those of their students. As many of the interviewees in the case study demonstrated, when utilized effectively, the distinct elements of their social media ecologies can fit together to provide a powerful method of disseminating research, communicating with students and connecting with professional peers.

However, to achieve this, vigilance, conscientiousness and self-regulation appear to be crucial. The employees of MU indicated that on Facebook, personal-professional boundaries should be maintained at all times with respect to current students. For those in administrative roles, this applied equally to current colleagues. Conversely, Twitter, LinkedIn and blogging sites offered platforms that were perceived as more appropriate for interacting with students and professional peers. As more exposed public spaces for social interaction, it was on these sites that employees appeared to demonstrate the greatest awareness for the professional consequences of their actions; regulating their interactions with respect to the anticipated responses of a highly diverse imagined audience consisting of students, professional peers and the tabloid press.

As new forms of social media continue to emerge and appeal to the student body, it seems likely that Higher Education employees will need to seek increasingly novel ways to protect and promote both their own reputation and that of their institution. Although Facebook remains an important site of inquiry, the experiences of employees within Middleton University indicate that we should also broaden our focus to encompass other elements of the individual's social media ecology.

References

Binder, J., Howes, A., & Sutcliffe, A. (2009, April). The problem of conflicting social spheres: effects of network structure on experienced tension in social network sites. In *Proceedings of the SIGCHI Conference on Human Factors in Computing Systems* (pp. 965–974). New York: ACM.

boyd, d. m., & Ellison, N. B. (2007). Social network sites: Definition, history, and scholarship. *Journal of Computer-Mediated Communication, 13*(1), 210–230.

Braun, V., & Clarke, V. (2006). Using thematic analysis in psychology. *Qualitative Research in Psychology, 3*(2), 77–101.

Brown, V. R., & Vaughn, E. D. (2011). The writing on the (Facebook) wall: The use of social networking sites in hiring decisions. *Journal of Business and Psychology, 26*(2), 219–225.

The Economist. (2013, April 15). What is the Streisand effect? *The Economist.* Retrieved from www.economist.com/blogs/economist-explains/2013/04/economist-explains-what-streisand-effect

Ellison, N. B., Steinfield, C., & Lampe, C. (2007). The benefits of Facebook "friends:" Social capital and college students' use of online social network sites. *Journal of Computer-Mediated Communication, 12*(4), 1143–1168.

Facebook (2013). *Newsroom: Key facts.* Retrieved May 7, 2013, from http://newsroom.fb.com/Key-Facts

Farnham, S. D., & Churchill, E. F. (2011). Faceted identity, faceted lives: social and technical issues with being yourself online. In *Proceedings of the ACM 2011 conference on computer supported cooperative work* (pp. 359–368). New York: ACM.

GlobalWebIndex (2013, January 28). Twitter now the fastest growing social platform in the world [Blog entry]. Retrieved from www.globalwebindex.net/twitter-now-the-fastest-growing-social-platform-in-the-world/

Goffman, E. (1959). *The presentation of self in everyday life.* New York: Doubleday.

Hewitt, A., & Forte, A. (2006, November). *Crossing boundaries: Identity management and student/faculty relationships on the Facebook.* Poster presented at CSCW, Banff, Alberta, Canada.

Hogan, B. (2010). The presentation of self in the age of social media: distinguishing performances and exhibitions online. *Bulletin of Science, Technology & Society, 30*(6), 377–386.

Kaplan, A.M., & Haenlein, M. (2010). Users of the world, unite! The challenges and opportunities of social media. *Business Horizons, 53*(1), 59–68.

Kietzmann, J. H., Hermkens, K., McCarthy, I. P., & Silvestre, B. S. (2011). Social media? Get serious! Understanding the functional building blocks of social media. *Business Horizons, 54*(3), 241–251.

KPMG. (2011). *Going social: How businesses are making the most of social media.* Retrieved from www.kpmg.com/global/en/issuesandinsights/articlespublications/pages/going-social.aspx.

Lampinen, A., Tamminen, S., & Oulasvirta, A. (2009, May). All my people right here, right now: Management of group co-presence on a social networking site. In *Proceedings of the ACM 2009 international conference on supporting group work* (pp. 281–290). New York: ACM.

Lewis, K., Kaufman, J., & Christakis, N. (2008). The taste for privacy: An analysis of college student privacy settings in an online social network. *Journal of Computer-Mediated Communication, 14*(1), 79–100.

LinkedIn (2013). About LinkedIn. Retrieved September 6, 2013, from http://press.linkedin.com/about.

Madge, C., Meek, J., Wellens, J., & Hooley, T. (2009). Facebook, social integration and informal learning at university: "It is more for socialising and talking to friends about work than for actually doing work." *Learning, Media and Technology, 34*(2), 141–155.

Marwick, A. E., & boyd, d. m. (2010). I tweet honestly, I tweet passionately: Twitter users, context collapse, and the imagined audience. *New Media & Society, 13*(1), 114–133.

Masum, H., Newmark, C., & Tovey, M. (2011). *The reputation society: How online opinions are reshaping the offline world.* Cambridge, MA: MIT Press.

McLuhan, M. (2003). *Understanding me: Lectures and interviews* (S. McLuhan & D. Staines, Eds.). Cambridge, MA: MIT Press.

Mount, M. K. (1984). Managerial career stage and facets of job satisfaction. *Journal of Vocational Behavior, 24*(3), 340–354.

Orna, E. (2004). *Information strategy in practice.* Aldershot, England: Gower.

Pollock, N. (2000). The virtual university as "timely and accurate information." *Information, Communication and Society, 3*(3), 349–365.

Postman, N. (1970). The reformed English curriculum. In A. C. Eurich (Ed.), *High school 1980: The shape of the future in American secondary education* (pp. 160–168). New York: Pitman.

Selwyn, N. (2009). Faceworking: exploring students' education-related use of Facebook. *Learning, Media and Technology, 34*(2), 157–174.

Simon, S. (2013, March 18). Students bare souls, and more, on Facebook "confession" pages. *Reuters.* Retrieved from www.reuters.com/article/2013/03/18/us-usa-facebook-confess-idUSBRE92H0X720130318

Skeels, M. M., & Grudin, J. (2009). When social networks cross boundaries: A case study of workplace use of Facebook and LinkedIn. In *Proceedings of the ACM 2009 international conference on supporting group work* (pp. 95–104). New York: ACM.

Valenzuela, S., Park, N., & Kee, K. F. (2009). Is there social capital in a social network site? Facebook use and college students' life satisfaction, trust, and participation. *Journal of Computer-Mediated Communication, 14*(4), 875–901.

Whitchurch, C. (2006). Who do they think they are? The changing identities of professional administrators and managers in UK higher education. *Journal of Higher Education Policy and Management, 28*(2), 159–171.

Wilson, R. E., Gosling, S. D., & Graham, L. T. (2012). A review of Facebook research in the social sciences. *Perspectives on Psychological Science, 7*(3), 203–220.

Index

Lightning Source UK Ltd.
Milton Keynes UK
UKOW01f0104041017

310368UK00019B/321/P